MONSTERS

MONSTERS

Evil Beings,

Mythical Beasts, and

All Manner of

Imaginary Terrors

DAVID D. GILMORE

UNIVERSITY OF PENNSYLVANIA PRESS

Philadelphia

Copyright © 2003 University of Pennsylvania Press
All rights reserved
Printed in the United States of America on acid-free paper

10 9 8 7 6 5 4 3 2 1

Published by
University of Pennsylvania Press
Philadelphia, Pennsylvania 19104-4011

Library of Congress Cataloging-in-Publication Data

Gilmore, David D., 1943–
    Monsters : evil beings, mythical beasts, and all manner of imaginary terrors /
David D. Gilmore.
        p.   cm.
    ISBN 0-8122-3702-1 (cloth : alk. paper)
    Includes bibliographical references and index.
    1. Monsters. 2. Animals, Mythical. I. Title
GR825 .G55   2003
001.944—dc21   2002028505

To Aggie and Jules,
and all the monster-slayers

CONTENTS

PREFACE

Like so many other eternal adolescents, I am fascinated by imaginary monsters—especially the luscious ghouls and extraterrestrials in sci-fi literature and Hollywood films. They always inspired both dread and attraction in me, or perhaps empathy is a better word. So, given this morbid interest, the present book may represent a coming to grips with a juvenile obsession that has endured well into middle age. The appeal of monsters reaches a peak in childhood, when all prudent boys and girls check under their beds at night for demons, but it lingers well into adulthood. In those who are seriously weird—a category I admit belonging to—it evolves into a luxurious repertory of fantasies, anxieties, and phobias.

I think the immortal monster is irrefutable proof, if such were needed, for the existence of Freud's aggressive instinct, the reality of an impulse toward violence. As my research has shown, people everywhere and at all times have been haunted by ogres, cannibal giants, metamorphs, werewolves, vampires, and so on. In Africa people believe in were-lions, and in the South Seas there are man-eating were-sharks, not to mention cannibal ogres among the American Indians and the bellowing ape-men of the Far East! Since these nightmares are universal, they must reveal something about the human mind. Monsters share certain characteristics no matter where they appear: they are always aggressive, gigantic, man-eating, malevolent, bizarre in shape, gruesome, atavistic, powerful and gratuitously violent. In rendering their fantasies in art and folktale, people have been both troubled and relieved.

The evidence indicates that monsters are more complicated than being reducible to the uni-dimensional id forces of sex and aggression. However terrible, they are not just metaphors for beastliness: their vast powers inspire veneration as well as repugnance. While we struggle against them, monsters also instill awe and even a grudging respect. This stark dualism— half horror, half reverence—inspired me to write this book.

Delving into the topic, I sought and received advice from many sensible people who indulged me as best they could. Among those who helped were Howard Bloch, Stanley Brandes, Uradyn E. Bulag, Jeffrey Jerome Cohen, John R. Colombo, Marc Edelman, Richard Gottlieb, Marie-France Gueusquin, Anita Moskowitz, Susan C. Rogers, John Shea, Aimeric Vacher, and Bonnie Wheeler. Lee Stern, quite fortuitously, tipped me off to the existence of the Park of Monsters in Bomarzo, Italy, and provided some charming photographs he had taken there. Federico Zanatta helped with some Italian translations on the same topic, and Francesca Zanatta tracked down and sent me materials in obscure Italian journals.

In Spain, Salvador Rodríguez Becerra was heroic in confronting monsters and demons in fiestas throughout the peninsula from Jaca to Seville, and in penetrating the lair of the famous Tarasca dragon of Toledo. He was also a source of much knowledge and wise insights as well as a splendid guide to local gastronomy. Our Spanish helpmates, María del Carmen Medina Roman, and Sol Tarrés Chamorro, supplied endless enthusiasm and practical assistance, as well as superb field notes and photos for which I am eternally grateful. In addition, Ms. Medina offered herself up to be swallowed by the ferocious Tarasca of Las Hacinas during carnival, and so experienced first hand being inside the belly of the beast!

In Toledo I received splendid support in locating the Tarasca in its current lair from Gerardo Fernández Juárez, Juan Estanislao López Gómez, and Fernando Martínez Gil. The latter also supplied me with marvelous photos of the beast in action. Also of great help to me in Spain were Julio Porres de Mateo and José Guillermo Afán Conde. My old friend, the wise and courtly Carmelo Lisón Tolosana, provided unstinting support and comfort during the brief time I spent in Aragon. For their help in shepherding the manuscript into finished form and locating so many wonderful pictures, I want to thank Peter Agree, Samantha Foster, and Bruce Franklin of the University of Pennsylvania Press.

Finally, I want to thank my children, Agatha Emily and Julian Jay, for their forbearance in putting up with my irascibility, which at times was truly monstrous. Aggie also assisted in translating some difficult material from French. Jules informed me knowledgeably about monsters in young people's literature while researching his own school project on sea serpents —like father like son. I want also to commend my colleague at Stony Brook University, Fred Grine, Chair of Anthropology, for providing me enough leave time to complete the fieldwork.

Last but not least, the following institutions provided generous research grants that permitted me to go to Spain and complete the writing: the National Science Foundation, the Program for Cultural Cooperation between Spain's Ministry of Education, Culture, and Sports and United States Universities, and the American Philosophical Society's Franklin

Fund. I am also indebted to Stuart Plattner of the NSF, who went beyond the call of duty and graciously permitted various changes to my original budget to allow for the contingencies of the research. As I was in the final stages of my research I got word that I had received a J. S. Guggenheim Fellowship—a most prodigious honor for which I am humbly grateful. The Fellowship permitted an undisturbed conclusion of my work.

To all those mentioned above and all the others who dared look into the abyss with me, I give my heartfelt thanks.

Whoever fights monsters should see to it that in the process he does not become a monster. And when you look into an abyss, the abyss looks back into you.

—*Friedrich Nietzsche*, Beyond Good and Evil

The constitution of the monster implies that taboos have been transgressed to promote adventures into the realm of impossible possibilities. . . . It is an evasion at once liberating and intoxicating, lifting from life all barriers confining the species. And so, the monstrous is exciting.

—*Jean Brun, "Le Prestige du monstre"*

1

WHY STUDY MONSTERS?

The dream of reason produces monsters.
—Francisco Goya, "Caprichos"

he mind needs monsters. Monsters embody all that is dangerous and horrible in the human imagination. Since earliest times, people have invented fantasy creatures on which their fears could safely settle. Examples from Western lore are Frankenstein and Dracula, all those dragons of the Middle Ages, Hollywood's ghouls and extraterrestrials, and of course the sharp-toothed bogeymen that hide under children's beds (and adults' beds, too). Classic works, from the Grimm brothers to recent psychological studies (Bettelheim 1976; Beaudet 1990; Carroll 1990; Warner 1998), demonstrate the rich variety and primal power of the imaginary evil creature as a cultural metaphor and literary device in folklore, fiction, art, dreaming, and everyday fantasy.

Monsters are not confined to a single tradition. Such nightmares haunt "primitive" peoples all over the world. Mythical monsters made an especially rich vein among Native Americans, for example. The Algonquian-speaking Indians of Canada, including the Ojibwa, Cree, and Saulteaux, are still obsessed today with what they call the Windigo, a man-eating giant with a heart of ice (Teicher 1960; Bishop 1975). Sightings of the Windigo inspired mass panics as recently as the 1960s, emptying out entire villages. In British Columbia, the Athabaskans feared the Wechuge—a cannibal woodland ogre (Ridington 1980). The Yuroks of California believed in all manner of devilish creatures and bogeys (many still do). One is the Wo-gey, a hideous homicidal demon. Older Yurok still have nightmares about the "vicious ones," horrid sprites. Many other Indians believe in giant reptiles and birds of prey that eat children whole and underground serpents that swallow people up (Buckley 1980: 155–56).

In New York State, the Iroquois are still bedeviled by malignant creatures called "stone giants." These are powerful demons, half-human in shape.

They lie in wait in dense forests, where, protected from human weapons by a skin of impenetrable slate, they eat hapless hunters. No arrow can harm them. Indestructible and unstoppable, they are, as usual, violently predisposed toward humans and of course enjoy a customary snack of human flesh (Fogelson 1980: 141).

In southeastern United States, Cherokees fear the uktena, a man-eating aquatic serpent. Although uktenas look like rattlesnakes, they have horns on their heads (Hudson 1978). Like many comparable monsters in other belief systems, utkenas live on the periphery of the Cherokee universe: in the high passes in remote mountains and in the deepest parts of the rivers that slice through Indian territory. They are able to spew forth fire and smoke, and so dreadful were they that even the sight of one would cause a man to fall ill. If a person happened to sniff the poisonous breath of a uktena, it would cause instant death (Hudson 1978: 62).

The uktena, incidentally, reflects a widespread archetype that reappears in many Native American cultures as a pond or lake demon. It of course can be found in deathless incarnations in European lore as the mysterious Kraken, a continuation of sea monster legends that go back at least to the ancient Greeks. Among classical writers, for example, the sober Aristotle pondered the terrible sea serpents and other marine terrors of the ancient Mediterranean that he and his countrymen believed responsible for most shipwrecks (Bright 1991: 2). Without the slightest possibility of cultural diffusion, it is obvious we are dealing with almost identical ideas among disconnected peoples, revealing some deep human thread.

Like these others, the people living in sub-Saharan Africa also fear monsters. For example, there is Mokele-Mbembe. Held in awe by the Congolese Pygmies and sought after unsuccessfully by European explorers, this imaginary beast (or cryptomorph) is a two-legged, dinosaur-like behemoth. It haunts the Congo River and its estuaries, eating travelers and panicking whole villages (Eberhart 1983: 3) This prehistoric leftover is only one of what has been called a huge monster menagerie of central Africa (Nugent 1993: 213–14), which includes man-eating devils, outsized beasts, and *chipekwes*, the latter described by the natives simply as "big monsters." In Kenya the horrible Nandi bear is said to have the appearance of a giant chalicotherium (an extinct prehistoric herbivore), except that it is carnivorous. Like other monsters, the Nandi bear eats human beings, supposedly cracking open the skull of its victim to extract the brain (Grant 1992: 47).

Further north, among the Egyptian Nubians along the Nile, there survives a belief in serpent-beasts called *aman doger*, "ugly water beings." These creatures come out of the river at night to prey upon human habitations. They are described as ugly, black, animal-like, masculine in gender, and having human-like desires. Their manner of predation is to attack the nose of the victim until he or she dies of suffocation, and they also eat small children (Kennedy 1970: 441–42).

In Arab North Africa, according to accounts collected by Frenchman Joseph Desparmet in the early part of the twentieth century (1909), Berber peasants in the Atlas mountains believed in cannibal ogres, or *ghouli* (from which we get the word "ghoul"). These evil spirits infested the broken countryside of the entire Maghreb area, making travel dangerous. Derived from the Arabic concept of jinn, or genies (which are mentioned in the Qur'an), these creatures were famous for their appetite. Desparmet tells us that in 1907 there was wholesale hysteria due to sightings of ghouli massed in the area around the town of Blida, and many panic-stricken women and children stayed behind locked doors for months (1909: 2–3). The same fears abound even today.

Moving further east, folklore roils with giant serpents, fire-blowing dragons, hideous demons, and other weird, threatening creatures. Many Far Eastern legends center on the depredations of fire-belching demons that local warriors must confront or else the society will be destroyed. The apocalyptic man-versus-monster formula is a prominent feature in both Tibetan and Japanese folklore (Kiej'e 1973; D. White 1991), and is probably as much a source as the Hollywood precedents for the Japanese Godzilla genre. Among the Tibetans, there is still a thriving artistic tradition of monster and demon masks used in Buddhist exorcism rites. Further east, off the Asian landmass, the Micronesians and Polynesians had their own nightmare apparitions. Their folklore is full of ogres and oversized reptiles, as well as marine were-beasts such as were-sharks and were-octopuses, all of which gobble up humans with relish (Lessa 1961; Kirtley 1971).

Latin America, too, both before and after the Iberian conquest, has had gruesome monsters. Aboriginal folklore before the Spaniards featured "diabolical dogs," giant lizards, and flying half-human fiends that attacked people from impenetrable forests (Peniche Barrera 1987). One of these, a giant ogre called Tlacahuepan in Mayan, ate children and occasionally adults too. The *ekuneil* and *hapai-can* were giant Aztec serpents that caught people in their coils and sucked their blood (15). These beasts still haunt rural Latin America today and have been regarded by anthropologists as reflecting a mixture of aboriginal and Spanish beliefs (Magaña 1988; Isla 1998).

PREVIOUS STUDIES OF MONSTERS

Clearly the world was and still is full of awful monsters. In the West, because of their everyday presence in popular culture—spurred on by Hollywood fantasy films—we tend to take them for granted while not believing in their actual existence. We rarely stop to consider the psychological meaning of their appeal. While they differ in shape and size, all the mythical beings of the world's cultures have many features in common that, like so many other aspects of myth and folklore, cry out for a broad comparison. Both the Maya and Spaniards believed in monstrous reptiles and man-eating ogres, and the blend of the two cultures gave rise to seamless composites at home in both traditions. In other cases the similarities between diverse cultural traditions seem to point to some underlying commonalities in the human mind. These commonalities are not only anatomical and pictorial, but also behavioral and moral—even dietary!

Literary critics, philosophers, historians, and psychologists have attempted to pinpoint common themes that run through the diverse traditions. So far this work lacks a truly comparative basis, being largely confined to the Western imagination, especially Euro-American fantasy art, science fiction, and horror films (Atwood 1977; Mully 1980; Carroll 1990; Williams 1996; Andriano 1999). Yet even with this limited scope, the research has produced some provocative findings. These are many-faceted and not easily summarized, but most authorities agree that imaginary monsters provide a convenient pictorial metaphor for human qualities that have to be repudiated, externalized, and defeated, the most important of which are aggression and sexual sadism, that is, id forces.

However, it seems to me that so much is fairly obvious. As I said in the Preface, I have always believed—perhaps based more on intuition than anything else—that the endless fascination with monsters derives from a complex mix of emotions and is not simply reducible to the standard Freudian twins of aggression and repression. The point of this book is to show that for most people monsters are sources of identification and awe as well as of horror, and they serve also as vehicles for the expiation of guilt as well as aggression: there is a strong sense in which the monster is an incarnation of the urge for self-punishment and a unified metaphor for both sadism and victimization (after all, the horrible monster is always killed off, usually in the most gruesome manner imaginable, by humans). We have to address this issue of dualism, of emotive ambivalence, in which the monster stands for both the victim and the victimizer. What other forces does the monster embody in the human consciousness aside from pure aggression? Why do we need all these monsters to express these emotions?

OBJECT OF THIS STUDY

One compelling reason to pursue a study of monsters is that they figure so prominently in world folklore (Campbell 1968; Mode 1973). In the archetypal Culture Hero myth, which is found all over the world, some brave champion goes forth to test his mettle in a climactic battle of good and evil, the latter always embodied as some monstrous beast. The Minotaur, Medusa, the Basilisk, Grendel in *Beowulf*, and Saint George's dragon are examples of the bestial villains of Western culture, but there are countless others in every tradition and in every literature from the Stone Age to the Computer Age (Rose 2000).

In early modern Spain, for example, Cervantes made fun of this genre when Don Quixote battles windmills he mistakes for the giant ogres of medieval romance. Involvement with the monster-nemesis figure, in Joseph Campbell's (1968) terms the "monster-tyrant," begins with the earliest stirrings of religious feeling, in one of the world's oldest symbols, the sphinx. This fixation with monsters is well documented as a major topos running through classical antiquity, especially among the ancient Greeks, who saw corroboration for their legends in the megafaunal fossils they found exposed in promontories around the Mediterranean Basin (Mayor 2000).

Even more compelling is the fact that the very idea of the monster springs up with the same aesthetic-intellectual impulse that gave rise to civilization itself. Art historian Heinz Mode argues that visual portraits of menacing creatures occur at precisely the same time as does literacy. He claims that the consciousness of such ideas, as far as archeology can tell, occurs as a product of the earliest known civilizations, in the period around 3000 B.C. Aside from some equivocal figures in European cave art (to be discussed in the next chapter), the first unequivocal and identifiable monsters are to be found in early dynastic Egypt and Mesopotamia, and possibly a little later in the Indus Valley in present-day Pakistan (Mode 1973: 12). Indeed monsters arise with civilization—with human self-consciousness.

WHAT IS A MONSTER?

Before describing monsters, let us first clarify terminology. People every-where use "monster" glibly to describe whatever they find loathsome, ter-rifying, or dangerous, so we should be specific. For purposes here, by *monster* I will confine usage to supernatural, mythical, or magical products of the imagination. I will not include heinous criminals or mass murderers like Hitler or Stalin (justifiably "monsters" in a metaphorical sense), nor will I include physical abnormalities, freaks and birth defects, or other real anomalies or deformities (referred to as "monsters" in the Middle Ages and Renaissance: Friedman 1981; D. White 1991). Additionally, for purposes of cultural comparison, I will exclude witches and sorcerers, because, like our serial murderers, they are only human beings who have gone bad, rather than fantasies. For the same reason I exclude revenants like ghosts and zombies, which are, once again, only dead (or half-dead) people come back to haunt.

Restricting our study to imaginary beings, then, we note that these are usually represented in fiction, art, and folklore in strikingly conventional and patterned ways. Most often they are grotesque hybrids, recombinations uniting animal and human features or mixing animal species in lurid ways (Harpham 1982; Andriano 1999). Such a formal definition of monster would include human metamorphoses like werewolves and vampires, as well as man-eating giants like the Algonquian Windigo and the Athabaskan Wechuge mentioned above, shape-shifters like Jekyll-Hyde, European dragons, and the various ogres of Micronesia (Hames 1960: 91–95). We would also include giants like the Gorgons and Cyclops of classical antiq-uity, since disproportionately huge size so often defines monsters, and ter-rible cryptomorphs like Grendel in *Beowulf* and the yeti or abominable snowman of Himalayan folklore. For our purposes, then, monsters, are imaginary, not real, embodiments of terror.

Other key elements are "mystery and menace" (D. Cohen 1970: 1). In her study of fictional ogres and monsters, literary critic Ruth Waterhouse develops what she calls a paradigm of the Monstrous, based on the follow-ing criteria. First there is large size and deformity, but there is also the qual-ity of inherent *evil*, that is, unmotivated wickedness toward humans (1996: 28–29). Another literary critic, Joseph Andriano, who has also written per-ceptively about monsters, in art and film, suggests that the main criterion of monsters is that they are dangerous objects of fear, but that this fear includes "the primal fear of being eaten" (1999: 91). To judge from what

St. George and the Dragon by Paolo Ucello (1397–1475), emphasizing the mouth both as weapon and as target of human aggression. Giraudon/Art Resource, NY.

we have already observed about the customary monster diet, this observation about being eaten is important. As we will see, eating human beings is as critical an aspect of monsterhood as bigness, physical grotesqueness, and malice.

Mythologist Joseph Campbell offers us other useful observations, and these may serve as parallel criteria: "By a monster I mean some horrendous presence or apparition that explodes all of your standards for harmony, order, and ethical conduct" (1968: 222). For Campbell, a monster is an imaginary being with a portmanteau morphology combining animal and human traits in frightening ways or mixing up animal categories, as in the generic dragon that combines lizard, bird, and snake—an icon in European mythology. For Campbell and others, monsters are defined not only by their size, their malevolence, or their tendencies to eat human beings, but also by their morphological oddity and, especially, the joining of known organisms into weird, unnatural forms that shock. Hybridization, or "reshuffled familiarity" (Harpham 1982: 5), remains a critical element in all analyses, demanding special attention. In a book on medieval monsters, the French cultural historian Claude Kappler (1980) includes such criteria as unnatural asymmetry of parts, substitution of anatomical organs by unnatural forms, and mélange or recombination of human, animal, and plant life into impossible composite organisms. He refers to such bizarre confabulations as an "agglutination of images" (1980: 283).

Historian Rudolf Wittkower confirms this by telling us that throughout the European Middle Ages and Renaissance what was considered monstrous was whatever combined various naturally occurring flora and fauna into weird combinations, whether in the imagination or as a mistake of nature, especially those so-called prodigies that united the animal with the human; during this entire thousand-year period, monsters were defined as composites, half-human, half-animal (1942: 197). In an analysis of medieval monster books such as the *Liber Monstrorum* (*Book of Monsters*), historian Douglas Butturff notes that in the literature of the Middle Ages the distinguishing characteristic of monsters is that they are a hybrid of man and beast (1968: 24). Of course this relates to the European tradition only, but the concept finds resonance in the other traditions we will be looking at, from the most "primitive" cultures to the present age.

Also stressing morphological mélange, Heinz Mode offers one definition of monsters that is perhaps worth quoting in full:

Thus we define a "monster" as a new shape resulting from a combination— usually in visual form, but sometimes only in words—of characteristic components or properties of different kinds of living things or natural objects. It is therefore characteristic of the "monster" that it does not occur in nature, but belongs solely to the realm of the human imagination, and also that its shape forms an organic entity, a new type capable of life in art and in the imagination. (1973: 7)

More recent observers generally begin with a criterion of visual bizarreness, but they add some important considerations. In his informative study of the horror genre in modern fiction, the philosopher Noël Carroll summarizes what he calls "monstrosity" or "horrific beings" in a useful way relating not to form, but to the emotional response of audiences. Speaking about what makes for the thrill in the horror genre in fiction and film, he argues that horribleness in fiction depends upon the presence of some dangerous entity which is extra-mundane, and therefore capable of superhuman destructiveness, and which inspires terror in the observer. He goes on to define such horrific beings as not only terrifying and threatening and bizarre in appearance and behavior, but also big enough to be overwhelmingly powerful and, above all, malevolent. But perhaps the most important criterion in his eclectic definition is what he calls ontological "fusion":

One structure for the composition of horrific beings is fusion. On the simplest physical level, this often entails the construction of creatures that transgress categorical distinctions such as inside/outside, living/dead, insect/human, flesh/machine, and so on. . . . A fusion figure is a composite that unites attributes held to be categorically distinct and/or at odds in the cultural scheme of things in unambiguously one, spatio-temporally discrete entity. (1990: 43)

ETYMOLOGY

Literary interest in monsters begins with the ancient Greeks, especially Aristotle, who wrote extensively about them in *The Generation of Animals*. The word he and other Greeks use for abnormal creatures is *teras*, meaning a warning or portent (Friedman 1981: 108). This usage gave rise etymologically in the Middle Ages to the suitably monstrous word *teratology*, which was the biological study of organic malformations, freaks, and anomalous births, a pseudo-science of prognostication or divining, which attained an exalted status in the Middle Ages, persisting at least to the mid-twentieth century, as in Étienne Wolff's *La Science des monstres* (Fiedler 1978: 250). However, the English word "monster" derives from the Latin *monstrum*, which like *teras* meant a prodigy or portent, stemming from the root *monere*, meaning to show or warn (Cawson 1995: 1). The Latin *monstrum* refers etymologically to that which reveals, that which warns, a glyph in search of a hierophant. Always alert to portents, the ancient Romans tended to use *monstra* to mean all abnormal phenomena regarded as warnings or omens of the will of the gods, not just monsters, and, as such, the Latin term constituted a very important element of the Roman religion, which was obsessed with divining celestial tempers and intentions through appearances in nature.

In the ancient world, monstrosities, *monstra*, are named from an admonition, *monitus*, because they point out something by signaling or symbolizing. Clearly, from the beginnings of recorded time, monsters have been part of a semiotic culture of divination, metaphors, messages, indications of deeper meaning or inspiration. Although words have changed, the basic import of the concept as an intellectual, aesthetic, and moral problem has remained fairly constant. Following classical usage, in the writings of St. Isidore of Seville, a seventh-century Spanish monk who wrote extensively about evil, *monstrus* likewise reveals a divine source, God's will or design in the Christian sense. For such holy men as Isidore, monsters came under the headings of God's creations and therefore must have some revealed meaning: "monstrations" or warnings from God, directing attention to deviations from the true path in symbolic or allegorical form. We will discuss this at greater length in Chapter 3, which considers medieval interpretations of monsters.

In the Middle Ages and later as the linguistic hold of Latin lessened before the onslaught of the European vernaculars, the old Roman *monstrum* persisted and its semantics remained unchanged in the majority of glossaries and lexica. The twelfth-century commentator Arnulf of Orleans treated the word frequently in his glosses on Lucan and was well aware that it could mean a divine warning about moral excesses in present times. Even as late as the fourteenth century, Pierre Barsuire explained in his *Repertorium Morale* that "monsters are creatures from outside, beyond, or contrary to nature. . . . Such things therefore are called monstria, from monstrando either because they show or signify some future event or because they exemplify some moral or spiritual flaw" (quoted in Friedman 1981: 116).

Today, of course, much of this semantic and religious baggage has been lost, and we use the term to imply made-up creatures that are frightening, oversized, and repugnant, but there remains a very powerful sense in which monsters are still signs or portents of something momentous, carrying profound, even spiritual meaning beyond just frightfulness. And indeed, as we will see, the origins of the word reveal yet another aspect of monsters, which is the paradoxical closeness of the monstrous and the divine. For monsters contain that numinous quality of awe mixed with horror and terror that unites the evil and the sublime in a single symbol: that which is beyond the human, the superhuman, the unnameable, the tabooed, the terrible, and the unknown. The monster of the mind is both our foulest mental creation and our most awesome achievement. What does all this emphasis on signs and portents mean, all these layers of significance, all this profusion of symbols?

In the following chapter, we begin to organize our fascination with monsters into a systematic overview and an outline of an eclectic approach, guided by the insights of anthropology and psychoanalysis, into a theory capable of explaining this fascination. After this, we begin our descent into the dark abyss of the imagination that produces monsters in every culture and tradition in the world.

HOW TO APPROACH MONSTERS

Monsters—composite beings, half-human, half-animal—
play a part in the thought and imagery of all people at
all times.

—Rudolf Wittkower, "Marvels of the East:
A Study in the History of Monsters"

 n the study of culture and folklore monsters come to our attention most often as enemies of culture heroes in the various ethnic traditions, both past and present. Mythologists like Joseph Campbell and others (Gould 1969; Holiday 1973; D. Cohen 1970, 1982) have written much about the theme of the Epic Hero who goes out to fight monsters in order to rescue maidens or to save society as a whole. At various times, Campbell writes about the recurrent archetype of both the hero figure and the monster in the world's cultures. He points out that the figure of the monster-tyrant is well known to the mythologies, folk traditions, legends, and even nightmares of the entire world; he adds that the characteristics of these monsters are everywhere "essentially the same." Campbell also notes that the existence of monsters calls forth heroes who must perform the same function the world over, that of clearing the field for humanity. Many monsters remaining from primeval times still lurk in the outlying regions and, through malice or desperation, set themselves against the human community: "They have to be cleared away." The elementary deeds of the hero are clearing of the field of monsters (1968: 15, 337–38).

As the hero's constant and inevitable foil, the monsters of myth share many characteristics. But what *are* these characteristics? And why are they the same across cultural boundaries? How can we conceptualize and analyze this apparent sameness? That the human heroes of myth are so similar is not surprising, given that their mythic function is always to clear the field of dangers. The tales of heroism, too, follow standard narrations and moral lessons: the young champion marches forth, vanquishes monsters in marathon battles, and returns the conquering hero. And of course these champions in whatever culture have more or less the same character more or less: brave, adventurous, confident dragon-slayers or, in Campbell's Freudian view, exalted father-killers. But how are humanity's terrible foes—the evil beasts—conceived, and why do they always oppose order and goodness? Whence springs this *negative*—the brutality, violence, moral deformity, generic horribleness that make monsters so irresistibly interesting?

WHAT MONSTERS HAVE IN COMMON

By what criteria can we envision Campbell's essential sameness? A comparative study of monsters must combine what ethnologists call "cryptozo-oology"—the study of imaginary creatures—(Heuvelmans 1990; Coleman and Clark 1999) with a psychological inquiry into why humanity has a need to create scary visions to instruct and enthrall. A cursory glance at monster lore suggests common features that indeed attest to shared fantasies. These common threads will form the basis of our inquiry, and both a sociocultural and a psychodynamic perspective are necessary.

As we have seen, for most Western observers the monster is a metaphor for all that must be repudiated by the human spirit. It embodies the existential threat to social life, the chaos, atavism, and negativism that symbolize destructiveness and all other obstacles to order and progress, all that which defeats, destroys, draws back, undermines, subverts the human project—that is, the id. As Marina Warner puts it in her aptly titled book *No Go the Bogeyman* (1998), the bogeyman is always the spirit that says no. Yet the monster, in all its guises, is also and paradoxically awe-inspiring, admirable in a perverse way. As depicted in folklore and fiction, terrible monsters are impressive exactly because they break the rules and do what humans can only imagine and dream of. Since they observe no limits, respect no boundaries, and attack and kill without compunction, monsters are also the spirit that says "yes"—to all that is forbidden. There is, obviously, a certain ambivalence here.

There is also a dualism of geography to consider: the *place* of monsters in the landscapes of the mind. In every cultural tradition, monsters are said to live in borderline places, inhabiting an "outside" dimension that is apart from, but parallel to and intersecting the human community. They often live in lairs deep underground, in an unseen dimension as it were, or in watery places like marshes, fens, or swamps. Or else they infest distant wildernesses of which people are afraid, like mountain tops, oceans, gla-

"A Werewolf Attacks a Man." From *Die Emeis* of Johann Geiler von Kaiserberg.

ciers, or jungles. They emerge from these fastnesses at night or during abnormal cosmological events to shake humans from their complacency, appearing in darkness or during storms, earthquakes, famines, or other times of disturbance.

Then, of course, there is the narrative component to consider in the monster's sudden irruption into the world. The typical story of attack shows a recurrent structure, no matter what the culture or setting. As Campbell and many other students of myth have discovered, the story is basically threefold, a repetitive cycle. First, the monster mysteriously appears from shadows into a placid unsuspecting world, with reports first being disbelieved, discounted, explained away, or ignored. Then there is depredation and destruction, causing an awakening. Finally, the community reacts, unites, and, gathering its forces under a hero-saint, confronts the beast. Great rejoicing follows, normalcy returns. Temporarily thwarted by this setback, the monster (or its kin) returns at a later time, and the cycle repeats itself. Formulaic and predictable, the dialectic is predictable to the point of ritualism (Andriano 1999).

The predictable narrative is so widespread in myth, its symbolism so ubiquitous, its moral messages so recurrent, its imagery so consistent, that it is odd (indeed monstrous!) that anthropologists have not followed the lead of other scholars in delving into the subject. As one literary critic writes, "The ubiquity of the monster dictates that its analysis will draw on a wide variety of subject areas, and critical studies of the monstrous reflect this range" (Williams 1996: 17).

RECENT RESEARCH ON MONSTERS

Recently, some postmodern scholars have examined the theme of what they call "the Monstrous" and "Deformed Discourse" in art and fiction. Most of these authorities affirm the above observations in different language but with a modified focus relating to political role. Postmodern research, mainly in Western literature and art, emphasizes the demonization of the "Other" in the image of the monster as a political device for scapegoating those whom the rules of society deem impure or unworthy—the transgressors and deviants (cf. Bann 1994; J. Cohen 1996). Deformed, amoral, unsocialized to the point of inhumanness, the monster in Western fiction, for many post-modern theorists, symbolizes the outcaste, the revolutionary, the pariah. For these theorists, then, the monster can only be seen as symbolizing human threats to Western bourgeois society, all that is subversive of, or threatening to, the prevailing political order: "the inimical other" (Fiedler 1978: 92). From this perspective, too, the impulse to create monsters stems from the need of the majority to denigrate those who are different, be they the lower classes, foreigners, or marginalized deviant groups.

Given the rich trove of political symbolism involved in monster imagery in Western culture, orthodox Marxist scholars have waded in. John Law, a historical sociologist (1991), sees the monster archetype in the European literary tradition (Frankenstein, Dracula, etc.) as symbolizing entrepreneurial capitalism. Such demonic beasts as vampires symbolize the awful energy that sucks the lifeblood from the masses. Restricting their scope to romantic European fiction, Marxists see monsters as symbolizing the anti-human power emanating from the predatory bourgeoisie of Leninist demonology. More explicitly, Marxist theorist Franco Moretti, in an article "The Dialectic of Fear" (1983), speaks of Count Dracula in Bram Stoker's novel as an embodiment of monopoly capitalism. Both are predatory, acquisitive, alien, and parasitical; the sucked blood equates to cash and the monster's depredations to the exploitation of capital. Deformed discourse—the emphasis on hideous misshapen, malformed images—relates them to the supposed deformations and distortions of human nature that capitalism causes in Marxist dogma.

To underscore the simile, Moretti refers to Marx's use of the term *vampiri* in *Das Kapital* to indicate the noxious economic activity of capitalism: "Capital is dead labour which, vampire-like, lives only by sucking living labour, and lives the more, the more labour it sucks" (cited in Grady 1996: 225). So for Marxist thinkers we have a one-to-one symbolism, monsters embodying the death-force of a single form of social and economic organization: late monopoly capitalism. Such a model, while perhaps useful for Victorian Britain, would be hard put to explain the power of the aboriginal Windigo among Native Americans, or the demons of Oceania, places where capitalism postdates monster lore by thousands of years. But then again, to be fair, these Western-confined theorists do not have the luxury of comparative data.

Taking all the above views into consideration is useful in understanding the complexities of monsters; however, my goal in this book is to integrate psychodynamic and social interpretations to gain insight into monsterhood in both capitalist and noncapitalist systems. As we have seen, monsters are universal, as universal as family or incest taboos, occurring in all kinds of societies and under all economic conditions, so the explanation of their role and function cannot be confined to a study of capitalist cultures, late monopoly or otherwise. Given this ubiquity, a Marxist or relativistic social-constructivist approach just does not take us very far.

Furthermore, and just as important, it is clear that no study of monsters and assimilated fantasies can proceed entirely without a psychodynamic referent (Dundes 1998). Assessing the powerful emotional tone always associated with monsters, the critic Rosemary Jackson argues that when people make up fanciful, dreamlike images, especially of monsters and demons, they are in fact recombining pieces of empirical reality, not inventing from scratch (1981: 6). The deformations imply repressed experience and the operation of unconscious processes, if only because of the energy imparted in creating the distortions and recombinations. These creative processes in turn, because they infuse reality with fantasy images, indicate a psychic dimension. "Fantasy in literature," she notes, "deals so blatantly and repeatedly with unconscious material that it seems rather absurd to understand its significance without reference to psychoanalysis and psychoanalytic readings of texts." It could not be put any more succinctly or persuasively.

Indeed, since Freud's time, we have come to know the monster of the imagination as not simply a political metaphor, but also a projection of some repressed part of the self. Whether the repressed part is called the id, Thanatos, animus, anima, or instinct, whether it encapsulates the repudiated wish or the sense of guilt, the monster of the mind is always the familiar self disguised as the alien Other. Accepting this advice to look within as well as without is not only logical but also ignored at peril. We can point out that folktales, myths, and other cultural productions, including public events such as rituals and rites, are, as semioticians have advised us, also symbolic texts—animated ones to be sure in the case of rituals and films, but still symbolic texts expressing inner feelings and fantasies. Understanding cultural texts and formulas also requires an awareness of depth psychology. A psychoanalytic approach is unavoidable in any serious approach to monster lore.

PRELIMINARY THEORETICAL FRAMEWORK

Accepting that a view both "outside" and "inside" the self is unavoidable in studying monsters, the approach I take here, then, will be a broadly eclectic one. I will open my study with a preliminary analytical framework of three major theorists: Sigmund Freud, Victor Turner, and Mary Douglas. There will of course be other thinkers to be considered, especially theorists of ritual like René Girard and Timothy Mitchell, and I will naturally make modifications when dealing with the ideas of theorists mentioned above. No one interpretation can claim pride of place.

As for Freud, psychoanalysis furnishes us with useful models of sublimation, projection, and displacement as tools for approaching the construction of monstrous images from human experiences. I realize Freud has been much criticized lately for theoretical positions at odds with current understandings, but here I am adopting his methods rather than standard psychoanalytic tenets. With the analytical tools Freud has given us, we can effectively conceptualize the psychic mechanisms at work in the creation and scene-setting of monster imagery. Freud's notion of "dreamwork," proposed long ago in *The Interpretation of Dreams* (1900), furnishes a workable model for analyzing the unconscious processes of visualization and objectification, and of condensation and symbolization, that figure prominently in the transformation of emotional states into pictorial tropes. Freud writes that the dream conflates and combines perceived images into one superimposed structure.

He explains it this way: the dream works by means of unification, "in which a 'collective figure' can be produced for the purposes of dream-condensation by uniting the actual features of two or more people into a single dream-image." For Freud, the visual collage, or collective image, physically juxtaposes, rather in the manner of a double-exposed photograph, two or more people into one person (or two or more objects into a single object). In the same way, the horrific fusion figure, the monster, is produced by a process of superimposition in the imagination, or on film as the case may be, of distinct types of beings into a grotesque and bizarre composite, which as we have seen is one of the criteria of all monsters.

Applying these ideas to fantasy and nightmare imagery, Freud's follower Ernest Jones provides some further insights to this phenomenon. Adhering strictly to psychoanalytic orthodoxy, Jones sees imaginary monsters as representing the primary sadistic eroticism of the infant. The inevitable cannibalism and fear of being eaten (which we have noted above is virtually synonymous with monster behavior) reflect primitive oral aggression, and the monster's fierce, unbridled power mixes erotic and hostile impulses (1971: 151). For Jones, monster imagery in fiction and fantasy is a dream-like manifestation of id forces, particularly sexual sadism, in visual and scenographic terms.

So far, so good. Beyond this modest and unobjectionable observation, however, but still in a strictly Freudian sense, we may add that the monster may stand for the Olympian castrating father of fantasy, and so the hero-myth simply works as an allegory for the Oedipal conflict in which the recurrent cannibal imagery serves as a metaphor for castration displaced to the entire body. As critic Leslie Fiedler notes, virtually all folklores of origins have a tribe of "monstrous patriarchal giants" who must be killed off by their children for humanity to survive (1978: 93). We will see this Oedipus-writ-large scenario ad infinitum in the mythologies of the early civilizations with heroes like Marduk, Seth, Thor, and so on. These culture heroes are always *young* warriors (sons); they always vanquish *old* and ancestral ogres, giants, dragons, and the like, many of which are depicted, like parents, as remnants from some distant past when the earth was young, that is, during the *infancy* of the human race. It seems, then, that there is no way getting around monster = Oedipus equation in pictorial form, as Campbell and other mythologists insist. But of course there is much more to it than a simple animation of universal symbols.

Although orthodox Freudianism can become reductionistic, psychoanalysis does permit us to appreciate the moral ambiguities and affective ambivalence of the nightmare images we are contemplating here. As projections of inner conflicts, these terrible images reflect both repressed desire and their opposites: guilt, awe, and dread in which the person feels both violent repudiation and a desperate empathy, as the monster inhabiting the dark dream inspires both terror and identification (as does the mutilating Oedipal father in classical psychoanalytic theory). The recurrent reappearance of the monster also brings to mind classic psychoanalytic notions of repetition compulsion, expiation, paranoia, and nemesis. The monster is so powerful an image, so universal, and so imbued with the Oedipal developmental cycle in all humans that it may even represent an autonomous instinct or drive.

Taking all the above into account, one may indeed argue that the monster that frightens the child and always returns in dreams and fantasies represents simultaneously an incarnation of the punishing superego and id forces which the child both identities with and struggles against. In this dualistic, contradictory, and starkly ambivalent sense, the monster represents an amalgam of opposing psychic energies, not just id but an alliance between id and super-ego. Surrounding the threatened ego, the composite monster unites the chaotic danger of the id and the punishing superego, the alpha and omega of the mental apparatus.

ANTHROPOLOGICAL APPROACHES: ETHNO-MONSTROSITY

If psychoanalysis is indispensable for capturing intrapsychic dynamics of monsterhood in all its Technicolor complexity and richness, then cultural anthropology furnishes us with the complementary heuristic tools for conceptualizing its cultural implications. In *Purity and Danger* (1966), anthropologist Mary Douglas provides an enlightening viewpoint on the relevance of monster imagery to group belief and behavior, especially in the community culture of tribal peoples.

Working with ethnographic concepts of danger and "un-naturalness," Douglas correlates notions of pollution and terror with the transgression or overthrow of established cultural categories. In her terminology, conceptually anomalous constructs like monsters, as well as anomalous but harmless animal species, hermaphrodites, or organic deformities, are "interstitial," by which she means existing between and in contrast to normally existing categories. Because they conflate or collapse cognitive boundaries recognized as the foundations of order, such deviations are frightening. They are frightening for many reasons: not just because of their ugliness and unfamiliarity, but also because they challenge the moral and cosmological order of the universe. Because they do this they are taboo—invested with magically destructive powers. /

Additionally, the focus Douglas puts on categorical schemes suggests a means to account for the usual emphasis on the monster as "un-natural," threatening, and impure, and consequently for its relevance to propitiation or expiation in community folklore, belief, and, as we will see later, in rituals. Abnormal and anomalous, the monsters of the mind violate the established taxa people use for basic understandings of nature. Ontologically intermediary, neither fish nor fowl, they do not fit into the mental scheme people rely on to explain the world. Being thus inexplicable, monsters are not only physically but cognitively threatening: they undermine basic understandings. By smashing distinctions, monsters offer a threat to the culture's very integrity as an intellectual whole, or more precisely to the assumption that such distinctions can de drawn in the first place (Uebel 1996: 266). In other words, monsters expose the radical permeability and artificiality of all our classificatory boundaries, highlighting the arbitrariness and fragility of culture.

Other anthropologists have also noticed the importance of mental monsters and their role in the philosophical and linguistic structures of pre-literate peoples. For example, in a cross-cultural study of lexical and faunal categorizations, British anthropologist Edmund Leach writes that the imposition of order in socialization leaves "certain objects in interstices of categories," that is, abnormalities that fall into the cracks of belief systems (1982: 4). Such inevitable anomalies include the sacred, deformities, and supernatural monsters. As deformed mirrors reflecting fears and anxieties, such anomalies, Leach proposes (presaging Douglas), offer a richly variant perspective into the cultural order.

All this gives us a clue why monster effigies are so useful in folklore and in community rituals when people gather to share stories and experiences. Transcending normal limits and domains, the monster-figure appears to be invincible or unstoppable; embodied as a giant beast, it becomes a perfect metaphor not only for the limitless power of evil, but also for dissolving of the boundaries that separate us from chaos (Fernandez 1986). The monster then represents all that is beyond human control, the uncontrollable and the unruly that threaten the moral order—a metonymy that seems psychologically acceptable to audiences both young and old. This fits into

Douglas's claim that culturally impure objects are generally taken to be invested with magical powers as "taboo" objects, and, as a result, are often employed in rituals as objects of both veneration and persecution (see also Carroll 1990: 34).

VICTOR TURNER: OBJECTIFICATION IN RITUAL

At this point, we pause to consider the role of monstrous images in the folk rituals we will later explore. The object here is to compare these rites with their dragons and demons to monster imagery elsewhere and to ascertain the common narrative features in the rituals, imagery, and mythology. And here we must turn to the work of Victor Turner. In his publications on the African Ndembu (1967, 1977), Turner also helps us further understand how ritual works in this model of cultural transgression and danger.

Having studied ceremonies among many societies, Turner argues persuasively that all societies have pressure points or "nodes of affliction" (1967), where internal contradictions and conflicts abound. These inner conflicts in the culture create an uncomfortable uncertainty in people that must be relieved to ensure the smooth functioning of the body politic. By its very nature, culture is also at least partly founded on the repression of instinct, and the resulting discontent bubbles beneath the outwardly calm surface. Basing his ideas on pioneering work on rites of passage by Arnold Van Gennep (1960), Turner argues that rituals and rites perform the function of relieving these tensions in pre-industrial societies (and in industrial ones, too). The performance of a ritual presents the people with a *liminal* time—a temporal punctuation in everyday reality, a conceptual "time out"—when the people can work out and reconcile these ambivalent or contradictory tendencies and impulses in their culture. At such times, new and unexpected formulations emerge out of the people's unconscious and take on monstrous forms that contradict and subvert reality. Turner writes that the power of liminality is to be found in its release from normal constraints, making possible the deconstruction of the normal constructs of common sense, ordinary objects are transformed into novel creations, some of them bizarre to the "point of monstrosity" (1977: 68).

From this perspective, the creation of monstrosities, recombinants, anomalies, and so on frees humans from their day-to-day location in the world of common sense. In the act of recreation of elements of the world, the weird recombinants permit visionary experiences and insights into both the world and the self. Monsters and dragons are compounded from various *discriminata* of the culture, each of them originally an element in the common sense construction of the social reality. In a sense they have the pedagogical function of stimulating people's powers of analysis and revealing to them the building blocks from which their hitherto taken-for-granted world has been constructed. In a way they reveal the freedom of the imagination, the free play of humanity's cognitive capacities. Monster construction encourages creativity, synthesis, and art as well as analysis (1977: 69). It is from this mental ferment, as the French philosopher Gilbert Lascault (1973: 102) has suggested, comes the *bricolage* (Claude Lévi-Strauss's term for inventive scavenging) that creates the monster out of scraps of reality.

This is the same cognitive process, turned inside out, that interprets and evaluates the strictures of the known world and the self. As monster maven Jeffrey Cohen explains it, the monster is never created out of nothing, but rather through a process of fragmentation and imaginative recombination in which elements are extracted from various forms in nature and then reassembled as an entity that can then claim autonomous existence in consciousness (1996: 11).

The somewhat simplified account above of Douglas and Turner points us in some interesting directions. We can see that monsters are both interstitial (Douglas) and liminal (Turner); as such they are conveniently concrete and animistically embodied as visibly organic *things* that by their very weirdness impinge strongly and unforgettably upon our consciousness.

RITUAL VIOLENCE

The final leg of my model derives from the work of French theorist René Girard, who in his masterful book *Violence et le sacré* (*Violence and the Sacred*, 1972) makes an important distinction between "original violence" and "ritual violence." This can help us better understand the role of symbolic violence in the relation of monster to community. In ritualized violence, such as occurs in gothic fiction, horror movies, and village festivals, the hypothetical *victime émissaire* (scapegoat or sacrificial victim) acts as a symbolic target for the therapeutic displacement of pent-up aggressions. Girard calls the ritual monster or devil a "mimetic creature," that is, a mythical being which symbolizes evil in order to cleanse the society of its own guilt and terror. The process of converting feelings into effigies is what Girard refers to as "projection, polarization, and magico-persecutory thought," a psychological model for ritual scapegoating that Hispanicist

Timothy Mitchell uses effectively in his study of symbolic violence in Spanish folklore and rites, and which we will also incorporate into our analysis of rituals.

In a series of publications, Mitchell shows how in Spanish ceremonies, violence is turned into a two-way street, with the community both potential victim and victimizer (1988, 1990, 1991). A similar process occurs in the *corrida* (bullfight), where the *toro bravo*, or fighting bull, the official stand-in for violence and chaos, both attacks and is attacked. Like the fighting bull, the ritualized monster is feared, hated, admired, and beloved all at the same time.

HOW TO APPROACH MONSTERS? CAREFULLY

To conclude: in the chapters that follow we will take a look at horrible monsters as they appear in various cultural contexts from prehistoric Europe to aboriginal North America. We start with a historical overview of monster lore in Western culture in antiquity and the Christian era. Then we move on to preliterate societies, including aboriginal North and South America, Asia, and Oceania, where ogres and cannibal giants reign. Then we turn to slightly more domesticated ritualized monsters in Spain and to a lesser extent in France, especially the Tarasca, the serpent-dragon of Corpus Christi. Finally, we attempt to place all this fearsome material in single perspective and to derive some conclusions about what monsters mean.

MONSTERS IN THE WEST, I
The Ancient World

When, on the road to Thebes, Oedipus met the Sphinx,
who asked him her riddle, his answer was: man. *This*
simple word destroyed the monster. We have many mon-
sters to destroy. Let us think of Oedipus' answer.
—*George Seferis, Nobel Prize Acceptance Speech, 1963*

onster lore in the West shows change and flux from the earliest times, as one would expect, but there is also continuity under the surface. By West I mean the European-derived traditions including those of the Americas: what is commonly referred to as the Occident. For current purposes, however, I will include the Middle East, for this is the cradle of the Judeo-Christian tradition from which much of Western mythology derives.

From its earliest stirrings in the archaic cultures of Europe and the Middle East, an "innate awe of the monster" (Wittkower 1942: 197) shines forth like a beacon in Western religions, philosophy, literature, art, and, perhaps most brilliantly, in folklore. Taking the standard chronological markers—prehistoric, ancient, medieval, Renaissance, modern—we can trace the development of monster imagery, observing both change and continuity. The current chapter explores ancient times from the Paleolithic to the Roman Empire; the next chapter covers the Christian era.

PREHISTORY: CAVE IMAGES

Monsters in Europe are as old as humanity itself. Before emerging from a world of illusion and enchantment into one of science, our ancestors needed some way to rationalize the forces of nature that threatened them as well as a way of mastering the frightening forces within. From the earliest times, Western peoples seized upon the most obvious metaphor for explaining the power of the unknown by attributing it to superhuman creatures combining the most frightening traits of members of the animal kingdom, including the most frightful, man himself (Daniel 1964: 44).

As noted in the previous chapter, monstrous images make their appearance along with the advent of modern humanity in Europe, a critical threshold approximately 30,000 years ago. This onset marks the beginning of what archaeologists call the Upper Paleolithic, a chronological coincidence that attests dramatically to the innate awe of monsters that Wittkower speaks of. According to Paleolithic art historian André Leroi-Gourhan (1982: 54–55), "monstrous forms" decorate the walls of prehistoric caves throughout southern France and Spain. These strange visual forms begin to appear in the early Magdalenian period (approximately 25,000–20,000 years ago) just after the advent of *Homo sapiens* in western Europe, that is, when people like ourselves appear and replace the Neanderthals. This is indeed the dawn of humanity as we know it in Europe.

Some of these drawings and scratchings on cave walls (called parietal art), well as a few sculpted objects scattered about (mobiliary art) may have expressed primitive people's awe of man-eating wild animals and the inimical forces of nature. But the parietal images tend to recombine such natural forms in bizarre and imaginative ways, showing an aesthetic inventiveness indicating some degree of visual dexterity in expressing fantasies symbolically as living creatures. These austere figures, although rare compared to naturalistic depictions of game animals like bison and elk, are nevertheless numerous and widespread throughout cave dwellings. In both pictures and in sculptural representations, monstrous images are in fact a constant in visual art in the Upper Paleolithic (Leroi-Gourhan 1982: 54).

Leroi-Gourhan believes that such forms, because of their very ambiguous and undoubtedly symbolic nature, represent the first evidence of the metaphysical side of the human imagination. They are therefore of supreme importance in understanding our psychological origins—our very nature as a thinking animal. Many composite figures in the French caves have the human body as a kind of base to which are attached animal appendages or antlers and horns; some have animal heads (the bison-man at the cave of Le Gabillou, for example, and a half-reindeer carved into on a stone at La Madeleine). Another parietal image shows a distorted human face with an curious animal-like snout (in the cave at Les Combarelles).

One most extraordinary humanoid monster is a drawing at the Pergouset site in France that shows what appears to be a human body with the head replaced by a snake-like tube emerging from the shoulders. The cave wall

The "sorcerer" of Trois-Frères, cave painting, 12,000–10,000 B.C. Author's drawing after Campbell (1968), plate VII.

in the area of this odd figure is literally covered with what Leroi-Gourhan (55) calls monstrous engravings: an amoeba-like figure somewhat reminiscent of the tube-headed human, and superimposed upon this a vaguely head-shaped figure of unclear meaning. Close to this assemblage is a large quadruped-like creature with a very long neck topped with a head quite like that of a horse or deer. Similar images with a simpler head can be seen the in the nearby caves of Altxerri and Le Gabillou and in caves in adjacent parts of France.

These are intriguing visual images, but they are ambiguous. Probably the first instance of what we can call a true monster, adhering to the criteria spelled out in the previous chapter, is the so-called sorcerer of the Trois-Frères cave site in the French Pyrenees. This mysterious polychrome shows some kind of half-man, half-beast creature, with staring, glowering eyes, powerful looking humanoid legs, and a weird head bearing horns or antlers (Lascault 1973: 94). The figure also displays a very prominent penis. What the meaning of this and other painted cryptomorphs might be, and what social or religious function they served in prehistory, is anybody's guess. Possibly they represented some kind of primitive hunting magic or pictoform propitiation. But despite the acknowledged ambiguity of form and function, the beast of Trois-Frères shows that imaginary beings combining human and animal elements are among the concepts to be rendered from human consciousness as visual notations.

For Leroi-Gourhan the troglodyte images prove that early people were like us in their capacity for symbolic thought. Like us, the stone-age hunters must have had the ability to imagine impossible combinations and to create such ideas as images. There may also have been an element of fear or religious awe involved. It seems indeed that such an psychological process is the very definition of *Homo sapiens* as an imagining species. Arguing just this point, Leroi-Gourhan concludes his discussion of cave art by saying that images of monsters provide evidence for a true creative impulse. These weird cave productions

shed some light on the imaginary in their period. If it were necessary to defend the attitude of artists toward symbolic thought, and to prove that they possessed oral traditions of the fantastic, then the monsters would be suitable for providing useful evidence. (55)

MONSTERS IN THE CRADLES OF CIVILIZATION

If monsters arise at the dawn of humanity, along with symbolic thought itself, they flourish with the first ancient civilizations, evolving into a rich bestiary by the time of the Pharaohs. In fact one may say that monsters are more than incidental in the rise of literate culture; even more, monsters have a critical and fundamental role to play in the rise of civilization itself, not only in Europe and the Middle East, but everywhere.

Art historian Heinz Mode (1973) has shown that monster-like beings crop up in the very earliest formative civilizations as integral components of the mental schemes that underlay the developing social order. Pictures and sketches of eerie composite creatures occur in the earliest fragments of religious art in both ancient Egypt and Mesopotamia, and in some cases as descriptions in written form as well, as for example in the Sumerian epics, which are full of dragons, hairy ape-men, and assorted goblins of the sort we will see repeated through human history. These Ur-monsters are actively engaged, albeit in a negative way, in the formation of the world.

Possibly the earliest examples of true monster art in plastic form that have come down to us are the Egyptian sphinxes. These proliferate wildly in classical antiquity. A primordial symbol (indeed, Nietzsche called the sphinx "the symbol of symbolism"), it is usually presented as a composite beast with a woman's head atop a mélange of dangerous animal parts, often with lion's claws or eagle's talons. It always looks fierce and forbidding, often guarding some treasure or sacred object. In ancient times there were numerous kinds of sphinxes. The most familiar was the androsphinx, a lion with a human head, usually female. A close cousin was the criosphinx, a ram-headed lion. Another variant, the hierocosphinx, was a hawk-headed lion, also formidable (South 1987: xxxi). Sphinxes occur in rich abundance in Egyptian painting and statuary by the third millennium B.C., the huge statue guarding the Great Pyramids being the most famous. They also flourish in the Middle East, in Assyria and Babylonia for example, and in neighboring areas of Asia, where they adorn statuary and architecture.

Already imbued with the ambiguity that monsters will demonstrate throughout the ages, not all these sphinxes were represented as malevolent beings in ancient lore. Some, if approached properly, could turn benevolent or be useful to man, guarding buried treasure or assisting in certain tasks such as locating missing objects, thus showing a basic moral ambivalence. However, by a large measure, most of them were dangerous or hostile to man, gratuitously one may say, often quite lethal, some holding entire villages hostage or murdering large numbers of people with abandon (Lehrer and Lehrer 1969). The latter occurs, for example, in the case of the roadside creature that menaces Thebes in the Oedipus legend. This beast poses impossible riddles to passersby and kills them when they fail to answer correctly (for an account of the myth, see Bulfinch 1970: 123–24). Traveler Oedipus of course answered the sphinx correctly, though with unforeseen and tragic consequences. In most such classical sources, sphinxes are depicted not only as dangerous or frightening, but as the very "embodiment of evil" (Scafella 1987: 180).

But such monsters as sphinxes bring forth the necessary heroes to defeat them, and because such heroes make civilization by the example of monster-taming, without the former there would be no civilization at all. In fact, one may say that monsters and heroes arise simultaneously in virtually all the ancient cosmologies as paired twins, indeed as inseparable polarities of a unified system of values and ideas underlying order itself.

Historian Norman Cohn (1993) has written a masterful study of myths of the epic hero in the early Old World cultures from Egypt to the pagan Norse. He shows how in each case local religions—one may say the social system itself, which was buttressed by religion—rested on an allegorical origin-myth of a man battling a monster. In every case a young warrior-god who represents harmony and order as well as nationhood goes forth to battle a "chaos-monster" (as Cohn calls it) that threatens the world. In the aftermath of such

"Oedipus and the Sphinx." Greek amphora, bequest of Mrs. Martin Brimmer. © 2002 Museum of Fine Arts, Boston.

apocalyptic confrontations, civilizations emerge, prosper, and flourish, and humanity takes its rightful place as master of the earth. The monster myths exclaim our ownership over the world and justify the present order.

These ancient hero types are familiar to us; we know them and revere them in legend and in sacred texts. But what about the monsters they fight? How do we know these creatures? Representing the internal and external forces that threaten the world, monsters are indeed curiously alike, almost identical. Their sameness occurs in many dimensions. Let us start with the idea of a form, a morphology. The texts invariably represent monsters as grotesquely repellent, but with a limited pictorial repertory: they are giant, writhing, reptilian creatures, or else they are loathsome half-human hybrids combining the worst of animal features with debased human traits such as cannibalism, wrath, and cruelty. Their lairs, too, are depicted with stunning and dreadful regularity: they inhabit the dark bowels of the earth or dark caves, or else they lurk in deep seas, bottomless lakes, or fens.

Providing dozens of examples of such conceptions with almost routine imagery, Cohn calls this narrative of man-versus-monster the universal "combat-myth" of civilization's origins. He says it is virtually universal as a founding principle. Such a vision underlies each and every ancient civilization as a cosmological starting-point (see also Rose 2000: xxv).

Among the most ancient Egyptians the principal chaos-beast was called Apophis or Apep in the texts. He is depicted as a giant writhing monstrosity. Beyond measurement, he dwells in a dark netherworld and constantly threatens the ordered world with devastation. Apophis is not only monstrously big—literally covering acres of land—but also all-powerful. Indeed, he is god-like in this respect, but his terrible might is used for evil purposes, not for good. He is always described as "he of evil character," and "he of evil appearance" (Cohn 1993: 21).

Confronting this paragon of deviltry is the young Egyptian Seth, the first in a long line of monster-beaters. A warrior above all, Seth battles and finally vanquishes the chaos-monster, saving the kingdom and emerging as history's first monster-slaying, world-preserving hero-god. Seth's monumental struggle with Apophis is a cataclysmic confrontation of good and evil and the subject of a vast celebratory liturgy collected in a work called *The Book of Overthrowing Apophis*, a secret text kept in the royal temple and ostensibly a source of potent magic. It is perhaps the first in a long line of didactic monster-hero literature.

These Egyptian liturgies, probably recited or chanted repetitively, seemed to have been intended for use as a kind of prophylactic, aiming at destroying the primordial monster for good and preventing his reappearance: "He is no more in the land. . . . He is fallen and overthrown," say the scriptures hopefully. The text also instructs on the construction of miniature wax models of the creature, which are then to be ritually destroyed in anxious times. Nevertheless, as in the case of most such terrible monsters, Apophis is not forever killed, despite all this. Like most monsters of the mind, he is immortal and always reemerges to challenge humankind in a never-ending cycle of violence.

But the Egyptians had more monsters than Apophis in their imaginary bestiary. Their monsters and demons came in all shapes and sizes, each one more terrible than the next. Indeed, as the Egyptians saw it, *ma'at* (stability, right order) was perpetually threatened not only by Apophis, but also by legions of smaller spooks dwelling in the abyss under the earth, or lurking in remote badlands or in the deserts or deep waters, and which were collectively the minions of *isfet* (disorder, chaos). From Pharaoh to slave, throughout life and even after death as they navigated the netherworld, each Egyptian was stalked by a whole army of ogres.

One of the most fearsome of the underworld creatures was Amun. He is represented in Egyptian mythology as a monster with a lion's body, the hindquarters of a hippopotamus, and a crocodile's head. Called the "devourer of the dead," Amun ate the hearts of all those who were judged unworthy at the final judgment in the great hall of Osiris. Although they took the monstrous to new pictorial heights, the Egyptians were not alone in their fascination with weird creatures. Their neighbors the Mesopotamians were equally enthralled.

MESOPOTAMIAN MONSTERS

Within the Fertile Crescent, beside the rivers Tigris and Euphrates roughly corresponding to present-day Iraq, two related tribal peoples developed civilization simultaneously around 3000 B.C. In the north were the Sumerians and the south the Akkadians. Around the 1750 B.C. they were united under King Hammurabi into the empire of Babylon; they were later conquered by another people from the north, the Assyrians. Sharing beliefs regarding cosmology, these Mesopotamian peoples confronted a host of chaos-monsters, all wholly devoted to destruction and implacably hostile to mankind, and only held off by the power of their great hero-god, Marduk. The well-known Babylonian epic, the *Emma Elish*, recounts the adventures of the hero Marduk in dealing with these many terrors and defeating them one by one.

Principal among the enemies of mankind faced by the warrior-god was Tiamat, depicted as a female monster and the living spirit of primeval chaos. Reflecting the ambivalence of monster imagery—part god, part demon—she starts out as a creator-goddess. But in the later texts she is portrayed as a composite behemoth rather like the Egyptian Apophis, with a scaly reptilian body, bird's legs and talons, and the horns of a bull (Hogarth and Clery 1979: 15–16). The changeful Tiamat was the tip of a demonic iceberg in Mesopotamia, surrounded on all sides by lesser ogres, gargoyles, and apparitions. Other Babylonian epics tell, for example, how civilization was menaced by teeming hosts of monsters that rose from the primordial sea within the bowels of the earth, endowed with the destructive powers of those chaotic waters.

One of these was Labbu, a gigantic sea beast, said in the myths to be three hundred miles long and thirty miles high. A typical sea monster, cognate to the Hebrew Leviathan, Labbu waded ashore every now and then to devastate the earth, devouring people and animals and frightening even the gods. But it gets worse: the library of the last Assyrian king, Ashurbanipal, includes a list of demons and kinds of demons with their distinctive attributes. Most of them are of Sumerian origin. There is Namtaru: son of Enlil and queen of the netherworld Ereshkigal, he is the messenger of the king of the netherworld Nergal. Then there is a female demon named Lamashtu, a barren and frustrated virgin. She attacks pregnant women and women in labor and kills their babies. She is commonly represented as a naked woman with the head of a lioness and feet like the claws of a bird of prey. The hot wind that brings sandstorms from the desert is the work of another ogre, Pazuzu, who is imagined as a winged monster with four claws and a deformed head (Cohn 1993: 44).

The list goes on and on. Aside from these looming beasts, there were also numerous smaller, human-sized monsters that enjoyed attacking individuals in particular situations—in lonely places, or when asleep, on travels, or in childbirth. Like most monsters worth the name before and since, these smaller Mesopotamian beasties were wont to tear people apart and eat them. As in Egypt, the Babylonians were stalked and plagued by ferocious specters. Vampire-like, legions of Babylonian succubae ripped open people's throats, drank their blood, and devoured their flesh. They dripped deadly poisons from their jagged maws; their razor-sharp claws were polluted and lethal.

Bronze Pazuzu from Iraq, ca. 800–600 B.C. Courtesy The Oriental Institute of The University of Chicago.

OTHER WEST ASIAN TRADITIONS

Between the two great cradles of culture, the Nile and the Fertile Crescent, lay a third cultural nucleus that the Bible calls the land of Canaan and is known to archeologists and historians as the Syria-Palestine area. This land was inhabited by Semitic speakers who were called Canaanites down to about 1200 B.C. and later on referred to as Israelites. In this general area, according to recent archaeological finds, was the metropolis of Ugarit (ca. 1700–1200), situated on the Syrian coast opposite the Mediterranean island of Cyprus. It was a strategically important trade site visited by peoples from the all over the Middle East and the eastern Mediterranean. A large number of Ugaritic myths date from the period between 1380 and 1360. These include rich monster lore.

The main Ugaritic monster was Yam. In a typical ambiguity, however, Yam, like Tiamat was also a spirit of the sea and reflected the sea's unruly and tempestuous nature. Although therefore a kind of god—reflecting once again the duality of chaos-monsters and their ambiguous relationship to humans—Yam was also said to be a destructive chaos-monster like Apophis: a negative force arrayed against order. Hideous and evil, he was depicted as a "wriggling serpent," a "dragon," and a "tyrant with seven heads" (Cohn 1993: 124).

Opposing this formidable spirit stood the stalwart young hero Ba'al. A brave and vigorous god, he was, according to the texts, "the mightiest of heroes," and also possessed of godlike qualities. He was also "he who mounts the clouds," because, like other divine warriors-heroes, he was the god of rain and storm. In the Ugaritic myths, Ba'al recounts his great deed in slaying Yam, boasting:

Did I not destroy Yam . . . ?
Was not the dragon captured [and] vanquished?
I did destroy the wriggling serpent,
the tyrant with seven heads.

Later in the epic poem, Ba'al is himself reminded of his victorious struggle with Yam:

you smote the Leviathan the slippery serpent,
and made an end of the slippery serpent,
the tyrant with seven heads. (cited in Cohn 1993: 124).

The Hebrews also had their monsters, which were again early creations of a mysterious God. In the Old Testament, for instance, we are introduced to the two giant creatures Leviathan and Behemoth, the former a sea monster, the latter terrestrial. Without giving any other description, the Hebrew Bible says:

Behold now behemoth, which I am made with thee; he eateth grass as an ox.
Lo now, his strength is in the loins, and his force is in the navel of his belly.
He moveth his tail like a cedar; this sinews of his stones are together.
His bones are as strong pieces of brass; his bones are like bars of iron. (Job
    40: 13–18)

These biblical verses are the main account for the mysterious Behemoth. In apocryphal literature and Jewish legend, Behemoth is a typical chaos-monster, a negative force of formidable strength, made by God for unfathomable purpose. Expressing the monster-thought so typical of the early civilizations, the word behemoth itself derives from the plural of the Hebrew *b'hemah*, "beast." Like monsters before and after, the scriptural image conflates human destructiveness with animal aggression and raw power. In the apocryphal book of Enoch the two creatures, Behemoth and Leviathan, are described in quasi-human terms as follows:

And in that day will two monsters be separated, a female named Leviathan to dwell in the abyss over the fountains of waters. But the male is called Behemoth which occupies with his breasts an immeasurable desert named Dendain. (cited in Williams 1996: 186)

The two sacred creatures encapsulate monsterdom as two halves of a universal metaphor. Behemoth is the epitome of all land monsters, just as Leviathan is the apotheosis of the sea's terrors. From Leviathan's nostrils comes smoke, from its jaws fire; like those of most sea-serpents, its body is covered with scales. But the source of the creature's monstrosity is its unnatural mixture of elements, earth and water, for while Leviathan is clearly a sea creature, perhaps a fish, it is also a sort of mammal, for it is often depicted suckling its young. The element of bizarre hybridization, organic boundary-crossing, is clearly manifested.

NORTHERN EUROPE

Lagging chronologically in cultural development, northern Europe produced its own set of primal demons much later that the Middle East. But the northern beasts were equally fearsome and omnipresent, and likewise there had to be heroes who were courageous and strong to battle them. Among the Scandinavians, for example, the young god Thor defeated the chaos-beast of Norse lore, a writhing beast called the Midgard serpent. It is described in the Prose Edda saga (thirteenth-century Icelandic texts composed by Snorri Sturluson) as either a giant snake coiled under the earth or a "vast sea monster." The battle is long and furious, but the human once again prevails.

Fresh from his world-preserving victory over this monstrosity, the young Thor then must confront a host of equally satanic minions who rise up to challenge him. These include Hrungnir, an evil giant who challenges the gods, and many other demonic figures, described variously as half-human, half-animal, and usually man-eating. Like their Asian counterparts, the Viking warriors fought monsters as much as they fought men.

The early Celts also had traditions about heroes battling monsters. As in the Norse and Saxon cases, such marvelous feats were the basis of Celtic mythology. The Irish epics are full of the exploits of the hero Finn MacCool. One of his prime attributes is that he vanquished many monsters, great reptiles, and "phantoms," as in following lines from the *Duanaire Finn*:

What fell of monsters by Finn, till doom may not be reckoned: what he
   achieved of battle and of exploits all men cannot number.
He slew the monster of Lough Neagh, and the giant of Glen Smoil, and the
   great reptile of Loch Cuilleann . . .
He slew the serpent of Benn Edair: in battle it could not be mastered: the
   phantom and reptile of Glen Dorche fell by the hand of the prince.
He slew the phantom of Loch Leín, it was a great endeavor to go to subdue
   it: he slew a phantom in Druimcliath, a phantom and a serpent on Loch
   Rígh. (cited in Holiday 1973: 178)

SHARED TRAITS OF ARCHAIC MONSTERS

In compiling all this varied evidence from ancient Greece to Scandinavia, Ireland, China, and beyond, from archaic religion to religion, Cohn notes again and again the basic similarities, the astonishing stylistic and aesthetic and behavioral convergences of both the monsters and the heroes who fight them. The great heroes of the archaic civilizations—Egyptian Seth, Babylonian Marduk, Hindu Indra, Norse Thor—are "all alike," he says, which is perhaps not so surprising since the monster-slaying, world-saving champion would necessarily be braver, more dauntless, and stronger than ordinary men, as well as supremely virtuous. Not much room for variation there. But even more to the point: the monsters likewise "have much in common" (1993: 65). What about the endless parade of similar monsters? Cohn does not elaborate.

The parallels do not stop at conventions of form. An unmistakable genetic component also weaves a connecting thread throughout the corpus. For however awful, repulsive, and inhuman, these chaos-monsters are not unequivocally alien. In fact, in a curious way, the opposite is true. There is a paradoxical connection with humanity: an ambiguous organic link we will see again and again. No matter how grotesque, monsters are our lineal relatives. No matter what their cosmological provenance, the monsters constitute an elder generation to the young heroes who vanquish them. For example, Marduk, the Babylonian warrior-god attacks and, with his mighty thunderbolts, defeats Tiamat, the half-god, half-monster who is his mother (Hogarth 1980: 15). In the Indian Rig Veda, the serpent-monster is described in one verse as the father to the heroes who battle him, who are said to having their own origin "inside" or "within" him (Cohn 1993: 65).

Indeed, virtually all the ancient monster-enemies of mankind are primordial ancestors, conceived as mothers or fathers or both, parental figures who stand in a tormented relationship with the younger generation who overcome them. The same relationship occurs, of course, in the more familiar Greek myths of the Giants and Gorgons, who appear as evil parents, harbor the usual cannibalistic urges, and stand firmly in the path toward civilization.

So consistent is this ancestral theme in the ancient cosmologies we must surmise a common ethnic origin. But such a historical link is not necessary to explain the parallels, because if these myths have so much in common it is a result of expressing the same hopes and fears of human beings since the dawn of history. So, from the earliest moment on, we are confronted with an Oedipal theme: child against parent, monster and human one blood, linked by hatred and violence as well as patrimony—a thread that runs to the present day, as in the case of Dr. Frankenstein and his offspring. But men create monsters from nothing, from thought. So who is father to whom?

CLASSICAL ANTIQUITY: GREECE AND ROME

Ubiquitous in the early civilizations, monsters reach an apogee in classical antiquity, especially among the Greeks. Indeed the pictorial and literary representation of monsters was to reach its apex in the classical age, in the Aegean world influenced by Greece and to a slightly lesser extent in the Roman possessions, after thousands of years, during which time the Hittite, Phoenician, Syrian, Cretan, and Mycenaean civilizations all kept monster mythology alive. So common were representations of monsters in the ancient world, both in visual art and in literature, poetry, and song, that many ancients made fun of their countrymen's obsessions with them. For example, Lucian in his *True History* and Horace in his *Ars Poetica* both derided the contemporary taste for monsters, as did the art critic Vitruvius in various writings (see Mode 1973: 10–11).

In the classical Mediterranean world, monsters first appear in literary form in the Homeric legends, by 700 B.C. (possibly earlier), perhaps derived from Semitic prototypes, and they immediately proliferate into the richest reparatory of perhaps any ancient civilization. One of the first pictorial representations we have from Greece is a vase painting dating from around 550 B.C., depicting Heracles battling against the so-called "Monster of Troy," from whose fearsome jaws the hero rescues the maiden Hesione (Mayor 2000: 157). Already venerable by the eighth century, the Monster of Troy legend repeats the threefold narrative discussed earlier concerning the manner of the monster's interaction with humanity.

In this case, the fearsome giant suddenly appears off the coast of Troy after a flood, preying upon farmers, whom it catches and devours, in the neighborhood of the port of Sigeum. In a typical twist, often repeated in monster lore, Hesione, the king's daughter, is offered by way of propitiation, but instead the hero Heracles arrives in time to kill it and set the princess free. The monster shows the usual characteristics: immense in size, hideous in appearance, destructive, and innately malevolent.

The Greek vase painting depicts Heracles and Hesione in confrontation with the monster depicted anatomically in skeletal form, she throwing stones, he shooting arrows. As the painting clearly shows, two of her projectiles have hit home, one just under the eye and another lodged in the creature's dreadful, snapping jaw; one of the hero's arrows projects from the jaw as well. The whole montage has a nightmare quality, due to the sketchily ambiguous, specter-like representation of the beast. The Monster of Troy is the first in a long line of Greek fantasy monsters.

The "Monster of Troy," Greek vase painting, ca. 550 B.C. Courtesy Boston Museum of Fine Arts, Helen and Alice Colburn Fund.

Although probably deriving such fantasy figures from the horrific Middle Eastern prototypes discussed above, it was the Attic Greeks who gave the most lasting visual forms to people's innate fascination with evil and who expressed in most striking pictorial forms the horrors of man's nightmares. The myriad Greek monsters that follow are often the offspring of humans with animals or the product of human wickedness. Carrying such sins upon them, they represented the dark side of the classical pagan imagination, the thanatotic (death-drawn), as against the erotic fantasies in the age before Christianity. For the Greeks, monsters were made by the gods to horrify, persecute, and bedevil humans, and most of all to represent the ineluctable evils of human existence. Monster and man were eternal neighbors, metaphorically intertwined in ambiguous ways.

A GREEK CRYPTO-BESTIARY

The inventory of Greek monsters is indeed a virtually endless category. The most familiar are known to every schoolchild who has studied classical mythology. The briefest list would include the following. There were the Tritons, half-human sea beasts; the Satyrs and Silenoi, lustful goat-men who waylaid innocent maidens; the Centaurs, frisky half-horse, half-man hybrids, depicted as oversexed if not necessarily evil; serpents; and of course the terrible Minotaur of Crete, a cursed creature with a bull's head and horns, the hideous fruit of miscegenation of woman and god, who demanded sacrificial maidens to slake his lust. But there were thousands more, of every shape, size, and sex. Here we name just a few figuring prominently in classical mythology in alphabetical order.

The Basilisk is depicted as a malignant serpent with gnashing teeth who killed people with a glance. Its eyes shot out death-dealing rays. Pliny describes the Basilisk in his *Natural History*, written in Rome in A.D. 77, as follows:

It routs all snakes with its hiss, and does not move its body forward in manifold coils like the other snakes but advancing with its middle raised high. It kills bushes not only by its touch but also by its breath, scorches up grass and bursts rocks. Its effect on other animals is disastrous: it is believed that once one was killed with a spear by a man on horseback and the infection rising through the spear killing not only the rider but also the horse. Yet to a creature so marvelous as this—indeed kings have often wished to see a specimen when safely dead— the venom of weasels is fatal: so fixed is the decree of nature that nothing shall be without its match. (1971, 8. xxxiii)

Just as terrible was the Chimera, a title that has come down to us in English to mean a nonexistent thing, a mirage. The Chimera was a composite beast with eagle's wings, green eyes, and a dragon's tail described by Bulfinch as "a fearful monster, breathing fire" (1970: 124). Then there was the Geyron, a monster-giant eventually killed by Heracles in Tartessus near present-day Cadiz in Spain. Next was the exotic Griffon, or Gryphon, a powerful hybrid beast with a vulture's beak, white wings, red paws, and a blue neck. Its claws were said to be so large that people made them into drinking cups. The Greeks believed the Gryphon to dwell in the east, mainly India, and to guard gold treasure. Then there were the Gorgons, a race of homicidal giants, one of whom, a female, was Medusa the snake-haired. The Greeks also feared the Hecatoncheires, or "hundred handed." These were gigantic ogres with fifty heads and one hundred arms, each of great strength. Equally bizarre was the Hydra, a reptile with nine heads, each with a razor-toothed mouth, also killed by Heracles. The Hydra's monstrosity consisted not only in its multi-cephalic nature but also in its promiscuous mingling of realms sea and earth, and, in Homer, its ability to grow back its nine heads when lopped off by humans, and therefore to escape death.

As classicist Adrienne Mayor points out in her study of ancient crypto-morphology (2000: 196–97), many giant monsters were supposed to be multi-headed and many-mouthed like the Hydra and the Hecatoncheires, conforming to a widespread contemporary belief in a motif of anatomical superfluity denoting superhuman powers. In addition, most of these crypto-morphs embody the motif of mixed animal and human features or of blended animal traits, also indicating the composite nature of monsters in general in ancient cosmology. The emphasis on the monster's mouth is a common motif and which requires its own formal analysis.

Another composite in Greece mythology was the manticore. It had the body of a red lion, a human face, three rows of teeth in each jaw, a fatal sting like a scorpion's in the end of the tail, and poisoned spines along the tail that could be shot, like arrows, in any direction. Some classical monsters were fierce giants rather than composites, for example, the great python Aksar, which was said to be sixty cubits long, and the monstrous weasel Pastinaca, which killed trees by its powerful smell (Cawson 1995: 6).

Some Greek monsters were entirely airborne or part avian. The Stym-phalian birds were giant, death-dealing creatures. Their huge beaks and claws were made of hardest brass, and they could shoot their feathers as if they were arrows. In some accounts, these misshapen birds are described as vicious man-eaters, vampire-like. It was one of Heracles's twelve labors to rid the lake Stymphalus of these monstrous birds. Another multi-cephalic ogre was Typhoeus, a fire breathing dragon with a hundred heads that never rested. And, lest we forget, the first werewolf was an ancient Greek, an accursed soul named Lycaon, who tears up the scenery in the fable by Ovid and from whom we get the term *lycanthropy*, or werewolfery (J. Cohen 1996: 12–13).

Still other Greek monsters were amphibious or water-dwellers. In ancient times, the lakes, ponds, and rivers as well as the deep seas were full of demonic creatures. Among the many water monsters was the dragon of Chios, a huge sea beast that terrorized the island of that name, eating peo-ple and cattle. Another marine terror was the so-called sea monster of Ethiopia, killed by the hero Perseus in the rescue of the princess Androm-eda and subject of a famous Renaissance painting by Piero di Cosimo.

Perseus Liberating Andromeda, by Piero di Cosimo (1462–1521), detail. Courtesy Uffizi Palace, Florence. Art Resource, NY.

Not all Greek monsters were represented as male. In fact a large proportion of the theriomorphic creatures were specifically depicted as female. For example the snake-haired Medusa turned men to stone with a look. Just one of many, the Medusa was joined by various kinds of lamias, sharp-clawed sphinx-like creatures with a woman's upper body who attacked men and boys and sucked their blood. The lamias were said to inhabit all the deep forests and woods of the ancient world. But perhaps the most fearsome female monsters of all were the sea-dwelling Scylla and Charybdis. Living under the waves in the Strait of Messina, off the coast of Sicily, these two female scourges dragged down sailors making the crossing. Charybdis was represented as a man-eating, gigantic virago who pulled down whole ships in her maw. Her cohort, Scylla, blasted ships and sailors with her six dog's heads, nine rows of sharp devouring teeth and twelve muscular legs.

To further bedevil mankind, there were the Harpies and Furies, also presented as distinctly and disturbingly female. In Greek lore, the Harpies were foul-smelling half-human, half-bird women who attacked travelers, stole their food, and befouled everything they touched. In the Aeneid, Virgil's hero describes the harpies as the worst of the Stygian monsters:

No monster is more terrible than the Harpies, no plague, no wrath of the gods
more dire, surging upwards from the Stygian waters. They are birds with the
faces of young girls. Disgusting filth comes from their stomachs; their hands
have claws and they are always pale from hunger. . . . Suddenly, with a fearful
swoop from the mountains, they are upon us, and with a loud clang they flap
their wings, plunder the feast, making every dish filthy with their dirty hands;
with the foul stench comes a hideous scream. (cited in Rowland 1987: 156)

There were still other female monsters. Similar in appearance and foul-
ness to the Harpies were the Furies, also called Erinyes (meaning the
"angry ones"). These were three hag-like creatures who have the head of a
dog, snakes for hair and bat wings; they persecuted and pursued all those
poor souls whom the gods wished to torment. Like the sphinxes, Medusa,
and the Sirens, who also had birdlike qualities mixed with female traits, the
Harpies and Furies rained death and destruction everywhere. They were
psychopomps who carried off the soul to the underworld, the personifica-
tion of human guilt and fear.

Completing the picture of a dangerous world were specifically male figures, often with a bestial, satyr-like sexuality. These animalistic, hyper-
masculine spirits cavorted in woods and attacked passersby, raping females
and killing men. Then there were the Cyclops, a race of giant one-eyed cannibals living on remote islands in the Aegean. The most famous of these was
Polyphemus, who was blinded by Odysseus in the Homeric tale after eating a number of Odysseus's men. Satyrs, centaurs, and various other
zoomorphic combinations populated Greek myths and folklore. These
could be of either sex, but were usually presented as male and as both malicious and egregiously lustful.

A WORLD FULL OF MONSTERS

Greek travelers to foreign lands often came back with reports of dragons
and other fantastic monsters that they had personally witnessed, especially
in modern-day Turkey and India, adding to illusions and fears held by Hel-
lenes of foreign lands. One of these travelers was Apollonius of Tyana, an
explorer and naturalist, who traveled from Asia Minor to the southern
foothills of the Himalayas in the first century A.D. According to Philostra-
tus, who compiled a bibliography of Apollonius based on the sage's lost let-
ters and manuscripts, on his return to Greece he reported that the Asian
countryside was full of dragons and that "no mountain ridge was without
one" (cited in Mayor 2000: 130).

Trophies of these and other dragon quests were displayed for all to see in an unidentified city the Greeks called Paraka (possibly present-day Peshawar in Pakistan): "In the center of that city are enshrined a great many skulls of dragons," Apollonius assures us, according to Mayor (2000: 131). Rather than being purely imaginary, these dragon remains were probably the bones of extinct megafauna such as the large giraffe Giraffokeryx and the colossal Siratherium, a moose-like quadruped as big as an elephant and carrying massive antlers.

Instead of dismissing these beings as silly fables, many Greek authors wrote copiously about them, taking them quite seriously. Most authorities corroborated their existence with whatever evidence they could muster. Apparently, there was a need to believe in them even among the otherwise skeptical. For example, an early philosopher, Empedocles of Acragas (Sicily), who died in 432 B.C., wrote at length deploring the literal belief in monster myths and folktales in general among his countrymen. Yet, despite his doubtfulness in other matters of myth, in one passage in his surviving works, Empedocles discusses the existence of such creatures as described above, and decides that they are, or were, quite real.

Empedocles writes that in the infancy of humanity nature brought forth all manner of such weird hybrids, "endowed with all sorts of shapes, wondrous to behold . . . such as human-headed oxen and ox-headed humans" (cited in Mayor 2000: 215–16). Like most Greeks and Romans, this scholar apparently accepted all the monster stories as real, yet at the same time he disputed the Olympian myths about gods and derring-do. "It is hard to escape the conclusion that Empedocles was here seeking to provide a scientific explanation of composite creatures like minotaurs, centaurs, and so on, which featured so heavily in mythology," writes Susan Blundell, a historian of ancient philosophy at University College, London (1986: 41). Another classical scholar, W. K. C. Guthrie, concurs with this assessment: the Greek philosopher "was always glad to show that his . . . system accounted for phenomena known or believed in by his countrymen" (1965: 205).

The Romans and their subject peoples were equally enthralled by weird beings. As an example of the appeal of monster myths, Empedocles's work was taken up later by the first-century B.C. Roman naturalist Lucretius, who was an otherwise rational and scientific observer. Seriously considering the issue of monsters, Lucretius resuscitated and refined Empedocles's theory of extinct monsters in his own work, *On the Nature of Things*. In this massive tome, he repeats his predecessors' belief that nature has indeed produced "many monsters of manifold forms" (cited in Mayor 2000: 216).

So full of monsters was classical culture, and so pervasive the belief among otherwise skeptical philosophers in the Mediterranean world, that classicist Adrienne Mayor decided there must be some rational basis for the obsession. She spent some time researching the matter and found some justification for this idea in classical archaeology. Her book *The First Fossil Hunters* (2000) shows conclusively that the Greeks and later the Romans based many of their visual images on the megafaunal fossils they observed around the shores of the Mediterranean Sea. Because of local geological conditions in the Mediterranean basin, many huge bones of dinosaurs and of extinct mega-mammals like elephants and giant bears were visible to the naked eye, literally sticking out of promontories and quarries. Since these morphologically anomalous remains could not be identified with any living animals, the Greeks took them as evidence of the extinct monsters they so fervidly believed in.

The example Mayor uses as the starting point in her study is the Monster of Troy depicted on the vase discussed above. The picture resembles nothing so much as a fossil skull of a giant Miocene giraffe that flourished in the Mediterranean area, the Samotherium. Indeed, it is in the vase painting as a large animal skull eroding out of an rocky outcrop, probably reproducing its natural provenience as seen by the naked eye (Mayor 2000: 158–60). She also writes persuasively that belief in the Cyclops may have been buttressed by observation of skulls of Pleistocene dwarf elephants. These were common in the Mediterranean basin and had a large nasal cavity in the middle of the skull, which could very well have been mistaken for a single eye socket: "The great piles of bones on the cave floors might be the remains of ship-wrecked sailors—the savage Cyclopses were probably cannibals!" (35–36).

So perhaps more than some other ancient peoples, the Greeks had visual clues at hand to assist them in the task of imagining monsters. This indeed may explain the richness and diversity of their fabulous bestiaries and myths. However, as historian Rudolf Wittkower pointed out long ago (1942: 197), the Greeks simply gave new and anatomically artful forms to legends and myths shared by all the ancient peoples, from the Egyptians onward, inventing new symbols to express universal fantasies.

The Greeks tended to depict their monsters in patterned ways, adhering to aesthetic and behavioral standards that remained steadfast up to the Christian era. Their monsters were usually immense in size, with the usual hybrid shapes predominating, and superhuman in physical power. Such beings also usually combined human and animal traits in shocking or terrifying ways. The most common fantasy was to imbue animal-like monsters, or half-animal beings, with human malice and destructiveness. Another common feature was, as we have seen, the imputation of man-eating, or, more accurately, cannibalism, as in the case of the part-human monsters like the Cyclops.

Later the Romans took over most of the Greek prototypes and elaborated on them without much change or invention, continuing also the theme of heroic rescue. Indeed, according to some historians, the Romans surpassed even the Greeks in their morbid preoccupation with monsters and prodigies. Classicist Carlin Barton, in her book *The Sorrows of the Ancient Romans: The Gladiator and the Monster* (1992), writes that, more than all other people, the Romans of the late Republic and early Empire were entranced by the horrific, the miraculous, and the untoward to the point of "embracing the monster" as a central statement of their culture. Aside from their beloved gladiatorial games, a favorite Roman pastime was collection of monster artifacts, often as commercial hoaxes. For example, there was the Monster of Joppa, supposedly the remains of the monster killed by the Greek Perseus in his valiant rescue of the maiden Andromeda at Joppa (present-day Jaffa).

What happened was that, in A.D. 58, Marcus Aemilius Scaurus obtained skeletal remains he claimed were those of the Joppa monster and had them hauled to Rome, where they were presented with much fanfare as the centerpiece of the "marvels of Judea." Pliny tells us that the backbone was 40 feet (12 meters) long and 1.5 feet thick, with ribs taller than an Indian elephant. Mayor identifies these remains as probably those of a beached whale (2000: 138). She notes that such hoaxes were commonplace and attested to the continuing fascination with monsters, oddities, megamorphs, and all manner of inexplicable phenomena.

To summarize, the Greeks and Romans continued inherited traditions dating back to Egypt and Mesopotamia. One continuing thread from the Pharaohs to the Caesars, aside from the usual hybrid nature and malevolence of monsters, is the sense of their antiquity. In ancient days, monsters shared the feature of being genetically ancestral to humans: they were father and mother, or in some cases both, and unimaginably old. The monsters of the archaic civilizations are both the predecessors and the progenitors of modern humans and thus closely related. Owing to their implacable hatred toward their human offspring, the monsters provoke the first generational conflicts on record.

Later in classical antiquity, this genetic theme is repeated, but there is a slightly changed emphasis. As among their Middle Eastern predecessors, the Greeks and Romans also maintain a belief in ancient monsters ancestral to men as, in the case of the Giants and Gorgons, who must also be defeated by their heroic children. But in classical thought, the legions of everyday monsters, like the Minotaur, are often the product of miscegenation of humans and beasts or of humans and gods, or are begat by gods and are often the brothers of heroes. So the curious and fluid organic familiarity linking men and monsters continues in a slightly changed form, continuing a kinship as tortuous as it is inescapable.

A view of a preexisting world-of-monsters underlies the basic cosmological paradigm in classical antiquity. The Greeks and Romans thought this prior epoch was populated by huge and powerful creatures, dwarfing their present descendants. In those heroic times of yore, everything was larger, more powerful, and more impressive than today. Such a phylogenetic paradigm of temporal "shrinkage," as Mayor calls it (2000: 201), may be regarded as a kind of a metaphor for the parent-child relation in which, ontologically, extinct monsters symbolize the giant inhabitants of childhood: fantasized images of none other than one's own parents.

Like imaginary monsters, one's own parents are of course temporally prior and epigenetic, occupying a mysterious prelapsarian world of which we know little. They are also (as perceived by small children) immense in bulk, looming majestically above, all-powerful and dominating, and therefore unintentionally threatening. As Mayor points out, this element of gigantism combined with a sense of mystery and power was for the Greeks a defining feature of all monsters. In all the early religions, gigantism is identified as being both godlike, on the one hand, symbolizing the immensity of the divine, and on the other hand embodying hubris, monstrous pride.

And here once again we come to a major conundrum of monster lore, because the moral duality and the ambiguous nature of the monster signal a dualistic and troubled relationship to mankind. If the image of God incarnates the idealized father (and mother), then the monster, which parodies god, may be said to embody the demonized father (and equally demonic mother). And so we see an unsettling paradoxical unity of men and monsters, a strange but unbreakable genetic relationship. We now move on to examine the fate of monster imagery in the Christian era.

MONSTERS IN THE WEST, II
The Christian Era

*Dreams and Beasts are two keys by which we are to find
out the secrets of our nature.*
— *Ralph Waldo Emerson*

 e saw that the ancients regarded their monsters as closely—if paradoxically—related to notions of divinity. Like the Babylonian Tiamat and the Egyptian Apophis, the terrible beasts of the early civilizations predate not only humankind but also the very gods, encompassing within their deformed bodies an unformed universe. Or else, as in the case of the Cyclops, the Minotaur, and the Harpies in Greek mythology, they are begotten by gods gratuitously, or to bedevil or to instruct humans, or else as divine challenges for mortal heroes like Odysseus. With the advent of Christianity, these attitudes underwent subtle shifts in line with the new theological and eschatological assumptions about a beneficent God.

EARLY CHRISTIAN LORE

First of all, there was the problem for Christian thinkers of reconciling monsters of the imagination with an all-knowing moral deity, the contrast of good and evil posing an intellectual dilemma for theologians much in line with the clerical question of God's purpose in allowing evil into the world. The patristic fathers in the first few centuries after Christ experienced a great deal of ambivalence about this conundrum. Most tended to accept that monsters did exist in reality and to view them as essentially evil, as sworn enemies of God, and, specifically in light of Christian eschatology, as descendants of Cain or emissaries of the Devil, antediluvian remnants of pagan sinfulness that had to be wiped out by warriors of the cross. But the question still remained why God tolerated monsters, why they persisted into the Christian era. Herein lies once again a case of the basic ambivalence of monsters vis-à-vis humans.

As did the age of Greece and Rome, the following centuries teem with representations of grotesque beings, literary and folkloristic as well as pictorial. The Old English and Norse sagas, composed between the eighth and tenth centuries, are bursting with grotesqueries: man-eating ogres like Grendel in *Beowulf*, not to mention a horrid dragon in the same poem. The Scandinavian and Germanic sagas likewise roil with demons, half-human fiends, and, especially, man-eating giants like those that threaten Thor (J. Cohen 1999). One only has to look at the legions of hideous gargoyles on European cathedrals to appreciate how much a part of everyday life monsters had become by the Middle Ages—icons of spiritual ugliness and terror, ubiquitous metaphors for moral depravity, indelible images for the contemplation of churchgoers everywhere.

Medievalist J. R. R. Tolkien, a man obviously enchanted by fantasy, wrote an important academic paper, entitled "The Monsters and the Critics" (1984) on this subject. In this influential paper (less well known of course than the Ring stories) he explores the meaning of the monsters in the minds of early Christians in areas bordering the North Sea. He tells us that there was at this time a momentous change in the mental landscape in which marvelous beings dwelled, accompanied by a shift in the didactic function of monsters as expressed in works like *Beowulf*. To get an idea of the change in focus from the pagan to the early Christian era, as expressed in this epic literature, he invites us to compare the moral and thematic position of Grendel in the Anglo-Saxon poem to that of the Cyclops Polyphemus in Homer.

In both poems, written about a millennium apart, the culture heroes battle man-eating ogres. The opponents are depicted in both cases as prodigiously evil figures—not much difference there. They threaten men with dismemberment and death, and their man-eating proclivities are the sign of moral monstrosity. But there are important differences in the way these personifications are conceived and their fates rendered. Let us take *Beowulf* first.

GRENDEL

Although *Beowulf* was composed in Old English (Anglo-Saxon) between the eighth and tenth centuries, the action takes place primarily in what is now Denmark and Sweden. The plot is a simple adventure story with spine-

The Grendel from *Bulfinch's Mythology*.

tingling effects. Once upon a time, the terrible monster Grendel lived with his "troll-dam" (mother) in a misty marsh. This frightful creature emerges on moonless nights to stalk, butcher and devour the subjects of the local Danish prince, Hrothgar. Variously described as "shadow-walker," "death-shadow," "grim demon," "monster," or simply "fiend," Grendel is portrayed throughout as a half-human giant of superhuman strength who takes great delight in rending his victims limb from limb before snacking on their flesh. Aside from casual references to wolves and other wild beasts, the physical appearance of Grendel is otherwise never fully realized, this vagueness making his menace perhaps even more dreadful (Friedman 1981: 106).

Unable to cope, Hrothgar calls the champion Beowulf to the rescue, Beowulf being at the time the king of the Geats, a Germanic tribe living nearby in what is now Sweden. Accepting the challenge, Beowulf perilously crosses over the stormy seas. After many bloody battles—described in gory detail—he succeeds in destroying Grendel, in fact ripping him apart (in a nice touch, he hangs the bloody arm and shoulder on the wall of the Danish banquet hall avenging the monster's many dismemberments). Enraged, Grendel's mother naturally flies at Beowulf, only to be cut down in turn after an equally grisly struggle (which takes place underwater), concluding with the ceremonial decapitation of her corpse. Having rid the world of the two monsters in this particularly gruesome fashion, Beowulf returns to Sweden to reign more or less peacefully over the Geats for more fifty years.

However, toward the end of his life, danger again threatens in the form of a giant fire-breathing "worm" (*wyrm*, dragon), which menaces the kingdom anew. After a few unsuccessful encounters with this fire-spewing beast, Beowulf defeats it in an apocalyptic confrontation, but is mortally wounded. Borne off on a warrior's bier of honor, he thereupon enters into the legends of his people as a hero of the highest renown (Heaney 2000: x).

ODYSSEUS AND THE CYCLOPS

Turning to the Greek myth, we see initial similarities. In the *Odyssey* it is the one-eyed giant Polyphemus who plays the foil for Odysseus, and in similar dramatic circumstances. On the surface, Polyphemus is presented in the same metaphoric terms as Grendel: a ferocious and horrible monster with superhuman strength and nasty habits, including man-eating. In the relevant episode, Polyphemus captures the shipwrecked sailors and, as Grendel did with Hrothgar's men, proceeds to eat them one by one, saving Odysseus for last. However, the wily Odysseus is able to trick the Cyclops into getting drunk, and when Polyphemus lies down to sleep it off the hero puts out his single eye with a sharpened stake, enabling his escape. So the two heroic narratives involved are not dissimilar: hero-man vs. monster; hero wins after numerous trials; hero saves the people; etc.

But there is one important thematic difference. Polyphemus, although a typical monster in size and shape not to mention habits, is himself god-begotten and under divine protection. He is, after all, the son of the sea god Poseidon. In *Beowulf*, conversely, with its fervent Christian imagery, Grendel is described in no uncertain terms as a member of the clan of Cain, "whom the Creator had outlawed and condemned as outcasts" (in the Heaney translation, 2000: 9). Cursed and banished by the Almighty, Grendel is therefore an "inmate of hell," a "banished monster," and consequently an "adversary of God." The Old English poem leaves no ambiguity on this point. For the early Christians, monsters have come to symbolize pure unvarnished evil, at least at the conscious level, meaning that which is opposite to God, spiritual malignancy in a general sense. The real battle is between the soul and its adversaries. Monsters are awesome, yes, but not in any way admirable, except for their formidable (if evil) powers.

Tolkien notes that by the time of the northern European Dark Ages, with the moderating influence of the spiritual quest of early Christianity, the old monsters became images of the evil spirit or spirits, or rather the evil spirits entered into the monsters and took visible shape in the hideous bodies of such anomalies as Grendel, Grendel's dam, the wormy dragon, and all the other malign cryptomorphs that the human mind could imagine. The authors of the Anglo Saxon, Norse, and Icelandic sagas make clear that inhuman fiends like Grendel are the descendants of Cain. They are banned by God and are God's implacable enemies. They are heathens who have not accepted Christ; they are pagan holdouts, deniers of Christ.

And so, from being ambivalently portrayed as omens from the gods in pagan days, monsters became pagan enemies of Christ, the favorite foils of missionary saints and holy men. In early Christianity monsters became a visual trope to visualize God's opponents and were put in the service of the Catholic cause as theological "other," equivalent to the Prince of Darkness (Friedman 1981: 89; D. White 1991: 19). There are certainly unmistakable similarities between Grendel and Beowulf, not the least of which is their superhuman strength and bravery and their love of disemboweling enemies. The nagging question remained for churchmen as to why God tolerated the existence of such fiends in the first place. Or were all these monsters just a figment of the poetic imagination, a literary device to assist in pious devotions? Did the people of the time really believe in them as ontological realities that God tolerated? Ambiguities abound.

Given the central moral mission of monsters in the new religion, many Catholic theologians wrestled with such weighty questions and began to write their own interpretations of the epistemological implications of the existence or nonexistence of monsters. Why Grendel? Did fiends and dragons really exist? Important treatises specifically relating to this subject and its moral complexities were penned by such celebrated holy men as St. Augustine, in his *De Civitate Dei*, and, notably, by the Visigoth encyclopaedist St. Isidore of Seville, in his *Etymologiae* (ca. 673). Numerous other theologians considered the subject worthy of comment in the period between 500 and the tenth century.

The Christian texts devoted to monsters included the tract called *Wonders of the East*, written in Latin and translated into Old English, which takes up the question of the existence of unnatural beasts; the anonymous Old English "Letter of Alexander to Aristotle," which also considers this question; and many other fragments, all of which make specific reference to mysterious beings and their relationship to God and the Devil (Friedman 1981: 150; Orchard 1995: 34–36; see also J. Cohen 1999). By the eighth century, monsters had become a veritable cottage industry in Europe (excerpts from many original texts may be found in a lushly illustrated book by Joe Nigg 1999).

MEDIEVAL MONSTERS: BOOKS AND FRAGMENTS

So important had the conception of the monstrous in the scheme of God become by the ninth century, in fact, that the best minds of the time got together to ponder the subject, and after much consideration produced a number of treatises on supernatural creatures (Waterhouse 1996: 31). The most famous of these is probably the multi-authored Latin work *Liber Monstrorum* (*Book of Monsters*) written at various times between 900 and 1000. Before considering this curious text, however, let us first consider the contributions of Augustine and Isidore, for these are liberally cited as authorities in the *Liber* and form the basis of much contemporary thinking.

Responding to reports of fabulous beings dwelling in the far reaches of the earth, Augustine takes up the issue in chapter eight of the sixteenth book of *De Civitate Dei*, entitled "Whether certain monstrous races of men derived from the stork of Adam or Noah's sons?" He argues that if monstrosities exist as had been reported, they must be part of God's plan and great design, for God is omniscient (D. White 1991: 30). Referring to Genesis, he notes that therefore the monstrous races must be the inheritors of the curse God put on Cain. They are thereby "descendants of the disobedient offspring of the Biblical Noah"; that is, children of Ham and his sons (cited in Jeffrey 1980: 48) whom God suffers to exist for the edification of men.

According to medieval scholars like David Gordon White, Augustine therefore "sanctified" monsters in medieval Christian lore—a "revolutionary" view, as White calls it, at least as compared to that of some of his classical predecessors, for whom monsters were amoral at best (1991: 30). Monsters existed in reality for Augustine's theology, and their purpose in God's plan is to remind us of our sins. For White, this Augustinian view of monsters represents a carryover of the dualistic eschatological vision of early Christianity that assumes a great cosmic drama, a battle between Good and Evil, between God and the Adversary. Such a dualistic moral vision, Manichaean in its polarities, was a logical consequence of the biblical creation story in which God ordered chaos—Tehom, the Deep, the equivalent of the Leviathan of Hebrew lore, and all sea monsters—and in which the talking serpent of the garden of Eden was transformed into a seven-headed dragon in the last days (D. White 1991: 193). But whatever the basis of the thinking, there is an underlying structure of ambivalence about the meaning of monsters and their role in the world, just as there was among the ancients.

Somewhat later, in the early seventh century, the Gothic divine Isidore of Seville takes up Augustine's ponderings with equal fervor, writing a long taxonomy of monsters in his *Etymologiae* (622–33). In defining what monsters are, he includes such criteria as "superfluity of body parts," "composite beings," and "mixture of human and animal parts" (cited in Williams 1996: 107–8). Like his holy predecessor whom he cites copiously on the subject, he accepts the existence of monsters as proven. And he also regards them as being not outside God's plan, that is, not "contra naturam," but part of the intended creation in all its diversity and richness (Wittkower 1942: 168).

To paraphrase Isidore's declaration here, the monstrous is a contradiction not of nature but of human epistemological categories, "since the Creator's will is the nature of everything created." For the pious Isidore as for Augustine, monsters like people derive from God's creative powers to invent living forms. This procreative force, originating in God's will, extends to the human ability to know and to classify what it knows, as always, having a purpose, however enigmatic. Thus, no matter how horrifying to human sensibilities, the monstrous being forms part of this semiotic aspect of nature in that, unlike other signs that reflect the intelligible world, the monster "portends," "points to," and "de*monstrates*" the unintelligible world and its mysteries (Williams 1996: 13).

THE *LIBER MONSTRORUM*

The fragments constituting the *Liber* were composed by various hands between the mid ninth and early eleventh centuries, probably by both Old English and continental scribes (Butturff 1968: 1–3). The complete title of the scattered work is *Liber Monstrorum de Diversi Generibus*, or *Book of Monsters of Various Kinds*. It consists of five tattered manuscripts now residing in museums in Europe. The original text is in Latin, possibly a translation from the European vernaculars. With great earnestness, it addresses a number of questions about nature, God, men, and monsters. It starts out by replying to a hypothetical question:

You have asked about the hidden parts of the earth and if truly there were as many species of monstrous beings as had been reported in the hidden corners of the earth, beyond the deserts, and in islands of Ocean and in the remote hiding places of the furthest mountains. You have desired me specifically to speak of the three earthly genera that strike mankind with the maximum awe and terror.

That is, the monstrous progeny of men, the numerous hideous beasts and the hideous species of dragons, snakes and vipers. (cited in Friedman 1981: 150)

The *Liber* goes on to summarize early medieval wisdom on the subject, borrowing liberally from Isidore and hence from Augustine, and so buttresses a venerable philosophical tradition. The authors of the *Liber* tell us first that monsters exist in reality as a category or "genus," in a threefold plan composed of men, animals, and monsters. This last category consists of neither man nor animal, but something morphologically anomalous with traits of both, rather like Mary Douglas's interstitial anomalies. Subsumed under the heading of monster are curious beasts that are hybrid in shape; polymorphous, uniting many genera; gigantic in size; or with some other kind of prodigious or disgusting physiological deformity that is in itself symbolic of sinful excess or enormity. The *Liber* then enumerates the defining characteristics of monsters. Reflecting timeless notions about good and evil, these are instructive.

First, emphasizing the paradoxical relation of man and monster, the *Liber* asserts that the distinguishing characteristic of monsters is in fact their anomalous morphology (Butturff 1968: 24); or else they are the result of men having crossed over into the bestial realm by acting in some animal-like way. Such beastly transgressors are then transformed through the power of their innate evil into half-human creatures, that is, monsters. Second, the authors insist that monsters were always geographically distant to civilization, living in border places beyond the pale, "in the dark sea" or in remote and hidden lairs or on mountain peaks, from which they emerge to wreak havoc (Orchard 1995: 111). Rarely seen, monsters are the children of darkness, hidden away, fugitive, remote, exemplars of the dark, the unknown, the alien. As in *Beowulf*, they are always with us.

Next, as one might expect, the *Liber* continues the long tradition of seeing monsters as fundamentally hostile to the human race: they are defined as having unprovoked malice toward humans, an "immense hostility" (Butturff 1968: 11), as well as an implacable antagonism to the divine order. And of course, promoting yet another stereotype, the *Liber* depicts monsters as always being larger than life: they are by definition giants, "monstrously huge." And their size of course makes them more dangerous and more terrifying. Gigantism is itself regarded in the texts as a form of sinfulness: a challenge to the immensity of God, a double-sided metaphor implying hubris as well as power.

Finally, there is what historian Andy Orchard refers to as a continual "marine metaphor" in describing monsters. The *Liber* often describes them in terms associated with the ocean, with the vast depths, with watery places and misty marshes. All this of course corresponds to the biblical emphasis on the mysterious Leviathan, another ancient immensity, which stems directly out of the Hebrew tradition of the forms of the unknowable. In the Old Testament, as we saw above, the sea-dwelling Leviathan is the epitome of all the monsters in the sea, just as in the same tradition Behemoth is the epitome of terrestrial monsters and elemental opposites. In the Bible Leviathan is identified usually as the whale, but originally as the dragon in its origin as a sea creature (Williams 1996: 183–86).

The authors of the *Book of Monsters* were skeptical about classical sources. But they believed in monsters as God's revelations rather than as wonderful fables or simply metaphors for sin. The patristic tradition begun at the dawn of Christianity was that monsters were "emblems" or signals of God's plan, an important aspect of Christian eschatology, which can never be fully understood by mere mortals (Butturff 1968: 56). Regardless of proofs of their actual existence, monsters represented a figurative, not a literal truth. Monsters were terrible and evil, of course, but they were also in some mysterious way reflections of divine purpose. In this way they reflect the same moral ambivalence as in the Beowulf-Grendel equation, in which hero and monster are mirror images.

REGIONAL TRENDS IN MEDIEVAL EUROPE

What we encounter, then, in the formative period of the eighth, ninth, and tenth centuries, is a bifurcation in the perception of the Monstrous, reflecting doctrinal and epistemological undercurrents and controversies in Christian cultures of Europe, with marked regional differences, especially between Nordic and Latin. One tradition, common in the south and east of the continent and descended from the thoughts of Augustine, reaching an apogee in Isidore, holds up monsters as revelations or as integral parts of God's purpose. This revelatory biblical tradition continues—at least in the sense of ascribing an allegorical or metaphorical role to monsters. This is especially true of the *Liber Monstrorum*, which seems to accept monsters as divinely ordained or in some inscrutable way God's means of instructing about sin, evil, and righteousness. The writings in this tradition are mainly in Latin, produced by clerics, theologians, and holy men, and retain some of the ancient theories about monstrosity as a portent.

In addition, there is a sense in which this Latin tradition minimizes the opposition between humans and monsters, humanizing the latter, as it were. The difference between monsters and humans—if monsters were, as the biblical tradition would seem to indicate, descended from "one proto-plasm" of Adam's stock—was not so much one of kind as one of degree (D. White 1991: 194). All this leads to what may be called an ecumenical view of monsters: they are pitiful beings, worthy of sympathy, understanding, and rehabilitation. They are our evil twins, yes, but still our kin.

A somewhat contrasting view takes hold in northwestern Europe, possibly because of the Germanic peoples' later conversion to Christianity and the insecurity of the new religion in those remote places. For these marginal peo-ple, monsters symbolized the unmitigated and irredeemable evils associated with unrepentant heathenism, which was still a threat. Conveyed in works written in the vernacular, mainly by poets, and sung before warriors, this tradition is exemplified in the Norse and Teutonic sagas like the Icelandic *Edda*, the German *Niebelungenleid*, and Anglo-Saxon epics like *Beowulf*. Here monstrous humanoids like Grendel are embodiments of evil forces, the implacable enemies of God; they have no meaning in God's plan other than as mortal enemies to be destroyed. According to medieval historian David Jeffrey (1980: 53), this second tradition continues in the Germanic areas of Europe down to the nineteenth century, as reflected in works on folklore such as the *Teutonic Mythology* of Jacob Grimm (1882), which discusses monsters, giants, wood-demons, and incubi, all seen as pagan and unalter-ably evil, opposed to God's design. Nevertheless, despite the negativity, mon-sters still have a redemptive role: as foils for the good and the holy, for heroes of the cross who match monsters in ferocity and power. So the difference is perhaps less deep that it appears. In both traditions, as Nietzsche warned, the abyss looks back at those who so bravely peer into it.

THE HIGH MIDDLE AGES

In the European later Middle Ages, some other subtle shifts occurred in the appreciation of monsters. Many later medieval churchmen took an acute interest in *monstra* because these creatures had come to represent a metaphorical realm in which God's desire to instruct people was most unambiguously manifested in the form of visual objects. Many pious artists in the late Middle Ages and the early modern period, like Hieronymus Bosch, Pieter Breughel, and Mathias Grünewald, used ugly creatures as symbols to represent God's power over nature and His fecund imagination,

"Troop of Furies," detail, center panel, from *The Temptation of St. Anthony*, by Hieronymous Bosch (ca.1450–1516). Musee d'Arte, Paolo. Alinari/Art Resource, NY.

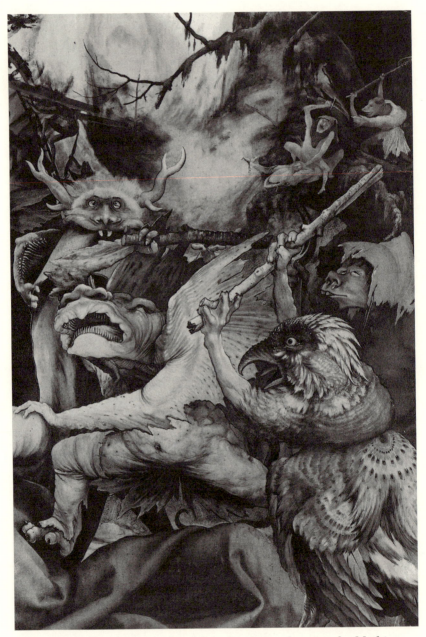

Temptation of St. Anthony, detail from Isenheim altarpiece by Mathias Grünewald (1455–1528). Giraudon/Art Resource, NY.

La Caputa degli Angeli ribelli (The Fall of the Rebellious Angels) by
Pieter Breughel the Elder (ca.1525–1569), detail. Giraudon/Art Resource,
NY.

their canvases teeming with fanciful organisms, half-human, half-animal,
all grotesque. Like the Devil, monsters reflect, then, a monitory tendency, a
warning to man, and can have positive uses in pointing out human frailty.

Some medieval thinkers, especially the Christian Neoplatonists (between
the tenth and fourteenth centuries) even came to regard monsters as things
of value, as instructive, didactic revelations to man from God. In David
Williams's words, these philosophers actually "valorized the grotesque and
the monstrous" as evidence of God's concern for humanity (1996: 108).
This viewpoint is evident, for example, in the fifteenth-century work *Liber
de Monstruosis Huminibus*, written by Thomas of Cantimpré (Wittkower
1942: 178).

The fascination with imaginary monsters grew apace in the high Middle
Ages. So powerful did it become among common folk that clerics began to

include within editions of holy books, including the Bible, long descriptions
of monstrous beings and demons that might be encountered by the average
churchgoer. Jeffrey (1980: 55–56) quotes one passage from a twelfth-
century German book of Genesis enumerating the various demons seen
cavorting in the land. It is worth repeating at length:

Some had a head like a dog,
some had their mouth on the chest
and eyes on their shoulders:
these were obliged to do without a head.
Some thought with their ears
(this is strange to hear!)
one kind had a foot
which was big and thick;
he ran swiftly
like and animal in the forest.
One kind gave birth to a child
which walks on all fours like a beast.
Some are marked (garbed) in beautiful colour,
some appear black and disgusting
beyond comparison
—the eyes glowed continuously,
the teeth were angled in the mouth
(and) when they flash them
they (would) frighten the devil.
Similarly did all their offspring
use their teeth as weapons.
Made as they were,
the order of creation must keep them on the outside.

So obsessed were the people of the period with the spiritual meanings
inherent in monsters and grotesque deformities—both imaginary and
actual birth defects—that many concerned clerics inveighed against the
time and energy their congregations were spending upon such idolatry.
These pious critics also attacked the artists and the architects who portrayed monstrous forms in churches and in religious art, as for example in
the numerous stone figures and proliferating gargoyles that adorned Gothic
church facades and interiors. The theologian St. Bernard of Clairvaux

(1091–1153) wrote an outraged letter to his parishioners in rebuking them for wasting their time contemplating the grotesqueries on church walls instead of paying attention to sermons. These people, he said, "spend the whole day gaping at every detail of these oddities" instead of meditating at their prayers (cited in Mode 1973: 11). "What is that ridiculous monstrosity doing?" he demanded (cited in Nigg 1999: 5). Monsters were becoming too emblematic of a whole age, too much on the mind of good Christians!

THE EARLY MODERN PERIOD

Monsters still consumed the Western imagination in the early modern period, even in the heart of Europe. One remarkable example of this enduring fascination in Europe is the magnificent statuary in the so-called Parco dei Mostri, or Park of Monsters, near Bomarzo, Italy, built by the nobleman Vecino Orsini (1523–85) in the mid-sixteenth century (Cresti and Cresti 1998). Also called Il Sacro Bosco, or the Sacred Wood, and undoubtedly the first theme park ever created, it contains a set of massive stone sculptures depicting bizarre organic forms, many deriving from classical lore, others from the imagination of the local artists and stonemasons (Bredekamp 1985). One such stone monster represents the Greek manticore, depicted as in the form of a scaly dragon and shown battling not humans, but various animals. Another massive sculpture depicts a giant cannibal head, complete with a cavernous mouth yawning open and a few symbolically gigantic teeth—irresistible as a tourist photo-op for willing victims. It represents the entrance to hell.

By the later Renaissance, however, there occurred another subtle shift in monster lore in Western Europe. Two parallel trends appeared. The first, sparked largely by the discoveries of the New World and other European explorations in distant lands, devoted itself to the contemplation of "monstrous races" thought to exist on the margins of Europe. Examples spawn by "Homo monstrosus" fantasies were such grotesqueries as the Blemmyae, supposedly people with no head and a face on their chests, the Sciapodes, who lived in the antipodes and who had one leg with a gigantic foot; the Cynocephalics, or dog-headed cannibal people in the tropics and in India, and so on (de Waal Malefyt 1968). A kind of proto-anthropology with racist and political overtones, this trend will not concern us here.

The other early modern trend was a growing concern for morphological freaks called "monstrosities" or "prodigies," that is, real deformities and, notably, grotesque birth defects. This morbid interest gave rise to various

Stone fantasy figure of manticore-dragon in the Parco dei Monstri (Park of Monsters), Bomarzo, Italy, mid-sixteenth century. Photo courtesy Lee Stern.

pseudo-scientific enterprises, one of which was a rebirth of the discipline of teratology, the study of monstrous births (Fielder 1978), a field that persisted until the middle of the nineteenth century. Also a legitimate medical specialty in the nineteenth century was the sister science of teratogeny, the study of monstrous embryology, the word having been coined by Etienne Saint-Hilaire in 1830 (Huet 1993: 108).

Fascinated by anomalies and errors of nature, people in the sixteenth and seventeenth centuries regarded physical mutations as signs from God, "legible deformities" (Pender 1996: 148). They were bestial, visible incarnations of the horror of our sins, sent directly by the Almighty to admonish Christians, to, as one late-sixteenth-century French teratological tract put it, "repentance and penitence" (cited in Daston and Park 1998: 189). There is clearly in this fascination an echo of medieval monster worship, with the same ambivalence about the moral status of the deformed object. However, since the "sciences" of teratology and teratogeny concern birth defects rather than imaginary or mythical beings, we will not spend more time on them here. The reader is advised to consult the fine works on this subject by Fiedler (1978), Daston and Park (1998), and Huet (1993).

ENLIGHTENMENT AND MODERNITY

Perhaps alarmed by all the attention given to monstrous things, real and imaginary, by the late seventeenth century the European churches began to crack down on such imagery in ecclesiastical art and architecture, leading to a kind of temporary suppression, at least as far as official iconography was concerned. Perhaps frustrated by the loss of fanciful creatures as officially sanctioned displacements, many people instead turned their attention at this time to human scapegoats. The most common of these, of course, were witches and, in central Europe, vampires and werewolves, leading in both cases to crazes and mass hysterias. In his study of early modern monster imagery, Gilbert Lascault, while arguing for the universal psychological functions of monsters, notes that, at least officially, the seventeenth and eighteenth centuries in Europe—the age of Enlightenment—constituted an age "without monsters" (1973: 45). This was perhaps true in the literate culture of the time, except of course for representations of the devil. Perhaps the lack of sanctioned monster lore drove the gullible to other forms of paranoid delusion. No wonder Europe and New England had witch hunts instead!

By the late eighteenth century, however, interest in imaginary beasts revived, spurred to some degree by scientific discoveries such as galvanism and electromagnetism. Literary monsters in particular make a comeback in the Gothic literature of the nineteenth century, led by Mary Shelley's *Frankenstein* (1818) and Bram Stoker's *Dracula* (1897). Much has been written about these two avatars of monsterhood (see Bann 1994), and I will only add a few relevant observations.

First, it is noteworthy that, like other monsters before and after, both examples of modern monsterdom are morphological hybrids breaching recognized boundaries. The Frankenstein monster is a composite being mixing the dead and living, and Dracula is a cross between human and animal (bat mostly, but sometimes a wolf). Like the historical monsters we have seen, also, both monsters are large in size. Although no giant, Dracula is represented in the novel and films as a tall man when in human form. Furthermore, both are capable of bloody violence against innocents, conceived

Frankenstein's monster. Publicity still from *Frankenstein* (1931).

in each case as inflicting bodily mutilation or eating human flesh. Dracula sucks the blood of his victims, shriveling and depleting them, while Frankenstein, although he does not eat humans, uses his powerful arms to rip people apart.

The spatial convention is respected in both stories as well. Both creatures dwell in dark border places, from which they launch attacks on ordered society: Transylvania is described in the Stoker novel as the most remote and unexplored spot in Europe, "an imaginary dreamscape" (Luciano 1987: 7). The vampire travels from there to bustling London in a casket filled with his native earth. The Frankenstein monster hides in Swiss forests like an animal, ultimately escaping to the most remote place on earth: the Arctic. In addition, Dracula adheres to the temporal fantasy, being the decayed remnant of a prior time (he is described as hundreds of years old, a fossil, a revenant from the time of the Turks). But turning this hoary convention on its head, Frankenstein's monster is "new": or at least he has been recently created from dead parts, put together by a spanking new science. Reflecting that curious twisted relationship of man and monster, it is the man, Dr. Frankenstein, who is ancestral (father) to the creature. The relationship, though reversed, is still organic.

MORE RECENT MONSTERS

Western science has by no means relegated monsters to oblivion. The need to believe still exists, even if it is only temporarily satisfied in fiction and hoax, as in the case of the famous Loch Ness monster. Yet folklore still recognizes the power of nightmare creatures to enter and agitate human affairs from Sweden to Spain. For example, many Russian rural people still believe in the Indrik beast, a violent, earth-shaking giant (Mayor 2000: 76). The analogous Swedish myth of the lindorm (a kind of scaly dragon) stirred Scandinavian blood up to the end of the nineteenth century. Found near Värend in central Sweden, the lindorm was said to be about ten feet long, but specimens of eighteen or twenty feet have been observed, according to Swedish folklorist Hyltén-Cavallius in 1883 (cited in Eberhart 1983: 11). This Grendel-like cryptid was said to be black with a yellow-flamed belly. It had a forked tongue and long, white, shining teeth. It eyes were large and saucer-shaped with a "frightfully wild stare." The Swedish source continues:

The monster-serpent is fierce and ill-tempered and his strength and pugnacity make him a dangerous enemy. When alarmed he gives off a loud hissing sound.

. . . His scaly body is so hard that even a scythe will have little effect on him. During the night he spits forth a poisonous liquid.

Until recently, rural Estonians believed in a water monster that is still summoned up to frighten children. It is described in a recent book on apocryphal beasts as a monstrous, fish-shaped creature of gigantic proportions that walks on feet on land but mostly it inhabits the waters (Rose 2000: 158). The so-called tarasque, a demonic ogre, still haunts the remote rural areas of southern France, scaring the wits out of gullible people, as does its analogue, the tarasca, in northern Spain (Rose 2000: 354). Every year on Corpus Christi, the Catalonians exorcize the tarasca in a festival in which the fire-breathing beast is ritually defeated by the townspeople (Warner 1998: 14)—a matter we will take up in Chapter 9.

In Britain, people still encountered hostile dragons until at least the middle of the seventeenth century. The home of one such beast was Henham, a little village between Bishop's Stortford and Saffron Waldon in Essex, thirty miles northeast of London. The Henham Dragon made its appearance about a quarter of a mile from the village in 1668, eating cattle and attacking people before it was finally killed by a concerted effort of townspeople. A pamphlet published the following year (1669) entitled, "The Flying Serpent or Strange News Out of Essex," describes the events as follows:

The first time that he was seen was about the 27 or 28 of May last, a gentleman's way lying by the place where this serpent keeps his station, as he rid carefully on, expecting to receive no hurt as he intended none, on a sudden this Serpent assailed his horse, affrighting the rider so much with his monstrous proportion and bold courage to give such an onset, that all in a maze he spurred his horse, who almost as much afraid as his master, with winged speed hafted away, glad that they had escaped such an eminent danger.

Being come home he acquaints his friends and neighbours with what he had seen of this monstrous serpent, especially makes it known to a neighbour in whose grounds this serpent doth lurk, wishing him to beware of his cattle, and to use his best indeavour for destroying it, least by protraction of time it might do much mischief when had I wist would be but small comfort to him for the losses he might sustain.

Not long after two men of the same parish walking that way, espied this serpent as he lay on a hillock beaking [basking] himself again in the sun, where they beheld his full proportion, being as near as they could guess 8 or 9 foot long, the smallest part of him about the bigness of a man's leg, on the middle as big as a man's thigh, his eyes were very large and piercing, about the bigness of a sheep's eye, in his mouth he had two row of teeth which appeared to their sight very white and sharp, and on his back he had two wings indifferent large, but not proportionable to the rest of his body, they judging them not to be above two handfuls long, and when spreaded, not to extend from the top of one wing to the utmost end of the other above two foot at the moll [tip], and therefore altogether too weak to carry such an unwieldy body. These men though armed with clubs and staves, yet durst not approach to strike this serpent, neither it seems was the serpent afraid of them, for railing himself upon his breast about the heighth of two foot, he stood looking on them as daring them to the encounter. (<www.henham.org/henham_dragon.htm>)

A contemporary woodcut shows a big, legless creature with a leathery skin and the suggestion of bodily segmentations. The ugly head, carried aloft on a long supple neck, has a rather large single eye and the tail is equipped with the usual broad-arrow shape. A stone carving of the monster is still visible on a pillar of Henham's parish church (Holiday 1973: 92).

Water creatures are still scaring people in modern-day Britain, and not only the famous Loch Ness monster of Scottish lore. One such preternatural event occurred in another lake in Scotland, in August 1969.

In the early evening, two long-distance truckers, Duncan MacDonnell and William Simpson, both respectable and sober, were returning from a fishing trip up Loch Morar in their motorboat. It had been a warm, sunny day, and the lake was totally calm. MacDonnell was steering when he heard a disturbance from the stern side of the boat and spotted something very large on the surface of the water overtaking the craft. A bare second later he felt an impact as the object struck the boat; the two men naturally ran to see what had hit them.

The boat, stationary now, was lying astern of what appeared to be a huge sea creature, the sight of which frightened the men to the extent that they grabbed a deer rifle and fired it into the thing. At this, it slowly sank out of view. Shaken but unharmed, the men came ashore. Fearing ridicule, neither divulged the episode to the press until the story leaked out a few days later through a third party. The men described the monster as about thirty feet long, the skin being scaly in texture and dirty brown in color. It had three humps standing about eighteen inches above the water line. Mac-Donnell claimed the thing had a long, flat snake-like head about a foot wide. Interviewed later, Mr. Simpson said "I don't want to see it again—I was terrified" (Holiday 1973: 179). This is but one of hundreds of water monsters encountered in the British Isles.

A MODERN AMERICAN MONSTER: THE JERSEY DEVIL

Closer to home for Americans, there is the famous story of the Jersey Devil. The story begins in colonial days, around 1735, when a woman living in the small town of Leeds Point in the Pine Barrens of central New Jersey allegedly gave birth to a deformed and grotesque creature. It was said to be a hideous monstrosity, an inhuman thing, with cloven hooves for feet, a horse's head, bat's wings, and a serpent's tail. This weird creature, which was first called the Leeds Devil and only later in the nineteenth century the Jersey Devil, scampered off immediately after birth to haunt the region for centuries to come. Other versions of the monster's origin have it appearing spontaneously from the wastes of the Pine Barrens or spawned by the Devil himself. People said they could hear it howling in the woods at night, and its appearance was generally thought to be a harbinger of evil.

Things reached a climax for the Devil in 1909, between January 16 and 23. The events of that year are chronicled in a book *The Jersey Devil*, written in 1976 by two local men, James F. McCloy and Ray Miller. According to the authors, thousands of New Jerseyans saw the Devil or its footprints during that week and testified to the fact. One fairly typical deposition was that of E. W. Minster of Bristol:

As I got up I heard an eerie almost supernatural sound from the direction of the river. . . . I looked out upon the Delaware and saw flying diagonally across what appeared to be a large crane, but which was emitting a glow like a fire-fly.

Its head resembled that of a ram, with curled horns, and its long thick neck was thrust forward in flight. It had long thick wings and short legs, the front legs shorter than the hind. Again it uttered its mournful and awful cry—a combination of a squawk and a whistle, beginning very high and piercing and ending very low and hoarse. (cited in D. Cohen 1982: 259)

The next morning the Devil supposedly flew menacingly over the local firehouse and attacked a man in Collingswood and a pet dog in Camden. Accounts of the these events appeared in newspapers across the United States (Coleman and Clark 1999: 120–21)

People continuously afterward found what they took to be the hoof prints of a weird animal in the snow, and the disappearance of chickens and some other larger animals was attributed to the depredations on the Jersey Devil. The legend continued. In December 1933, John Irwin, a summer park ranger in the Wharton State Forest of New Jersey and a respected figure in the community, was patrolling at night when he spotted a large sinister figure approaching him from the woods. According to the ranger's deposition, it stood on two legs like a human, was well over six feet tall, and had black fur that looked wet and matted. The report later submitted to the state police by Irwin's superior officer stated that Irwin "sat in his car only a few feet away from the monster. His initial shock soon turned to fear when the creature turned its deer-like head and stared through windshield. But instead of gazing into the bright yellow glow of a deer's eyes. John found himself the subject of a deep glare from two piercing red eyes." How closely this description fits the first recorded monster in human history: the bison-man "sorcerer" of Trois-Frères! Not much has changed in 15,000 years of human foibles.

The phenomenon of the Jersey Devil refused to disappear. As late as 1951, this mystery cryptid made another appearance, when a number of local people, mainly teenagers, reported simultaneous sightings in the area around Gibbstown. Farm animals were found dead and disemboweled. On investigation, the local police school authorities denounced the excitement as a mixture of hoax and hysteria (D. Cohen 1982: 259–60).

It has been pointed out that a large group of people still believe in the existence of wondrous beasts in the United States, Canada, and other Western countries. In fact, such inveterate "monster buffs" constitute a large and profitable industry in America, with their own earnest associations and scientific meetings and conventions (D. Cohen 1970:6). All of which brings us to the movies.

CINEMATOGRAPHIC BEASTS

Movies are the perfect medium for monsters because of the technology of special effects. The cinema has offered up a ravishing gallery of beasts, demons, extraterrestrials, and apparitions since the first showing of *The Golem*, a silent film about a Hebrew stone giant rampaging through Prague, directed by Paul Wegener and Carl Boese in 1919. In its monster heyday, more or less between 1948 and 1962, Hollywood produced over 500 films featuring sci-fi monsters (Luciano 1987: 1), beating out all other genres for sheer quantity—if not quality. The overheated imaginations of script writers and special effects artists ran wild!

Hollywood monsters need no introduction. Everyone has shivered before the likes of King Kong, Nosferatu, Godzilla, all the hideous mutations spawned by atomic radiation, weird invaders from outer space, and so on. Like monsters in literature and folklore, celluloid terrors are routinely hostile to humans and "anthropophagic" (as some film critics have put it) as a matter of course—a plot setting theme rarely questioned (Flusser and Rabkin 1987: viii). Numerous books have explored monster imagery in films, a much-beloved classic being *Famous Monsters of Filmland*, a three-volume selection of 450 photos of creatures designed to make readers shiver with delight and their flesh crawl with horror.

Rather than reviewing this massive genre, let us briefly consider a few recent paragons of filmic monstrosity. My own favorites are *Jaws* (1975), directed by Stephen Spielberg from Peter Benchley's novel; *Alien* (1979), directed by Ridley Scott; and *Jurassic Park* (1993), also a Spielberg film, from the Michael Crichton book. The first involves a monstrous squalus, the second a killer-beast from outer space, the third a nightmare dragon from the distant past. What do the shark, extraterrestrial, and T. rex have in common?

First, again, all are giants. Bursting horribly out after incubation within a man's stomach, the alien starts out as a tiny, lizard-like marauder, but quickly—supernaturally—grows intimidatingly huge. "It's big," one crewmen says fearfully after a few colleagues are slaughtered. The shark in *Jaws* is presented as over thirty feet long—much bigger than normal great whites, and there are tantalizing references throughout the novel to the mysterious *Carcharodon megalodon*, the extinct mega-shark paleontologists say may have reached fifty feet or more, providing an added frisson of terror (Andriano 1999: 22). Needing no introduction, the largest carnivore of all time, Tyrannosaurus rex, measures over forty feet in length and has dagger-like teeth six inches long. The inspiration for countless Godzilla-like reincarnations, its sudden appearance in the film at night during a hurricane is overwhelmingly terrifying, a thrilling masterstroke of the filmic genre.

Second, all three brutes are implacably hostile to humans, and their antagonism is only equaled by their ferocity. Third, in terms of morphology, all are "un-natural" composites or mutants: the space alien is depicted as a bizarre cross between a lizard and an insect with some human traits (intelligence); T. rex is of course a reconstructed dinosaur (living and dead matter again); and the shark combines animal savagery with human malice

Godzilla. Publicity still from *Godzilla, King of the Monsters!* (1956).

and vengefulness, provoking the taciturn shark-hunter Quint, before being devoured, to comment on its sinister, unnatural intelligence.

Fourth, all three monsters have primitive traits suggesting an irruption from the distant, evolutionary past. The man-eating shark conjures visions of a Cenozoic predecessor; the alien is some kind of archaic-looking reptile complete with an exoskeleton like an even more primitive invertebrate; and T. rex has been—well—extinct for sixty-five million years.

Fifth, in line with the usual spatial convention, these mega-beasts all lurk in dark, hidden, watery places, bursting out of hiding to wreak havoc. The shark of course, comes from the depths of the sea, but it is also described as attacking in murky waters; the extraterrestrial, drooling continuously from its ferocious maw, emerges from a slimy chiaroscuro nest on some unknown planet where perpetual twilight reigns; and T. rex initially attacks on a stormy night. Moreover, the action in *Jurassic Park* takes place on a remote Caribbean island. All three creatures therefore have associations with liquid: either water or slime.

Next, there is the familiar motif of eating human flesh. All three monsters are vicious carnivores that eat (or rend) human flesh with gusto. The three films lovingly display grisly remains or dismembered, half-eaten, or disemboweled victims, the horror enhanced by the graphic visuals. Adding to this theme is the scenographic emphasis on yawning mouths, cavernous throats, and bloody teeth, almost as defining features of the monsters. Given the virtuosic flexibility of films, this oral-aggression theme is taken to its imaginative limits. The horribleness of the space alien is compounded by perhaps the most cinematographically imaginative conceit in recent horror films: the retractable mouth-within-a-mouth, a murderous buzz-saw that pops out of the original maw, itself lined with razor-sharp fangs. T. rex of course is little more than a walking mouth lined with dagger-like teeth. Similarly, the monster shark is basically a rampaging mouth with fins.

Last, there are some narrative and emotive similarities. For one thing, although the monsters are all horrible and disgusting, there is, paradoxically, a measure of awe, even reverence about them. Gigantic, relentless, and terrible, the creatures seem to be both superior and inferior to humans. There is in each case as well a subliminal moral element: human wickedness is linked mysteriously but firmly to each monster. In *Jaws*, the greed of local officials lets the shark feed on swimmers; in *Alien*, evil multinational corporations protect the creature; and the hubris and venality of a fatuous millionaire are responsible for both the creation and the unleashed chaos of *Jurassic Park*. And, in each case, through its destructiveness, the unleashed monster instigates the mobilization of the right-minded of the community and its ultimate and redemptive unity.

PALEOLITHIC TO PRESENT

Horrible monsters have stalked the European imagination since people lived in caves in the Paleolithic, maybe even earlier. Who knows what our Neanderthal predecessors dreamed about? In the Western world, humans and monsters are essentially coterminous. What has changed and what has remained the same?

Today, people no longer regard monsters as their direct lineal ancestors as did the ancients. However, there remains the same close organic relationship between monsters and those who fight them. God made both people and monsters, heroes and demons; so in His eyes we are brothers and sisters. In the divine plan, monsters are still bound up mysteriously with human emotions and with sinfulness, personifying the errors of our ways. In the modern age, as in the cinema, greed and evil behavior (e.g., bad science) either produce monsters or abet monsters in their depredations. So Western monsters still reflect, embody, and thrive on human failings.

Additionally, throughout European history, monsters have always carried with them the whiff of a remote and distant past, either morphologically in an atavistic appearance, or metaphorically through some chronological inversion (e.g., T. rex). So in the same enigmatic way as in ancient Egypt and Greece, monsters are still symbolically ancestral to humanity, dredging into consciousness some deep-seated hint of superseded, archaic times dimly remembered. In the Norse and Anglo-Saxon epics this temporal theme is recapitulated by the notion of Grendel as a holdover from the previous age of pagan depravity. Aggressive and belligerent, these ancient, primitive monsters still challenge our heroism, bringing out the best and the worst in modern humanity.

Other traits have remained virtually unchanged throughout the ages. Monsters still emerge periodically from dark, hidden lairs, often but not always from underwater (after all, what is outer space, but an extension of the unplumbed depths, a disjunctive dimension). Of course monsters still relish mutilating people and feasting on human flesh. Their grim mouths, always lined with fearsome teeth or fangs, have remained the focus of obsessive fears and fantasies for people since antiquity. As Jeffrey Cohen says, "a fascination with monsters, dismemberment, and the materiality of the body is not the invention of late twentieth-century Hollywood," but goes back eons (1999: 63).

Too, in terms of personal characteristics (if one may so speak about imaginary creatures), monsters in the Western world are still depicted as being instinctively hostile, prone to attack without cause, gratuitously violent. In whatever age, these qualities mean that monsters must be confronted, defeated, above all, *engaged* if humanity is to survive; monsters are thus peremptory, inescapable, unavoidable, and cannot be ignored. Now let us turn to non-Western societies. We start with aboriginal America, specifically the Indians of central Canada, the land of the fearsome Windigo.

WINDIGO
Monster of the North

The Wendigo, The Wendigo!
Its eyes are ice and indigo!
Its blood is rank and yellowish!
Its voice is hoarse and bellowish!
　　　　　—Ogden Nash, "The Wendigo" (1936)

 any are the monsters that haunt the woods of North America, but none is more terrible than the Windigo—the very incarnation of terror. A fixture of native American folklore since aboriginal days, the Windigo (also transliterated Wendigo, Witiko, Wiitko, Wetikoo, etc., all stemming from roots meaning the one who lives alone, hermit) lurks in the forested backlands throughout central Canada. When this lonesome creature gets hungry for human flesh, which is often, it crashes through the forests, uprooting trees, stampeding game, and setting off whirlwinds. Within its hideous, malformed body, there beats not a flesh-and-blood heart but a pitiless block of ice. The Windigo is as cruel, murderous, and unstoppable as any monster conceived by the mind of man. Because the Windigo rules over such a swath of territory it is worth a chapter all to itself.

MEETING THE WINDIGO

One of the first anthropological accounts of the Windigo comes from the pen of the Pennsylvania anthropologist A. Irving Hallowell. An expert in North American Indian culture, Hallowell was a pioneer in the collection of folklore in the Lake Winnipeg area in Manitoba Province in central Canada, a cold and forbidding place in the winter. Interviewing countless Indian informants in the 1930s and '40s, he recorded thousands of bloodcurdling tales. Much of his ethnographic work was later collected in a classic anthol-

ogy, *Culture and Experience* (1974). His work deals with the psychology
and personality traits of the Algonquian-speaking Indians.

In one of the earliest first-hand accounts of the power of the Windigo
belief, dating from the early 1930s, Hallowell notes the association of the
monster and local environmental disorders, especially ice storms, gales, and
tornadoes, as well as the mass hysteria sparked among the Indians.
Describing one such event, personally witnessed, among the Poplar River
Saulteaux in the early 1930s, he writes:

One midwinter night at Poplar River, when a terrific gale was blowing, word
got around that a *wíndígo* would likely pass that way. All the Indians on the
north side of the river left their homes at once and congregated in a house across
the river. In order to protect themselves they engaged one of the leading
shamans to conjure all through the night in order to divert the *wíndígo* from his
reputed path. The Indians firmly believed that the cannibal passed without
harming them and part of the evidence they adduced was the fury of the wind,
which was interpreted as a sign of his presence. . . . To these Indians such monsters are quite as real, quite as much a part of the environment as the giant animals already mentioned, or, as in our culture, God, angels, and the Devil.
(1974: 257)

In terms of sheer geographical range as a belief, the Windigo reigns as
monster monarch of North America. It haunts a vast territory from the high
Canadian Rockies to the Arctic Circle in the north and the Great Lake
states and the Dakotas in the south. It lumbers across the continent as far
east as the Atlantic provinces of Canada, including French-speaking Quebec, ruling an area almost as large as the United States.

While the Ojibwa and Saulteaux Manitoba are perhaps the best-known
peoples ascribing to the existence of the Windigo, many sub-arctic tribes also
acknowledge it. These include the Micmac, the Algonquians, the Montagnais-
Naskapi, the Swampy and Woodland Cree, and, in the south, the Blackfoot.
Speaking mutually intelligible dialects, these otherwise diverse Indian peoples are sometimes lumped as the "northern Algonkian-speaking group" or
simply the "Northern Algonkians" (Bishop 1975: 237). By contrast, the
Algonquians' nearest neighbors, the Eskimo to the north and the Athabaskans to the west (the totem-pole building tribes of the Pacific Northwest
like the Haida and Kwakiutl) seem to be free of the idea, although they are,
as we shall see, troubled by other sorts of equally horrible bogeymen,

demons, and monsters. Going by other names, these are not so dissimilar to the Windigo.

After the first observations by Hallowell and some others, American anthropologists flocked to the region to investigate the Windigo phenomenon. A number of very good descriptive and interpretive works naturally followed. Probably the most comprehensive of these is a meticulous monograph published by the American Ethnological Society, written by Morton Teicher, entitled *Windigo Psychosis* (1960). Teicher's work ignited some excitement in academic circles, and good follow-up studies appeared shortly afterward in many obscure scholarly journals. These include papers by Raymond Fogelson (1965), Thomas Hay (1971), Charles Bishop (1975), Richard Preston (1980), and Robert Brightman (1988); however, after this scholarly flurry, interest seems to have died out among professionals.

Perhaps inspired by the enthusiasm of these field anthropologists, a number of Canadian creative writers, folklorists, and poets, both Indian and white, have subsequently compiled anthologies of Windigo lore and fiction (e.g., Colombo 1982; Marano 1982; Norman 1982). Much of this nonprofessional writing is anecdotal, without scholarly commentary or theoretical underpinnings, and all the more useful for the lack of bias or jargon.

IMAGERY AND REPRESENTATION

What does this North American specter actually look like? What shape, what physiognomy? Native lore is very diverse and endlessly imaginative on this score. Descriptions in the literature are fascinating and often horrific. Indian informants first emphasize its colossal size. So monstrously big is the Windigo, they say, that the mind cannot fathom or comprehend it: "your heart stops in its presence and you forget where your heart is" (Norman 1982: 4). But it gets worse. Already terrifying, the monster is said by informants to be full of rage, its nasty disposition making it all the more frightful. It is also said to be possessed of superhuman muscular strength, which it uses to strike down people (Parker 1960: 604).

So much for proportions and disposition. What about morphology? There are of course many regional variations in descriptions, limited only by imagination, but the best descriptions are noted by Teicher (1960: 2–3) and by folklorists Seymour Parker (1960), John Colombo (1982), and Howard Norman (1982). All rely directly on native sources, including first-hand interviews. In addition there are numerous sketches and paintings done by native artists giving their versions of the Windigo.

The Windigo is a particularly weird and abhorrent creature. We have already spoken of his (most are male) dimensions. Other grotesque deformations abound. Within his gigantic head is a cavernous mouth made more awful by the lack of lips. This odd feature requires its own explanation. Most Indian informants say that the monster is so hungry for flesh that he has eaten off his own lips! From this gruesome maw there protrude rows of jagged teeth through which the monster issues his fiery breath, making a sinister hissing that rivals windstorms in volume and is audible for miles around. It is in fact the whistling whirlwind of his foul breath that sends the Indians scurrying to safety, for the racket means a Windigo is on the prowl.

Anatomically, the creature is said to be human-like, at least in having two arms and legs, but is deformed and misshapen. His huge eyes are grotesque and repellant: they are yellow and protuberant like those of an owl, but they

(*left*) The Windigo eating beavers, by native artist Norval Morrisseau. Courtesy Glenbow Museum, Calgary, Alberta.

(*right*) Twin images of the Windigo, by Ojibwa artist Carl Ray. The upper figure shows the monster leaping in mid-flight, the lower clothed in ice. Courtesy Estate of Carl Ray and James R. Stevens.

are bigger and roll in blood. The monster's hands are massive and paw-like, ending in terrible claws twelve inches or more in length. His feet are a yard long and have only one toe, capped by a long dagger-like nail. The creature uses these blade-like appendages to slash and tear his victims.

The monster is also deafeningly noisy. The Indians say that when the Windigo opens his cavernous maw to let out one of his signature roars, the sound is tremendous, ear-splitting, "more reverberating than thunder" (Teicher 1960: 3). When he indulges in one of his cannibalistic rampages, the monster issues long-drawn-out growls and whistles that cause people to panic and flee in mortal terror. The earth shakes, the wind howls, and the

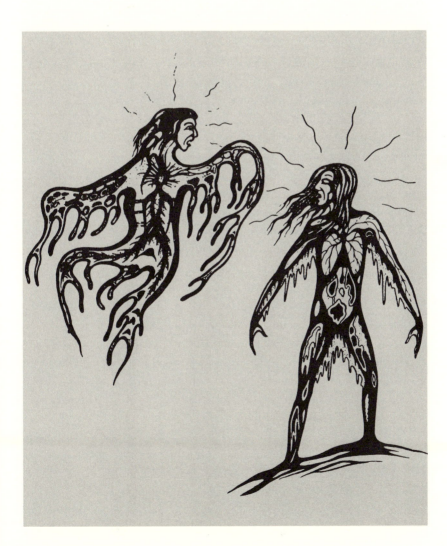

animals flee. The Windigo literally tears up the earth with his mighty bellows.

In proportion to his size and fury, the physical strength of the Windigo is described as prodigious. His destructive powers are superhuman and irresistible. The Ojibwa say the strength of his body is "omnipotent and fierce" (Parker 1960: 605). He can disembowel a man or a big animal with one swipe of his paw—a frequent enough occurrence, as the Indians will testify. He can devour tall men, grizzly bears, and horses in one gulp. Striding through the forest, full of windy fury and bloodlust, he lashes about with his mighty arms, ripping up tree trunks, snapping branches, and tearing up the surface of the earth, leaving a path of destruction as wide as that of a tornado. He will sometimes rip up a particularly big tree and use it as a club or a walking-stick.

The Windigo is virtually indestructible. Rain or snow cannot slow him; water cannot stop him. He can glide over the surface of lakes and rivers without sinking, and like a porpoise or a seal he can swim underneath the surface for hours without coming up for air. His speed and strength in water are so great that when swimming he raises titanic waves on either side, swamping and overturning canoes miles away.

As far as diet goes, the Windigo, as is customary for monsters, displays some disgusting proclivities. For everyday food, he likes mushrooms, rotten wood, moss, lichen, and other forest effluvia. Like an animal, he eats everything raw. He literally eats the forest from the ground up. These vegetable things, however, are just hors d'oeuvres. By far his favorite dish is meat, especially tasty human flesh. He can never get enough.

What about internal organs? The signature feature of the Windigo is his heart, which is made of ice. Impervious to all human weaponry, a Windigo can be dispatched by a human only by melting its frozen heart (Norman 1982: 73), although some Indians say cutting off the head may do the trick, if you can manage this feat! Some Indians extend this frosty metaphor to the entire body of the monster. For example, sometimes the Ojibwa depict the Windigo as a skeleton-like demon made entirely of ice. Other Indians say all the internal organs are made of frost.

The Windigo can be either male or female, although, as we have seen, most are represented as basically male and have traits the Indians associate with masculinity, such as anger, physical aggression, and large size. However, more important than its indeterminate gender is its isolation from human society, its separateness, alienness, remoteness. Males and females do not live together as couples. If two Windigos of opposite sex should happen to meet, the Indians believe, a violent battle will erupt and survivor eats the loser. Alternatively, the defeated Windigo is thrown into the fire and the body is reduced to ashes, all except for the icy heart, which is taken out of the fire and pounded to bits which are then thrown back into the fire to be melted (Teicher 1960: 2).

Clearly, like most monsters, Windigos are asocial beings, misanthropic, solitary, referred to as "hermit Windigos." For the Cree and Ojibwa the monster is "the outsider," "He-Who-Lives-Alone," or simply Upayokawit-igo, "the Hermit" (Norman 1982: 5).

How old is the Windigo? Indians say that the spirit of the monster is a timeless eminence that has "always" been among them like the skies and the waters. It origins, they say, lie in the distant, unknown, and legendary past. The Cree, for example, say that the Windigo arose when the first ancestral humans emerged from the primal slime in mythical times and were given shape by the gods and instructed to take over the land from wild beasts. Many Indians associate the monster with "the olden days," mean-ing the time not only before Western acculturation, but also before Indian culture itself took shape, that is, prehistoric times. The creature was pres-ent at the beginning of the earth and, like the gods and spirits, is eternal.

Aside from a taste for murder, cannibalism, and general mayhem, Windi-gos are held responsible for virtually all misfortunes and disasters that can befall humans. For example, if a hunter freezes to death in the forest, or a family starves, or a young person goes on a vision quest and disappears, the invariable explanation is an attack by a Windigo (Teicher 1960: 3). If a per-son sinks into a depression or becomes senile or demented, the Indians will say that a Windigo caused this to happen. The same blanket causality is ascribed to natural disasters like cold spells, lack of game, famines, and indeed all nature's inimical forces—Indians surmise that a Windigo did it. As we have seen, the Windigo is also held responsible for natural calamities like wind storms, frosts, and tornadoes.

"GOING WINDIGO"

To understand the Windigo in the Indian imagination, one must recognize that these horrific creatures are not separable from people. In fact, men (and women) can easily "turn Windigo," as the natives say, and become cannibals themselves—miniature replicas of the giant ogre. Indeed, accord-ing to Hallowell (1974: 257–59), the term means three things, all concep-tually interchangeable.

Windigo means first, the mythical monster itself. Second, it means an ordinary human being who has become possessed by the spirit of the monster and who, without changing shape in any discernible manner except supposedly to grow bigger, coarser, and hideously ugly, becomes prone to cannibal urges, going so far as to kill and eat his fellows. And third, in a more abstract sense, the word means the cannibal urge itself, as an acted-out crime or a fantasy.

When a human goes Windigo, certain observable changes happen. First, the affected person's size increases and he or she becomes coarsened and wild-looking, with a maniacal staring look. Then, the victim's heart freezes over and becomes ice, as they say; next he or she becomes possessed with demonic physical powers and animal cunning. And of course the victim is struck by irresistible cannibal urges, upon which he or she must act or die.

"Going Windigo" therefore creates a menace to all those around, including the victim's own family, so he or she must be wrestled to the ground and held down by ten strong men until pacified. The person must be bound up tightly and held over an open fire so that the smoke drives away the evil spirit. If this treatment fails, the human-turned-Windigo must be killed at once to prevent him or her from harming others, and especially, from actually committing an act of cannibalism, which is the most disgusting thing in the world to the Indians. As we shall see, numerous killings of human Windigos have actually been reported since the phenomenon was first documented over three hundred years ago (some of these killings are authenticated in tribal or police records, others probably are apocryphal).

So close is the connection between monster and human, so routine the metamorphosis, that most Indian legends depict the Windigo's origin as deriving not from an act by gods or spirits, or from nature, but from an Indian who was once transformed by magic or by gnawing hunger. In addition to being transformed by bewitchment or hunger, someone can "go Windigo" by committing some heinous infraction against group values, something considered the moral equivalent of cannibalism. In the Indian lexicon, such heinous acts would include the unprovoked killing of a fellow Indian, the breaking of a serious religious taboo, or the act of incest. If the transgression is bad enough, for example, if a person commits a premeditated murder within the tribe, or if one has a "cannibalistic thought," however momentary or fleeting, one may suffer the dreaded transformation (Carpenter 1980: 102).

The Cree Indians, for example, say that most Windigos were once just ordinary people who went bad. Many Indians believe that all Windigos, including the giant monster-spirit itself, are in fact doomed human souls having left their human bodies. That is, they say that the human and monster forms are metaphoric counterparts: physically and morally interchangeable, part and parcel of the same evil that permeates the world (see Norman 1982: 5).

Folklorist Robert Preston quotes one old Indian who repeated a myth describing the Windigo as being human in origin: "At one time in his life he was a human being born of human beings and perhaps quite normal for some years of his life" (1980: 122). A Cree elder told Howard Norman that "Windigos were all once persons. But once they begin to go Windigo, it gets worse and worse" (Norman 1982: 5). In one of those imaginative twists we have seen before, man is once again ancestral to monster, at least metaphorically speaking. Which is man, which is monster? There is a thin line between them. Indeed, there are many ways a human can go Windigo without even committing a transgression or having a single bad impulse. For example, without any conscious intent, an innocent person may be visited by the Windigo spirit in a dream or a vision. This involuntary experience is enough to transform one into a monster, for the Indians say that simply to dream of the Windigo is to become one upon wakening.

This may also happen during the vision quest that many adult males undertake. Like other Algonquian speakers, the young males among the Ojibwa and Cree must obtain a spirit helper through a dream-vision that is brought on by fasting and other sacrifices. This helping spirit is needed for a youth to pass into the status the Indians consider true manhood. If during his manhood quest the Indian youth is accosted by a Windigo in a vision, and if he does not reject the Windigo spirit forcefully enough, he then becomes a Windigo himself. He is then doomed to become a cannibal and suffer a terrible fate.

Man-into-monster metamorphoses, however, are most likely brought on by famine and starvation in the cold winter months when hunting is bad. If a person suffers severe hunger for a long enough period (meaning long enough to dull the moral sense and blur the mental capacities), then he or she may turn into a Windigo. This happens most often in the winter when food is scarce, leading to a native association of Windigo, food deprivation, and cold. This association probably explains the ice metaphor: the Windigo embodies the lethal cold and gnawing hunger that lead to cannibalism.

Going Windigo can happen in less ominous circumstances. A person who inadvertently eats a product of another human being—for example, mistakenly consuming someone's hair clippings or excretions in normal food—will then develop a taste for human flesh and will probably go Windigo. Teicher recounts the story of an entire family turning into Windigos and preying on each other because of hunger-induced hallucinations of this sort (1960: 23). Again, this happens most often in winter. Preston cites one story that highlights the routine aspect of man-into-monster transformations. It is worth repeating.

He [the unlucky hunter] goes out every day, trying to feed his starving family and himself. Their plight becomes desperate. A time comes when one of the party begins to look longingly though slyly at another. This person is tempted to kill, so as to eat. It becomes an obsession with him or her. At last—chance offering, it happens. The person kills and soon he (or she) is eating. He has passed from being a human to beastliness. The rest of the family realizes that they have a Wetikoo to cope with. All they have heard about such monsters comes into their minds. A great dread overwhelms them, the marrow in their bones seems to melt and they have no power to move or fight. (1980: 123)

A person may also turn into a Windigo through hostile enemy means. For example, this may happen to a man who is the object of sorcery by a member of an enemy tribe. Although going Windigo most often occurs to male hunters and their families after an unsuccessful hunt in winter, both sexes can be affected. Teicher's study of seventy well-documented cases from the late nineteenth century to the 1950s notes that forty involved men turning into Windigos; twenty-nine involved women, and in one case no sex was given (1960: 108).

Another Canadian folklorist who was piqued by the Windigo, Howard Norman, interviewed hundreds of Cree Indians in the early 1980s. He reports that all the one hundred and fifty older Cree people he interviewed agreed that a human could go Windigo under the slightest provocation. When that happens, a person's sense-perceptions of other humans are greatly altered by the inevitable cannibalistic urges; the affected person may then perceive another person, even a friend or relative, as food, as a "fat ptarmigan" for instance. Norman gives one concrete example that came to his attention: "Isaac Greys, a Cree elder," he writes, told how a man going Windigo "'began asking his own brother how it was in a nearby beaver lodge' . . . *in the lodge*! Because he saw his brother as a fat beaver and he wanted to eat him!" (1982: 37; italics in original).

WINDIGO PSYCHOSIS

The notion that people can turn into Windigos has given rise to the psychiatric concept of a culture-bound disorder known as "Windigo psychosis," whose symptoms are anorexia, vomiting, insomnia, and melancholic withdrawal into oneself. The Indians feel that the sufferer can be cured during the initial stages; but the more advanced stages, which are characterized by perceptual distortions causing the victim to see other persons as edible animals and by outbursts of violent antisocial behavior, are considered beyond native therapy. When the violent stage is reached, the afflicted person has to be killed by the community in self defense. The corpse is usually chopped to pieces and burned to melt the icy heart and forestall resurrection (Fogelson 1974: 4).

Another observer, Richard Preston (1980: 120), however, adds that although all Windigos are vicious killers, not all are necessarily cannibals. Some Windigos murder their victims without eating them. "Witigo," he writes, is not necessarily a cannibal; he may be only "a murderer of his fellows, urged on by dreams, melancholy, and brooding." Virtually all other observers except Norman (1982: 3), who cites the above passage without commentary, however, agree that Windigo and cannibalism are virtually synonymous. For Teicher (1960: 2–4) and Robert Brightman (1988: 337), the Windigo is "an anthropophagous monster" by definition. Empirical confirmation of the cannibal connection comes from Teicher's systematic study. He was able to reconstruct from written records and from Indian memories an exact profile of seventy authenticated cases of Windigo madness. Forty-four of these cases involved actual cases of cannibalism, and in the remaining twenty-six cases cannibalism was a fended-off threat; that is, the victim actually attempted to kill and eat another human being. Frequently, close relatives are attacked and cannibalized:

Of the forty-four cases where cannibalism occurred, members of the immediate family were eaten in thirty-six cases. In one case, "a friend" was eaten and in seven cases, no information was given as to the identity of the person eaten, although it was evident that cannibalism had actually occurred. (1960: 109)

In the twenty-six cases in which cannibalism did not occur, the Windigo psychotic was actually killed before he could act out his cravings, proving the force of the Windigo belief in the culture of the community.

A WINDIGO STORY

One brief Indian tale will demonstrate the hold of Windigo on the native consciousness. Condensed somewhat, "The Windigo at Berens River" (Colombo 1982: 195–97), goes as follows. Once upon a time, in the late nineteenth century, a small camp of Indians were living near a post by the Berens River. One winter day a hunter from this isolated camp, driven by hunger, went out trapping with his wife and children. A few days after their departure, the remaining people in the camp heard the trapper screaming and howling most piteously in the forest. They knew from their own premonitions that the man must have been possessed by the Windigo and had become a cannibal ogre himself. Some courageous people went to the man's trap line to investigate, and there they discovered the half-devoured corpses of the trapper's wife and three children. Everyone in the camp was immediately overcome by panic, running frantically hither and thither in terror. For they knew it would only be a short time before the homicidal man-beast would be at their throats. Something must be done before the monster was upon them.

The panicked Indians hurriedly convened a council and unanimously elected the most powerful brave in camp, a youth named Rotten Log, to defend them. A true culture hero, Rotten Log said, "I am the person without fear of man or beast," and he readied himself for the epic struggle to come. One other brave man agreed to help.

Later, in the forest, the two young braves built a fire and huddled nervously around the flames waiting. At last they saw the terrible creature striding boldly through the trees toward them. As the huge monster approached, whirlwinds started, the trees were torn up, and all the forest animals yelped and howled in terror. The two Indians were horrified to see that the demon had chewed off its own lips: its awesome teeth stood out like daggers. The face of thing was hideous to behold, and its teeth, arms, claws, and fingers were caked with blood and gore. Undeterred, the two heroes stood their ground.

Before they could react, the loathsome monster jumped over the fire and pounced on Rotten Log, trying to bite through his throat. However, the hero was prepared. He called on his helper-spirit and guardian, the great Mis-qua-day-sih, to save him, and the spirit responded: he instantly gave Rotten Log supernatural powers to equal those of the monster. After a titanic battle, Rotten Log and his helper emerged victorious and tied up the Windigo and put its enormous, grotesquely malformed body on a dog sled.

When they returned to the camp with their hog-tied captive at last, the other people, jubilant over their salvation, made a gigantic bonfire to melt the giant's ice heart. After being forced to vomit up the half-digested bodies of its previous victims, the Windigo was burned and finally died when his heart defrosted. The happy people then threw the massive burned corpse onto the flames in order to ensure the final destruction of its restless spirit. The terrible Windigo was finally dead.

ORIGIN AND TENACITY OF BELIEF

Perhaps because it seemed so close to Western models of monstrosity, with its eerie echoes of celluloid monsters like *The Predator* and the alien in Ridley Scott movies, the Windigo originally seemed to be of borrowed origin to many anthropologists, possibly a product of white contact. But this turned out not to be so. Accounts by Jesuit missionaries and others as far back as the early eighteenth century prove conclusively that the Indians had such beliefs before any serious acculturation took place. The Windigo belief is undoubtedly native, pre-contact, and unquestionably pre-Hollywood.

The earliest notice comes from a Jesuit's report in the mid-1600s concerning the Montagnais-Naskapi tribe of northern Quebec. At that time the Indians were being converted by French Jesuit missionaries. In the winter of 1634–35, Father Paul Le Jeune, a French Jesuit, wrote that an Indian man in the Three Rivers area had gone insane and had tried to eat his brother, wife, and sister-in-law, who had considered killing him out of concern for their safety. This man was described as being half-mad with cannibalistic rage, promiscuously homicidal, and physically uncontrollable—all typical symptoms of Windigo possession (Bishop 1975: 239). While the Frenchman does not mention the word Windigo or any of its variants, it is clear that he is reporting on a case of classical Windigo psychosis.

Another serious outbreak occurred in 1661, which was likened by the same priest to a plague of "veritable werewolves" (Colombo 1982: 7). Father Le Jeune also mentions in the same report that other Indians had reported to him that a number of entire families had been eaten by "Devils" (his word), and that the Montagnais, fearing for their lives, avoided hunting in the neighborhood of Cape de Tourmente and Tadoussac because cannibalistic monsters had appeared in these places (241). Although the good father again does not report the Indian name used by his informants, it is clear this is a case of Windigo hysteria.

Reports abound in the eighteenth century, and the Algonquian word Windigo, or variants, appears in another Frenchman's report by the 1720s (Colombo 1982: 8). In 1748, English explorer Henry Ellis (1721–1806), writing about native Ojibwa beliefs, reported that the Indians he knew were suffering from fear of a supernatural monster: "They likewise acknowledge another Being, whom they call Wiitikka, whom they represent as the Instrument of Mischief and Evil; and of whom they are very much afraid; but however we know of no Methods made use by them to appease him" (cited in Colombo 1982: 9). Colombo and others report historical cases through the eighteenth and nineteenth centuries (these stories continue with very much the same plots, narratives, and dramatis personae up to the 1970s). In careful analyses of such historical data, most recent anthropologists have therefore concluded the concept of the Windigo as completely aboriginal and not a product of white contact or of some kind of post-contact cultural or environmental change or social trauma (Bishop 1975; Brightman 1988).

Whatever its origin, belief in the terrible Windigo still lingers today among the Indians, many of whom still believe. And it still exerts enough power over them to have significant behavioral consequences. For example, there were numerous outbreaks of mass Windigo hysteria right up until the middle of the twentieth century. Indeed, a revelatory incident occurred in 1950, as reported by Canadian journalist Beth Paterson in a local newspaper. In the early part of that year, over a thousand Saulteaux people living at Island Lake, 326 miles northeast of Winnipeg, were completely disrupted—"thrown into a state of total panic and trepidation" in the journalist's words—for an entire summer by the rumor that a Windigo was on the prowl in the vicinity. The Indians huddled together for protection and avoided going into the forests, which hobbled local economic activities for weeks (cited in Teicher 1960: 4).

Writing just a few years earlier about the Montagnais-Naskapi in Quebec, a local geographer reported that "numerous terrifying spirits still range the forests. . . . Windigo, the giant cannibal . . . who lives on human flesh . . . no one among them would dare to doubt the existence of the cannibal giant Windigo." About 100 miles northwest of Sioux Lookout in Northwestern Ontario is a small lake called Packwash Lake. Teicher reports that the contemporary Ojibwa believe that a Windigo resides there and claims at least one life each year. "Their fear is so intense that the area is studiously avoided" (Teicher 1960: 4). Colombo (1982), Marano (1982), and Norman (1982) report on sightings and panics up to the 1980s. Even today many older Indians pay homage to the Windigo, hurrying indoors when the wind howls and whispering ominously about apparitions and shadows in the forests.

So intense is the fear among the local Indians that some whites living with them have come to appreciate and even echo the Indian beliefs—even some sophisticated people. Indeed, the Windigo, as melodrama and metaphor for terror, has worked its way into much mainstream Canadian fiction to a surprising degree. In a paper entitled "Canadian Monsters" (1977), author and critic Margaret Atwood considers this issue, writing that much of the outdoorsy fiction written in Canada features supernatural monsters that represent the huge untamed northern wilderness and the psychological "Other," both of which are greater and less than human nature. She adds that there is a very strong tradition of what she calls "semi-human heroes" fighting monsters in modern Canadian fiction, and that much of this literature follows the inspiration of Indian folklore, in particular using and interpolating Windigo traditions (Atwood 1977: 109). Fascinating anthologies by Norman (1982) and Colombo (1982) provide numerous examples of modern stories and anecdotes on the subject. Even some American poets have paid their respect to the Windigo, sometimes in a humorous vein, as in the ditty by Ogden Nash cited above. Having introduced the bellowing beast, the poem continues with macabre glee:

The Wendigo!
The Wendigo!
I saw it just a friend ago!
Last night it lurked in Canada;
Tonight, on your veranda!
As you are lolling hammockwise
It contemplates you stomachwise.
You loll,
It contemplates,
It lollops.
The rest is merely gulps and gollops.

★ ★ ★

What is most important to keep in mind about this aboriginal Indian myth is how closely it conforms to European models, despite the dubiousness of transatlantic diffusion. The Windigo is gigantic, ancient, mute, unstoppable, ancestral to man, ferocious, supra-human in the sense of being simultaneously godlike and demonic, a repository of all our worst fears, an incarnation of pure malevolence as conceived by the human mind, as well as reflecting a certain degree of superstitious awe and veneration. Most saliently, this Canadian beast is a voracious, insatiable cannibal, as are monsters everywhere. Windigo drips with blood and gore.

In appearance Windigo closely resembles Grendel and the other Western demons we have met, for it, too, it a giant creature, bizarrely hybrid in anatomy, half human and half beast, uniting the worst features of both and having the feral cunning that so terrifies the human mind which relies upon superior intelligence as protection from a savage nature. Also like Grendel, the Windigo lives on the margins of society, is at home in water, and has a vague, nightmarish mobility, suddenly emerging from dark mists. Its behavior is similar to Grendel's, and whatever obvious differences may exist between the two may be ascribed to local conditions, such as the Windigo's association with freezing cold, winter darkness, and famine. The Windigo calls forth local heroes who resemble Beowulf in their superhuman powers, and the monster likewise gives moral meaning to man's struggles with nature and with his own appetites.

Although the Windigo is perhaps the best known of the American monsters, it is only one among many terrible creatures and weird beings that haunt the native imagination. We now turn to other American apparitions, starting with the Windigo's junior cousin, the Wechuge, a formidable creature in its own right.

6

AN AMERICAN MONSTRUARY

I have seen no more evident monstrosity and miracle in
the world than myself.
— *Montaigne*, Essays, *book II, no. 11 (1580)*

he Windigo is pretty much localized to the Algonquian-speaking tribes of central Canada—a few thousand souls in all. Anthropological evidence indicates that the neighboring peoples did not borrow or reinvent the Windigo per se in their belief repertory. For example, the closest neighbors of the Algonquians, the Arctic Eskimo (Inuit) to the north and the Athabaskans on the Pacific Coast in British Columbia to the west, have no cannibal monster called by any of the cognate terms that may be transliterated Windigo.

This difference in the mythological repertory of these neighboring tribes has cast some doubt on the conventional wisdom of ascribing the Algonquian belief to an environmental cause. Given the harshness of local conditions under a stone-age technology, many anthropologists assumed that the root cause lay in the extreme cold and frequent starvation during the long, brutal winters of sub-arctic Canada. These ecological pressures are said to drive the Indians to desperation with hunger, and in extreme cases to lead to cannibalistic fantasies and other malnutrition-induced hallucinations and pathologies.

Such an interpretation seems logical, but a moment's reflection puts it in doubt. The reason is obvious: the Eskimo and the Athabaskans experienced similar climatic conditions. In the case of the Eskimo, indeed, conditions during the long bleak Canadian winters were much worse. So the origin of the Windigo belief must lie somewhere else in the human mind. Nevertheless, the Eskimos and Athabaskans had their own demons to contend with. The Athabaskans, for example, a people in some ways like the Algonquians in technology and culture, maintained (and many still maintain) a strong belief in evil half-human creatures they describe as woodland ogres with

man-eating tendencies. Their main beastie was the Wechuge, a semantically empty morpheme of uncertain origin. Although differing in important
details of appearance and behavior from the more famous Windigo, the
Athabaskan Wechuge is analogous in form and viciousness, and perhaps
even derived in part through cultural diffusion from the memorable Algonquian model.

Neither the Wechuge itself as a cultural construct nor the possibility of
diffusion from Algonquian-speakers has been researched systematically by
anthropologists. In my opinion, given the inherent fascination of these concepts (and their impact on behavior), this is truly an egregious (indeed
monstrous!) omission for which I have no explanation. The only serious
writer about the demonic world of the Athabaskans is Canadian ethnolo-
gist Robin Ridington. For many years in the 1970s and '80s he lived among
the Dunne-za (also named Beaver Indians), an Athabaskan-speaking tribe
living along the Peace River in British Columbia. The following discussion
borrows from his work.

WECHUGE: WINDIGO JUNIOR

First of all, how intense are monster beliefs in general among these
Athabaskan peoples? Are they as obsessed as their neighbors with ogres
and with cannibals? The answer is a resounding yes. Ridington goes so far
as to say that the Dunne-za believe strongly in a host of man-eating monsters, and that this belief is even more deeply ingrained than among the
Algonquians (1976: 109). As we will see as we peruse the vast parade of
monsters around the world, ethnographers think their own people are the
epitome of creativity on this score, but the truth is that each and every culture teems with such imaginings!

Although there are other bogeys in the Dunne-za catalogue (some are
discussed below), their principal fright has always been the Wechuge. The
Indians conceive of this creature in a metaphoric frame slightly different
from that employed by the Algonquians to envision the Windigo. According to local storytellers, the Wechuge is a remainder of the distant past, a
physical remnant of the earth's infancy, a time of primordial darkness when
monsters dominated humans. In those remote times, they say, many man-
eating giant animals swarmed on the face of the earth hunting people, who
were at that time in an uncultured state like babies, weak and not yet the
masters of the earth they would later become.

This situation obviously made life difficult for the Dunne-za. They were too frightened to do much else than cower in their miserable caves. Finally, after eons of abject subjugation, a local hero rose up to help the people conquer the earth. This hero was a young warrior named Saya. With the help of some watchful good spirits, he subdued the swarming man-eaters through many titanic battles, which are of course detailed in numerous myths, and drove the monsters underground so that the people could live freely and establish a rightful human hegemony—as the gods had intended (1980: 173).

However, like some monster-slayers we have met in other places, the hero Saya was somewhat negligent, failing to kill all the monsters and giants. Some of these terrible creatures escaped his arrows and still remain alive today, although they no longer take the form of giant monsters, and because the people today are able to fight back, they no longer dare tread openly on the earth's surface. Rather, they persist in the physically reduced and insidiously disguised form of Wechuges. Lessened in size but not in evil or malice, these evil leftovers roil hidden in the dark netherworld underneath the surface of the earth, awaiting opportunities to rise up and make mischief for humans. Like all good monsters, the Wechuges lust voraciously for human flesh. Given these proclivities, they emerge periodically to wreak havoc.

Let us consider appearance and behavior. What do these Wechuges look like? Interestingly, the Indians say that although they are fairly large compared to normal humans, they are not necessarily giants. Nor are they so grotesquely awesome in appearance as the overwhelming Windigo. Instead, they look rather like ordinary people—if outsized, rough-looking, and of sinister mien. But they have certain unmistakable feral traits that give them away. These signs include too-large and too-pointy teeth, chewed-up bloody lips, wild staring eyes, a general savage and hirsute look, and, of course an insatiable appetite for human flesh. Not as powerful or dominating as their Algonquian cousins, the Wechuges use tricks and guile rather than brute strength to subdue their victims.

In terms of internal organs, Wechuge is said to be very much like the Windigo. The Dunne-za say that the Wechuge's innards, including the heart, are made of ice. Like the Windigo, this smaller monster has to be held down and roasted over a fire so that the interior ice melts before it can be killed—preferably, again, by decapitation.

As in the Windigo psychosis, the Dunne-za believe that men (and also women) can turn into Wechuges. They believe that this happens with appalling frequency. When people undergo the change, they become murderous cannibals, and like the human-Windigo of the Algonkians they have to be killed before they can butcher and eat their fellows. The transformation is triggered when people break important taboos, transgress cultural boundaries, or simply lose control of themselves in some irreversible way. For example, if a person is led by hunger to fantasize about eating human flesh, this by itself can trigger the metamorphosis. If a person commits a crime judged to be heinous by the culture, such as murdering a fellow Indian or committing incest, he or she stands a good chance of becoming a Wechuge. All this recalls the Windigo syndrome.

Another curious situation that can trigger the transformation is what the Indians call becoming "too strong." This condition is a constant worry and a subject of continual discussion and vigilance. It happens when a person becomes prey to unbridled emotion of almost any kind, be it sexual passion, rage, or hunger. The Dunne-za say that such a peremptory emotion wipes out the affected person's reason, his or her humanity. Then this psychological lapse permits the Wechuge spirit to possess the weakened victim, and the transformation into a cannibal beast is assured.

As mentioned above, Wechuge represents the native conception of "the past." The Athabaskans say that, since the monster is a remnant of prehistory when monsters ruled the earth, the man-into-monster metamorphosis is actually a regression to that gruesome time—a clear metaphor for the unquenchable power of atavistic impulse. The Indians told Ridington that this kind of reversion was their most powerful fear in a world that harbors many dangers (1976: 115). The Dunne-za are not the first people to think that being in the grip of a commanding passion is the same as turning into a beast, reverting to a pre-human condition, or, in their own idiom, becoming a cannibal monster. Nor are they the first to embody this idea of regression metaphorically in the shape of a bogey.

So far, we can see many parallels between Windigo and Wechuge that may (or may not) imply cultural diffusion from the Algonquians. However, as we have seen, the Dunne-za add an interesting fillip to the Wechuge repertory aside from the creature's smaller size and more innocuous physiology. A sense of the mythic past exists among the Algonquians, but is less emphasized in their monster lore. The latter believe their Windigo to be eternal, dating from the origin of the world, and so in that sense a living link to mythical times. Employing the same temporal metaphor, but going a little further, the Athabaskans say that the appearance of the Wechuge signals that the affected person has actually—not symbolically—regressed to the times of yore. They say that when a man turns into a Wechuge, the metamorphosis is equivalent to a moral and physical return to that primitive world, and that ancient world then becomes a living force in the present. Through this temporal trope they provide a outlet for their fears by telescoping time in moral terms (Ridington 1976: 122). The metaphor of monstrosity here has both a psychological and a temporal referent: monsters represent primitive instinct over which civilization spreads a thin veneer.

WOLVERINES AND OTHER BEASTS

The Wechuge occupies pride of place in the Athabaskan bestiary, but it has much company. The same Indian groups also believe in were-animals and other dangerous hybrids. The main were-animal is what they call the wolverine man. The Athabaskans recognize three distinct ontological forms of this carnivore. First are the natural, weasel-like animals smaller than wolves but tenacious and hardy. Second, is the "giant wolverine," a mythical man-eating forest creature which, like the Wechuge, has roots in the distant past when people were eaten by giant beasts. Last are what the Indians call "wolverine-men." These are bad Indian people who have undergone mystical transformations as a punishment for some sin.

The three forms of wolverine have different psychological import. The natural wolverine, while a cunning competitive hunter of game, is not feared. The giant wolverine, being a monstrous man-eater, naturally inspires terror. Like the Wechuge, it lives in the dark forest, emerging occasionally to trap humans as food. Sightings are frequent in winter and cause panics among Indians similar to those we discussed above. The third type, however, the were-creature, wolverine man, poses a greater danger to society. This is because any man can turn into such a beast at any time and then go on a rampage, killing and devouring his fellows. The metamorphosis happens in the same way in which a person turns into a Wechuge. The victim does something to compromise his or her essential humanity: commits a crime against another member of the community, feels cannibal urges, or becomes "too strong" in his or her emotions (Ridington 1980: 114). The Indians can never be sure if the object of their fears is a human changed into a wolverine man or the giant wolverine itself, and there is a some vagueness in their descriptions of such encounters, a shadowy quality about what was seen. All this adds a certain indiscriminate anxiety to their daily lives, for the monster may appear suddenly from a shadow or from behind an ordinary object.

Ridington relates the following story by an old Indian friend, which tells of one such sighting and the hazy, indistinct, dreamlike impressions left thereby. "Once upon a time in April," the tale begins, "in late winter, when there were monsters, one old medicine man felt *nagata*, the feeling that something bad was going to happen" (180). Although the other Indians scoffed at this premonition, the wise old man persisted in warning people that something terrible was coming after them. On the sixth day, the old-timer predicted that the monster would come that day. And come it did.

The people said it was a really big monster, bigger and faster than anyone thought possible, moving fast through the forest like a wolverine, only "it was huge." When they saw it advancing upon them, the women of the tribe began to cry piteously and all the children began to howl, for they were deathly afraid it would eat them all (no actual description of the monster is ever given in the tale). However, the old shaman, knowing all sorts of magical tricks, managed to charm the beast and afterward, after much study, found out that it was the spirit of a bad Indian who had turned into a wolverine man. Finally, having been bested by the shaman, the ashamed monster left the camp to hunt other humans elsewhere. The storyteller continues:

One Indian, named Tsuke saze (the old man's nephew), followed the monster to track it. He saw the tracks of the great big monster and he started following them. All day he followed those tracks. He saw that they were coming from where his relatives were camped and he thought than the monster must have eaten all of them. But it soon got dark and still he hadn't seen the monster so he went back to his camp. He told the people, "All day I followed the tracks of *Onli nachi* (the Wolverine Giant), but I couldn't catch up with him. Maybe he didn't want me to see him. His tracks were coming from where my relatives were camped. Maybe he ate them all." That's how the story goes. That is the end of the story. (Ridington 1980: 182)

What makes the story most chilling are the indecisive features—the fading tracks, the lack of confirmation of fears about cannibalism, and the monster's mysterious disappearance. As elsewhere, the monster is an integral part of the native landscape and as such, ubiquitous, everywhere and nowhere.

STILL OTHER CANADIAN MONSTERS

Because of the anthropological interest they have aroused, Windigo, Wechuge, and perhaps wolverine man are the most famous aboriginal North American demons. But many other weird creatures inhabit the northland imagination, not only among Indians but also among Europeans—of both English and French stock and both educated and uneducated. Let us peruse some of the eerie folklore of our northern neighbors.

In rural areas of white French Canada, for example, there is a belief in the dreaded loup-garou, or werewolf, to send shivers down people's spines. Hairy and feral, the loup-garou lurks in the dark forests of Quebec and is said to be a combination of human and animal. Its worst trait—maneating—is legendary. Repeating European motifs (werewolves are well known in western European folklore and of course in Hollywood horror films), this notion is probably an Old World import, although some American Indians held similar beliefs in were-coyotes, were-bison, were-serpents, and suchlike changelings. Considering the fact that Windigos, Wechuges, and their ilk were also thought to be troubled humans having undergone feral transformations for some evil deed, the European were-animal as a precept (the notion that people can turn into beasts under certain conditions), is not too far removed from Indian beliefs.

Also in French-speaking Canada, there are monster beliefs among the Montagnais, a tribe living near the St. Lawrence River in Quebec. The Montagnais believe in a maritime female monster they call Gougon. She dwells near the Bay of Chaleurs on the St. Lawrence and is said to be taller than the mast of the tallest ships and powerful as the wind. Like Scylla and Charybdis, she delights in carrying off and devouring sailors (Bishop 1975: 242). The English-speaking eastern Canadians have their own favorite bogeys and monsters. In Newfoundland, the third-generation Scots speak about a demonic apparition, "Raw Flesh and Bloody Bones." A forest creature, Bloody Bones probably represents an autochthonous concept in the New World, as there seem to be no European antecedents. A bipedal monster, it resembles a human skeleton. It rampages at night, devouring humans with its big, bloody teeth.

On the northwest Pacific coast of British Columbia, the Kwakiutl and other tribes of Vancouver Island have monster beliefs. As reported by anthropologist Wayne Suttles, many people believe in a cannibal woman called D'Sonaqua. They say that, in a travesty of motherhood, this scourge devours youngsters who stray into the woods. Many older Kwakiutl also still fear the "basket ogres" and "woodmen," evil spirits who dwell in the deep forest and take people away to feast on (Suttles 1980: 251). Also in the Pacific Northwest, many people, Indian and white, speak of the Sasquatch (also called Bigfoot), familiar to urban Americans through news reports and movies. This reclusive, hairy, half-simian cryptomorph resembles the Abominable Snowman, and is not necessarily aggressive but not to be trifled with. It is said to live in forests and to be twice the size and have four times the strength of a normal man.

Suttles is one of the few serious scholars to write at length about Sasquatch and those who believe in it (1972, 1980). Tracing it back to native beliefs, he notes that Sasquatch, well known to white Americans, is only one of a whole class of monsters the Indians of British Columbia call *slalakums*, which are said to be everywhere, haunting every nook and cranny of the world. These cryptomorphs may attack people, causing a serious disorder called "soul loss," meaning that the victim is possessed, loses self-control, and may fall prey to any number of dangers. An encounter with a slalakum does not necessarily result in death, but it supposedly makes people crazy from fear. Some people have to be institutionalized after the experience as incurably insane.

The folklorist John Napier (1972) consigns the Sasquatch to what he refers to as the rich "Goblin universe" of western Canada and northwestern United States, a huge inventory of imaginary creatures, evil demons, and man-eating bogeys said to prowl the northern backlands in search of human victims. Another such forest goblin, according to Napier, and ascribed to among whites rather than the Indians, is the "Boo-bagger." It is said to look like a human-bear hybrid and to be a menace to hikers and backpackers in the woods. According to local authorities this threatening figure is entirely covered with long black hair; it has been described by those who have seen it (and survived) as "a big hairy monster" looking for all the world like a cross between a man and a grizzly (18). Perhaps this entire northwestern monstruary is ascribable to the mental effects of the heavy forestation and the misty climate on the cold-addled mind. But who can guess the cause of such imaginings in so enlightened a land? The distinction between native and white lore is negligible.

Still, the Canadian bestiary is incomplete. The next best known monster in the northern imagination after the Windigo is a marine creature called Ogopogo, often referred to as the Okanagan counterpart of the Loch Ness beast and one of many Canadian water serpents. Living in western lakes,

Bigfoot. Photo Patterson/Gimlin, ©1968 Dahinden. René Dahinden/
Fortean Picture Library.

this mega-reptile is said to be a hundred feet long and to gobble up men
and boats. Similar beasts are also reported from the various maritime
provinces, such as a giant (fifty-foot-long), fast-moving, shark-like creature
with a long mouth like an alligator's lined with menacing teeth. Cold Lake,
on the border between Saskatchewan and Alberta, is said to harbor in its
waters a white humpbacked creature the size of a whale, called Kinosoo by
the local Indians (Carpenter 1980: 101). The aquatic man-eating sea serpent the Cherokee call uktena, which we met above, is also widespread in
Canadian Indian lore (Fogelson 1980: 139), possibly reflecting diffusion.

According to Canadian folklorist Carole Carpenter, who compiled a long
compendium of local lore, the common feature of these apparitions is their
association with evil. She writes that "Evil is a, if not the, primary characteristic of many Canadian monsters—either they bring or do evil or they
appear as a result of evil having been done"(1980: 102). She also mentions
another common denominator in the spatial and cognitive marginality we
have mentioned often before. The Canadian ogres, giants, cryptomorphs,
and were-animals dwell in remote "wild places" of that huge, cold, and
underpopulated country. They live in the depths of seas or in the deepest

lakes, or in the dense, uncharted forest, on mountains, and in other eerie places (102). To this we may add another common feature: all the monsters above, are, like the Wechuge, connected to the distant past: atavistic, morally backward, and physically primitive—reptilian, simian, or serpentine.

THE ARCTIC

We now continue our journey further north. In the remote northern areas of Canada and Alaska, the Eskimos are without either a Windigo or Wechuge. But not to be outdone, they have invented their own goblins and beasts, some of which are just as dreadful. Tundra, ice, and snow do nothing to dampen the capacity to conjure monsters.

One of these arctic creatures, called Kudloopudlooaluk, is a kind of slithery sea serpent. Eskimo children are warned not to play too close to the water, or else the Kudloopudlooaluk will drag them under and eat them. There is also in various Inuit traditions a creature called Sewdna, a monstrous sea hag, whose deformed fingers become the first seal and walrus in Eskimo myths, and whose temper is fearsome. In appearance like a deformed witch, she is credited, like Scylla and Charybdis, with vicious storms and other marine disasters (Carpenter 1980: 101). The Eskimo world is in fact populated with all manner of amphibious monsters, which in Inuit are generically called *turngak*, "those we fear" (Graburn 1980: 199). Another is Nulayuuiniq, depicted as a monstrously large cannibal infant, who inhabits the Hudson Bay area (Rose 2000: 234).

Other Eskimo myths feature rather typical aquatic monsters. One Canadian traveler named Duncan Pryde, a government agent who lived with the Copper Inuit of the Northwest Territories for many years until about 1970, wrote a book about his adventures exploring the inland areas near Hudson Bay (1972). In one passage he describes how one summer in the 1950s he ventured by kayak up the north-flowing Perry River with Eskimo guides to explore the furthest reaches of the arctic wilderness, only to be abandoned on the shores of McAlpine Lake. The natives considered this area to be haunted by a man-eating water-serpent and ran off in terror. He describes his experience:

Testing myself, I traveled farther and farther. Sometimes I headed down the coast to the east, almost to Gjoa Haven. . . . I was very interested in this lake, because the Eskimos said a huge monster called *Iqaluaqpak* lived there, the Loch Ness monster of the Canadian Arctic. No Eskimo would paddle a canoe or a kayak on McAlpine because it was well known that *Iqaluaqpak* swallowed such unwary visitors whole, kayak and all. (1972: 175)

UNITED STATES INDIAN LORE: THE YUROK

When we return south and cross the U.S. border, monster lore flourishes, despite the warming trend. The Yurok Indians of northern California, for example, have a demonic galaxy that they spend endless hours discussing and defending against. We have already introduced the wo-gey. This term includes a whole series of malevolent goblins who, like the Wechuge, are supposedly remnants of a "beforetime," when people were weak like children, had no hero to protect them, and, like the Dunne-za, were terrorized by beasts. Some wo-gey have human-like physical traits combined with superhuman powers; others have undefined or animal-like shapes.

Counted in the generic wo-gey class is the water panther. A demonic feline, this beast takes the shape of a cross between a bird and a giant lizard. It attacks and devours travelers. Other members of the genus are the so-called Porpoise Brothers. These devilish twins live in the center of the earth, emerging at the surface occasionally to trap and eat people unlucky enough to cross their path (Bishop 1975: 155). Another wo-gey is called the Long One. A gigantic, horned, serpentine monster, it is a killer and destroyer, gratuitously attacking and devouring people crossing the Klamath River in boats. Still another large class of Yurok bogeys is made up of giant reptiles called *sok*. These are said to attack and eat people out of malice.

According to Bishop, most of these Yurok monsters are conceptually complex constructs, and some have a dual nature. One the one hand, they are malicious like monsters everywhere. On the other hand, when treated properly and sympathetically by humans, they can be tamed and become paradoxically beneficial. All the Yurok monsters, however, are in Bishop's view essentially wild and "antisocial" beings, associated in Yurok thought with areas that mediate between cosmographic levels (that is, they come from unexplored, in-between places). As such, they naturally frighten people because of their very weirdness, if not their nasty habits and bizarre or threatening mien. Last, they are all, in a strict sense, conceptual anomalies or prodigies (Bishop 1975: 157). All these traits inspire both fascination and dread among the Indians.

Although they are beset by monsters at every turn, the Yurok, like other New World peoples, have some help from their magnificent culture heroes.

Their own savior's name is Pulekukwerek, literally "he who destroys monsters." Like many other valiant heroes, Pulekukwerek has some monster-like traits himself. He is outsized just like his monster foes, has the same superhuman strength, and, in a final touch, has a sharp horn growing out of his buttocks, giving him the nickname "sharp pointed one behind" (Bishop 1975: 167). So in appearance the hero has the look of a monster. Once again, hero and monster share some traits, aside from being abnormally strong and fierce.

MONSTERS OF THE AMERICAN GREAT PLAINS

Further south, between the Mississippi and the Rockies, we find diverse monsters. The Arapaho, for example, believed in a creature they called Raw Gums, described as a hideous cannibal giant with teeth as big and as sharp as a wolf's. His capacious mouth is bloody-red and his gums are raw from eating human flesh (Rose 2000: 234). Further east, New York state also has its monsters, besides the "stone-clad" giants of the Iroquois introduced in Chapter 1. According to anthropologist Anthony Wallace (1972: 288), the Allegany Seneca of northern New York (a branch of the Iroquois), as late the mid-nineteenth century believed in the existence of many squirming subterranean creatures. As in so much Indian mythology, these beings were thought to predate human existence and to emerge periodically from their caves to cause pestilence and death among the Indians. As in Athabaskan lore, most but not all of these chthonic creatures had been vanquished at the beginning of "real" time by various culture heroes. Like the Wechuge, those remaining still pose a continual threat to life and limb. Many Indians still harbor such beliefs, or at least like to frighten their children with such stories. The ground seethes underneath with demons.

In addition to these underground dangers, some tribes living in the Great Plains believed in a gigantic bird of prey, the Thunderbird. When this monstrous bird flapped its awesome wings, it caused thunder and windstorms, and it swooped down from its mountain aeries to carry off children, which it fed to its young. The Thunderbird belief, or variants, like that of the Windigo, predates white contact and is both ancient and aboriginal. In 1675 the French explorer Jacques Marquette discovered a rock painting on the Mississippi River near modern Alton, Illinois, that depicted a huge, weirdly shaped bird known locally as the *piasa*. Marquette described the local Indian conception of these birds as being as large as a calf; they have horns on their heads like those of a deer, a horrible look, red eyes, a beard like a tiger's, a face somewhat like a man's, a body covered with scales, and so long a tail that it winds all around the body, passing above the head and going back between the legs, ending in a fish's tail. (cited in Eberhart 1983: 81)

Other midwestern tribes such as the Sioux, Arapaho, Cheyenne, and Dakota are famous for Thunderbird myths, the origin of the name for numerous North American commercial products, such as the famous sports car and the infamous jug wine.

THE HOPI: A COMPENDIUM OF MONSTERS

Continuing south, we move to the deserts of Arizona. Occupying a dozen or so villages between Keam's Canyon and Tuba City in northern Arizona, the Hopi are a community of shepherds and corn-growers. They are also known as the Pueblo Indians, and in academic anthropology they have become rather a model of a pacifist tribal culture, made famous by Ruth Benedict and others for their Apollinarian solemnity, ceremonialism, and moderation. In this theirs contrasts markedly with the warlike cultures of the Plains Indians like the Sioux and Cheyenne mentioned above.

The present area of the Hopi abuts the lands of the much more numerous and well-known Navajo tribe, with whom they have had some arguments over real estate in the past. The Hopi are ethnically and culturally related to the Zuñi of New Mexico. Today, of course, like most other Native American Indians, the Hopi are acculturated to white civilization and have lost many of their aboriginal byways, but many of the older Hopi still cherish old traditions, especially ancient myths, hero legends, and an elaborate system of beliefs about supernatural beings and the interference of demons and bogeys in human affairs.

The colorful mythology of the Hopi, largely preserved by diligent anthropologists, reveals them as people obsessed with all manner of monsters and evil spirits. Hopi tradition, like so many others in aboriginal North America, tells of how the present world originated only after the defeat by tribal heroes of horrible chaos-monsters who once held the world in thrall and fed off humans. The outlines of the narrative are virtually identical to those of the literate cultures of the Old World; only the dramatis personae and some of the narrative details differ. Hopi folklore also shows how these victorious culture heroes must constantly safeguard the people even today by confronting relics of the past that rise up from the bowels of the earth to bedevil mankind. In order to grasp the cultural context of man and monster in the Hopi narrative, we will start with the Hopi myth about the origin of the present world.

In the beginning of the world, the Hopi passed through a series of realms before arriving in the American southwest. In each of these prior worlds, they faced trials and tribulations set for them by the spirits. In oral tradition, a goddess named Huruing Wuhti, or "Hard Substances Woman," was the mythical progenitor of the human race, creating humans and animals out of cuticle rubbed from her body. This miraculous origin from dead skin or dirt is not specific to the Hopi but a common creation myth paralleled in many other southwestern cultures. In the Hopi variant, the newly minted humans, after being spawned in this way, were left by the goddess to find their way to a good life, passing from world to world with the help of various culture heroes and helpful animals who assisted them in their journeys.

In the beginning, the path of the Hopi was blocked because horrid monsters, giants, and demons prowled the worlds. These adversaries naturally made life miserable for the people. It was up to two young brothers, the Pöqanwhoya twins, grandsons of the motherly Spider Woman—herself a fixture in Hopi mythology—to defeat them and facilitate safe passage. Full of good humor and tricks as well as bravery, these charismatic twins were always playing a Hopi game called shinny (a stick and ball contest). They brought grass and trees into existence as they ran around playing, and they gathered mud to make the great mountains of the world and the soil from which the corn crops could grow (Courlander 1971: 23). The brothers also shot great lightning bolts, splitting open the earth, making such landmarks as the Grand Canyon and filling other canyons with clean rushing waters. Then they turned their attention to the horrible monsters and giants that roamed the earth and terrorized humankind. They were determined to exterminate them, in service to their old grandmother, Spider Woman, and for the benefit of all the tribe.

One of the creatures menacing the Hopi was the Tsaveyo monster. Terrifying tall and preternaturally strong, he wore a buckskin cape and carried a quiver full of deadly arrows. In one hand he carried a mighty bow and in the other a large stone ax with which he crushed humans with powerful strokes. Having a bizarre appearance, he looked like a giant grizzly bear with human appendages. Like the grizzly, Tsaveyo was a ravenous man-eater. Undaunted, the brothers killed him after many stratagems and battles, and at this victory the people rejoiced.

Another kind of monster the Hopi encountered in their mythical journey through the prior worlds were the So'yokos, man-eating ogres that looked like malformed human beings—ghouls with dripping fangs. There were hundreds of these beings in the next world in which the Hopi migrants arrived. Again the brothers came to the rescue. With great swings of their mighty weapons they killed these demons too, and once again the people rejoiced. But the battles of the Hopi had only begun. They journeyed to other worlds, seeking game, water, and tranquility. At the next place, they came across wandering earth-giant monsters called Cooyokos. The chiefs of all the clans sent messengers to the two warrior twins to ask for their help again. The young brothers arrived post haste. Upon their arrival they saw a Cooyoko threatening a village. Always up to the challenge, the youths put their playing sticks aside, took their bows from their backs, and killed the Cooyoko with lightning arrows. Then they went on playing stickball until they found another horrible monster, and they killed him also. They searched out and killed the Cooyokos one by one and killed them all, until none were left.

But still the brothers' work was not done. Four more individual monsters in the next world had to be slain before the people could be masters of the earth: Nata'shka, Cha'veyo, Wukochai'srisa, and Kwa'toko. The first two were humanoid creatures with great bulging eyes, sharp beaks, claws, and a bag or pouch of some kind on their backs in which they carried victims away to eat. Wukochai'srisa was a gigantic composite of man and elk with monstrously large antlers. Kwa'toko seems to have been a half-man, half-animal hybrid not clearly represented in either oral or pictorial form, also depicted as a man-eater (Parsons 1969: 395). All four terrors were slain by the heroic twins with the usual magical lightning bolts.

Despite these great feats, the primordial Hopi world was not by any means yet rid of dangerous monsters. Many So'yokos still remained hidden in the deep earth, waiting for opportunities to attack. Like the Windigo and Wechuge, these noxious remnants had to be confronted by the ever vigilant twins. One such confrontation is related in the oft-told folktale "How the So'yoko Monsters Were Killed by the Pöqanwhoyas." The tale, related in 1980 to Ekkehart Malotki (1983: 1–20) by the famous Indian storyteller, Herschel Talashoma, is, typically, both inspiring and gruesome. A paraphrase:

In a time not so distant to today the Hopi people were living in the mesa settlement of Oraibi in Arizona. The people of the village kept disappearing after going out into the bush to gather firewood or water. These unfortunates never returned, and the people, putting two and two together, realized that they were under attack by cannibal monsters from earlier worlds. Fearing the worst, the boys' grandmother told them to go and see what they could do to stop these depredations. Reluctantly (for they were as usual enjoying a shinny game at the time), the two adolescents did as they were told, journeying out into the wilderness and, indeed, discovering the source of the disappearances to be a So'yoko monster who was in the habit of capturing and eating wayfarers.

Given the nature of things in Hopi folklore, the Pöqanwhoyas twins were hardly surprised to discover that this monster was a human metamorph: their own missing uncle, horribly and atavistically changed into a cannibal ogre because of his bad behavior in the present world. Indeed, Hopi legends are full of humans turning into animals and monsters and vice versa: the dividing line between living forms and mythical concepts, as between temporal epochs, is as tenuous and permeable as the geological boundaries between the four worlds of Hopi mythology (Courlander 1982: xxxii).

The two boys let this monster-relative capture them without seeming to put up too much of a fight. Licking his chops at such an easy catch, the fierce uncle-ogre bound the twins with thick twine, put them in a cane basket, and carried them off to his lair, where he and his equally foul So'yoko wife, who was already lighting a fire in anticipation, prepared the usual banquet. "What a feast we're going to have!" the thrilled monsters chortled (15). Bound hand and foot, the boys remained quiet and passive, and it looked bad at this point for them and for the entire Oraibi Hopi tribe.

However, as usual, the heroic twins had once again outsmarted the ogres. Before their capture they were prescient enough to chew on a special medical plant that imbued them with superhuman strength and the ability to resist being roasted in a fire. Jumping out of the cooking pot at just the right moment, the two heroes attacked the cannibal beasts and a memorable hand-to-hand battle ensued, ending only when one brother grabbed the monster's giant bow and quiver and shot dead both So'yokos, husband and wife, with well-aimed giant arrows. At this point, the triumphant twins debated what to do next. After a brief discussion filled with the usual self-congratulation (they are always portrayed in the myths as egregiously—indeed monstrously—

arrogant and boastful), they decided to cut off the So'yokos' heads and, disguised as monsters themselves, play a trick on their grandmother. "Why don't we scare our grandmother?" they said gleefully (19).

So the boys made lurid costumes out of dead So'yokos' head, hair, and skin, put them on, and scared their old grandmother out of her wits on their return. So frightened was the old woman that she ran about the house "urinating and defecating from fear," finally collapsing in a heap. However, being good-hearted, the twins revived her, and seeing the brave act they had done, she forgave them. All was well again—at least for the time being.

So the Hopi people were saved yet again from the looming threat of maneating monsters by the valiant twins. "And this is the way the Pöqanwhoya brothers destroyed those monsters for the Oraibi people," relates the Indian orator, Herschel Talashoma. "And this, I suppose," he continues, "is the reason there are still people living in Oraibi today. And here the story ends" (21). But of course the story does not end here for the beleaguered Hopi. There will be further monsters to contend with and further stories to tell. Occasionally a horrible monster will rise up from the earth to threaten the people once again, sometimes in response to human frailty or error.

Each Hopi mesa has its own series of tales of the continuing danger from the ubiquitous monsters. Some villages have their own local monsters of which they are very proud. One such tale was collected by folklorist Armin Geertz in Walpi pueblo, First Mesa, in northeastern Arizona. It tells of an entirely different sort of beast from those defeated by the twins—a vast dragon called the "Great Serpent." Like European dragons, it demands human sacrifice:

It is recorded in legends that at one time the Great Serpent rose in the middle of the court of an ancient village until his head projected to the clouds. As this monster emerged from the earth he drew after him an overflow of water that covered the whole land, and drove the inhabitants to the mountains. When a flood covered the earth, the chief of the village, speaking to the serpent, whose head was in the zenith, said "Why do you thus destroy my people?" The snake replied, "You have a bad man, or wizard, in your number who bewitches you. I will not return to earth until you sacrifice to me your son." Sorrowfully the chief followed this demand for the relief of his people and threw his son into the water, and the serpent sank into the earth, dragging after him the flood that he had brought. (Geertz 1994: 174)

A CELEBRATION OF MONSTERS: KACHINAS

As we know from prior experience, monsters are never defeated completely but always return. In fact, among the Hopi, monster stories are reenacted in pantomime every few years at what are known as the Kachina ceremonies. These ceremonies occur during the extended rites-of-passage for both girls and boys who have reached maturity and are to be initiated as adults in the tribe. (Some related Indian groups, such as the Tewa, only initiate boys in their life-cycle rituals.)

As the great initiation ceremony approaches, the Hopi children are purposely frightened with horror stories about the ordeal that awaits them, being told by adults that they will be chopped up and eaten alive by monstrous spirits called Kachinas who are coming to get them. Assembled in the center of the village, the adolescents are then literally attacked by these Kachinas, which are actually their fathers and other male elders dressed up in costumes, their faces hidden. At a signal by the ceremonial leader, the Kachinas rush forward to whip the initiates mercilessly on their backs, often drawing blood, and of course petrifying them with terror. The boys (boys and girls in some villages) are supposed to bear up stoically under the ordeal, because the Hopi believe adults must be able to control emotions and conquer fear, for example, the obsessive fear of demons. Some Kachina masquerades depict the very same ancient monsters the hero twins vanquished in the olden days, for example the Cha'veyo and Tsevay. Another very popular Kachina costume, called the Black Ogre, resembles the original So'yoko spirit. Others depict hybrid man-animal ogres, half-human witches, and assorted demons.

One particularly fearsome Kachina that never fails to petrify the children is the Soyok Wuhti, a female figure. This awesome creature, whose name in English is Monster Woman, appears during the main (Powamu) ceremonies as one of the many So'yokos who threaten the lives of the children. Dramatically dressed all in black, with long straggling hair, ogling eyes, and a wide, fanged mouth, she suddenly appears carrying a blood-smeared meat cleaver in one hand and a long jangling crook in the other—a truly terrifying image to the young initiates. Folklorist Barton Wright continues to describe her role thus:

When she speaks, it is in a wailing falsetto or with a long dismal hoot of "Soyoko'-u-u-u," from which her name is derived. She may reach for the children with the long crook and threaten to put them in the basket on her back,

Kachina figure representing Awatovi Monster Man, painting by Cliff Bah-
nimptewa. Courtesy Heard Museum.

or to cut off their heads with the large knife that she carries in her hand, utterly terrifying her young audience. On some mesas she may be the ogre that threatens a small child who has been naughty and bargains with a relative to ransom the child, but in others she is not. In some villages she leads the procession of ogres; in others she remains at the side, content to make threatening gestures. (1973: 74)

Monster Woman may be accompanied by Awatovi Soyok Taka, or Awatovi Monster Man. Like his female counterpart, he pretends to eat children.

Hopi artists have created a cottage industry of miniature Kachina dolls carved from wood and painted, as well as paintings. These are produced both for local use, as children's toys, and for sale to visitors to the mesas.

MESO-AMERICAN MONSTERS

Crossing the border now into Mexico, we find monsters following hard on our heels. Early Spanish writers were impressed by the rich imaginary bestiary of the native Mexicans they conquered, especially the Aztec and Maya, whose pictorial art was more developed than that of their neighbors. Such luminaries as Bernardo de Sahagun and Bernal Díaz del Castillo reported on such arcane matters in the fifteenth century, providing us with a glimpse into pre-Columbian monster legends. Other Spaniards detailed those of the Mayan peoples in the Yucatán and Guatemala. These notations are summarized in a book by Mexican folklorist Roldán Peniche Barrera (1987), who provides us with a fascinating glimpse into native concepts of the demonic.

The Aztecs, for example, believed in all kinds of monstrous giant serpents. Aside from those mentioned earlier, one of these, the famous plumed giant Quetzalcoatl, was both monster and hero to them (Peniche Barrera 1987: 135–36). Numerous lesser hybrids completed the Aztec imaginary bestiary. In their sacred book, the *Chilan Balum*, the Aztecs wrote about Hapai-Can, a great swallowing serpent (*serpiente tragadora* in Spanish), which sucks human blood and whose main diet is children. Another bloodcurdling beast was the *ekuneil*, or the great black snake. This was described as a monstrous serpentine creature like a huge anaconda that encircled and suffocated travelers. Still another was a two-headed giant python, which was said to have similarly violent propensities.

Not all Aztec monsters were serpentine in form. The Indians of central Mexico also feared numerous types of bipedal man-eating giants very similar in conception to those in Homer's *Odyssey* and in other classical sources

(Peniche Barrera 1987: 71–73). We have already mentioned Tlacahuepan, described as a humanoid ogre supposedly so big as to be able to hold a human in the palm of his hand. The terrified Indians made propitiation to this tyrant by sacrificing and butchering slaves captured from other tribes, whose free-flowing blood and still-palpitating hearts the monster greedily devoured. After scenting the blood, Tlacahuepan, like the giant in "Jack and the Beanstalk," lumbered forth to find his meal. Unless such gruesome sacrifices were made, the monster would eat any person who ventured too near (151–52).

Another terror was El Cráneo, the flying head. This was depicted in oral folklore as a large disembodied skull with chomping teeth that bit, tore, and swallowed humans. It was said to fly about at night, attacking people and animals. As in ancient Greece, not all pre-Columbian monsters were male. There was, for example, a ferocious water spirit whose native Aztec name, Chalchiuhicueye, translates as "she who wears a skirt of emeralds" because she had an jewel-encrusted scorpion's tail. Belying the beautiful appellation, this water demon was said to drag down boats and drown sailors, much like Scylla and Charybdis (46–47).

Many of these aboriginal beliefs have filtered down to the present little changed among central Mexican rural people. Anthropologist Julius Kassovic, for example, writes that even in the late 1970s many Indian villagers feared monsters and devils living in the *malpaís*, or badlands, whom they regard as the essence of all evil (1980: 188–89). These evil incarnations are both revered for their power and feared for their unprovoked malice toward humans. In this brief article, the anthropologist describes numerous ceramic objects and figurines villagers make today representing these swarming monsters. The villagers regard these beings with a mixture of awe and horror. There are hundreds of them in every shape and form.

SOUTH AMERICA

As we move to the cone countries, we find a plentitude of monster legends, some dating to pre-Hispanic times (Magaña 1988). For instance, in Toba Province, Argentina, live the Chaco tribe, a stone-age people, who were hunters-gatherers until recently. With mystical ardor, they believe in a monstrous figure which they call the "Pitet" (P. Wright 1988: 117–18). They believe it is ever-present, but invisible during the day, materializing and attacking at night. This curious beast is a typical hybrid in form: the Indians say it has the overall form of a bird, but with a deformed human body and human arms. However, it is made all of bone, so that it has the appearance of a bizarre skeleton. When in corporeal form at night, it flies about, using a deadly razor-sharp lance to slash and kill unwary people.

In northern Tucumán Province in Argentina, there circulate stories (some with a political twist) about the many mythic monsters that prowl the countryside at the behest of the landowning oppressors. The most feared of these is a giant "diabolical dog" (Isla 1998: 138). This monstrous canine supposedly eats up peons (workers) who make trouble for the rich. It is described by a local peasant man, who obviously has some political consciousness:

The most widely spread legend of the North is the one they call the "Familiar" dog. According to this legend, it is a gigantic dog that drags huge chains behind it while fire comes out of its eyes and its mouth. This demonic monster was the guardian of the fortune of the owners of the sugar plantations. People said that this dog fed on human flesh of the peons. Any people who had trouble with the owners, that peon disappeared, "eaten by the Familiar." . . . These stories and legends gave all of us the fright of a lifetime. (cited in Isla 1998: 138)

Other equally monstrous (but nonpolitical) creatures exist in Argentina's vast badlands. For example, there is another nocturnal beast the Indians of the Pampas call the Iemisch. This was described by an Italian immigrant named Florentino Ameghino in 1897 in a letter which he sent to his brother in Italy, along with a few bones supposedly from this creature. His rather lurid description:

This animal is of nocturnal habits, and it's said to be so strong that it can seize horses with its claws and drag them to the bottom of the water. According to the description I have been given, it has a short head, big canine teeth, and no external ears; its feet are short and plantigrade, with three toes on the forefeet and four on the hind, three toes are formed by a membrane for swimming, and are also armed with formidable claws. Its tail is long, flat and prehensile. (cited in Grant 1992: 49)

COMMON FEATURES OF AMERICAN MONSTERS

We end this chapter on American monsters by summarizing the common New World traits, both north and south. Despite variations, there are common denominators. These have been pointed out by a few anthropologists.

Raymond Fogelson (1980: 147–48) describes the major commonalities as follows. First, all the New World monsters are violent cannibals. Some eat people whole, like the Windigo; others chop people up into little pieces with a variety of weapons (e.g., the Hopi Monster Woman with her cleaver and the Chaco Pitet bird).

Second, American bogeys are large enough, powerful enough, and bizarre enough looking to be frightening if only by their appearance, which, like that of Grendel, is often mysteriously indistinct or bizarrely changeful. Third, they all have anticultural propensities, meaning they respect no behavioral limits, recognize no restraints, and break all the rules. Fourth, by their very existence they define the "natural" by providing a shocking contrast that is unnatural and confusing and horrifying. The last common feature Fogelson notes is geographical provenience. The monsters originate in the boundary between the known and the unknown, between human and animal, between civilization and wilderness. These borderline qualities make them all the more frightening to the people who believe in them. One may add that most of these monsters live deep within the bowels of the earth and are depicted as rising up to attack, or, in the case of the monster-avians like the Thunderbird, they inhabit the sky or mountain aeries.

To this useful list of shared traits we may add a few observations. First, the American monsters are usually described as being timeless and eternal, as having an anomalous relationship to human chronology. In most cases they hearken back to a primordial past when humankind was in its infancy and giant beasts ruled the earth. The monster images are "mythical" in the temporal as well as existential sense, having existed before humans when the world was "new" (Hallowell 1974: 76). For example, Windigo and Wechuge have "always" existed; they are precedent as well as ancestral to humans. It is also not surprising that all these primordial monsters are mute: they issue only roars, bellows, and other animal noises, as befits their animal-like provenance.

Many American monsters live in or near water. Most are aquatic or vaguely amphibious. If not fully marine, they lurk in marshy fens or god-forsaken wastelands. They all seem to have a paradoxically close, if adversarial relationship to humans because they are dependent upon humans for food. Men and monsters thus have a kind of perverse interdependence. Humans, meanwhile, at least in many North American legends, can turn into monsters, as illustrated in the Algonquian, Athabaskan, and Hopi cases. So the relationship is complex, reciprocal, and morally ambiguous.

Finally, there is a recurrent attitude toward the monsters which can only be described as bifurcated and contradictory. The Indians who believe in them (and some Canadian whites also) do not look at their monsters with a single-sided repugnance, but instead with ambivalence: reverence mixed with fear. In particular, Windigo, Wechuge, the Hopi So'yoko Kachinas, and, especially, the Aztec Quetzalcoatl, who is a full-fledged hero, are sources of respect and even religious veneration as well as fear.

Consequently, given the mixed emotions involved, these imaginary American creatures can only be described as being very like the ancient beast-gods of the Near East and Europe, because they are amalgams of the divine and the diabolical, horribleness and sublimity. American monsters, are, in short, like monsters everywhere, stark dualisms: evil and divine, more and less than human, repellent and fascinating. We move on to Asia and Oceania where the echoes are eerie.

THE OGRES OF ASIA

In a deeply tribal sense, we love our monsters.
— *E. O. Wilson*, In Mortal Disaster

e spoke earlier of a "combat-myth" that underlies many early state religions and serves as a basic cosmological principle. In these myths, a hero goes forth to challenge a beast that holds the world in thrall. The Egyptian Seth and Babylonian Marduk are among the earliest examples of monster-defying champions, defeating the terrible Apophis and Tiamat respectively. By destroying these tyrants, the hero ends human subjugation, liberating people from darkness and promulgating civilization. Central to the great traditions, the archetypal combat-myth instructs that only after vanquishing monsters can people achieve control over themselves and over nature. The hero's victory signals not only the beginning of "real" time, that is, time measured by a self-referential cultural index, but also the cognitive infancy and the moral starting point of the human race.

Not confined to the literate Western traditions, foundation myths crop up in most other cultures as well, as we have just seen. Not written down but transmitted orally, the same stories appear in myriad forms; some feature single heroes, others multiple saviors or, in many American legends, brothers —for example the ball-playing twins among the Hopi. In the general thrust of the narrative and its moral symbolism, the pre-literate cultures and the great civilizations are pretty much the same, as Norman Cohn suggests, attesting to the universality of the monster metaphor as a means of sublimating instinct.

As in the case of myth and pictorial art, the earliest writing teems with monsters. A classic example in a literate tradition outside the Occident is that of the Hindus, who are of course of Indo-European stock and through either ancestry or borrowing share many traditions with the European and Semitic peoples whose imaginary fauna we have already examined. Perhaps it is not surprising that the earliest South Asian texts should share many features with Greek, Roman, and other Western traditions and in fact to replicate the same epics, metaphorical situations, and, most important for us here, confabulations (D. White 1991: 29). We start our Asian journey in the subcontinent.

MONSTERS OF INDIA

Very much like its Western counterparts the Christian Bible and the Hebrew Talmud is the famous Indian epic, the Rig Veda, a holy Sanskrit book based on a pastiche of legend and myth. The formal basis of Indian cosmologies, the Rig Veda is full of stories about heroes and holy men who battle monsters. The text is literally bursting with mischievous beings who are always threatening to smash what appears to be a fragile civilization.

The main villain in all this is Vritra. This foul specimen has much in common with the Egyptian Apophis and others of their ilk. Vritra represents primordial chaos and is conceived in the texts as so huge as to be almost unimaginable, so formidable as to be unstoppable, and so powerful as to outstrip the very gods. He is, like the howling Canadian Windigo, described as noisy. Portrayed as a "screaming dragon," among other epithets (Cohn 1993: 64), Vritra contains all darkness and destruction within his deformed body. Incapable of words, he can only bellow and hiss. After oppressing the world for eons before real time begins, he is finally defeated with a final yelp by the warrior-god Indra in the usual climactic battle. Thenceforth, mankind is liberated, civilization springs up, the gods smile, and culture grows.

Rejoicing in such a world-shaking victory, the Indian hero resembles Thor, Seth, and all the other hero-gods. But aside from the contest and consequent triumph, the Rig Veda also tells of a world still swarming with little demons and mundane monsters not so easily vanquished in single-handed epic combat. Undaunted by Vritra's defeat, these residual demons, like the American ogres who lurk beneath the ground, remain in hiding to trouble the world of the Hindus and, given their evil, are always trying to overthrow the gods and hurl humanity into the pit. If they are not thwarted, the entire universe would disintegrate into chaos. In early Hindu India, this meant that everything that went wrong in life, from natural disasters like droughts, fires, and floods to personal misfortune and bad luck was laid at the door of these supernatural scourges.

As in North America, there was no limit to the evil doings of these demons. Indefatigable and malignant, they threatened life, property, health, and for-

وویه تهای حبری راکطین برای نکا هبانی سیتیا که رشته بود از ترس ماون کرختنه وراون سیتبا

Rāvaṇa seizes Sītā. Freer Gallery of Art, Smithsonian Institution, Washington, D.C.: Gift of Charles Lang Freer, F1907.271.131a.

tune. They attacked singly, in pairs, or in massed legions: "in pairs or in whole bands, demons prowled the land" (Cohn 1993: 74). As is usual in such perfervid imaginings, people conceived of these scourges in various shapes and sizes, all malformed and frightening, permuting at will. Some were said to be bizarre composites blending human and animal features in grotesque ways; some were said to look deceptively like normal men or women and to be of normal size but deformed, with yellow eyes or multiple heads, scaly serpentine skin, or wolfish or canine faces. Others were said to have exaggerated animal traits on top of a basically human anatomy: they were slimy reptiles but had human heads or arms, for example. Or else, totally abandoning any pretense at deception, they were entirely animal-like in form, appearing as diabolical dogs or oversized vultures.

Many could change shape at will, going out at night as beasts of prey and returning in humanoid form to escape detection. As usual, their home was the netherworld, the subterranean domain of everlasting darkness where evil dwells. As in ancient Egypt and Mesopotamia, in iron-age India every man and woman had to be alert at all times because the chthonic spirits were watchful, awaiting opportunities for mischief. People were most vulnerable when in some abnormal or handicapped situation. They were in special danger when sick, depressed, or, in the case of women, when pregnant or nursing.

Such was the monster-filled world of ancient classical India, but even today the danger of attack has not lessened. In the hinterlands of the Hindu world, not only in India proper but also in the bordering states of Sikkim, Bhutan, Nepal, and Bangladesh, monsters and demons still prowl the land in the minds of the uneducated. In India proper, the Sanskrit word for monster (*adbhuta*; that which exceeds or goes beyond the normal) is eschewed in favor of the more general *asuras*, a portmanteau Hindi term for all those who oppose the Vedic law, that is, outcastes, anti-gods, or, in the symbolic sense, demons, devils, and evil spirits. The same term is used for both pariahs who live on the periphery of Hindu society, such as polluted outcastes or murderers, and foreign invaders or barbarians—a broad usage that suggests a conceptual category of the invasive alien other in the political as well as metaphorical and psychological senses (D. White 1991: 19–20). But Hindu lore, the religious consciousness as well as the mythology, is full of weird creatures and macabre composites, evil spirits and demons, who, like the protean Hindu gods themselves, are inveterate shape-shifters, taking on incalculable incarnations.

One of the most famous monster-gods is a female figure: the bloodthirsty demon, Kali. This lurid image is familiar to Westerners as the gory, multi-armed, sword-wielding fiend of Hindu mythology. Flesh-eating and blood-drinking, she is the goddess of death, the taker of life, oppressive and frightening, the impersonation of terror. Kali is not the only she-demon in the Hindu pantheon, which is richly populated with gruesome females—among them the ghoulish virgin warrior Durga and her emanations Camunda, Mahisamardini, Yogi Nidra, and Ambika. Also a shape-shifter, the goddess Durga is one of the many forms of Devi (Bennett 1983: 261). The Anglo-Indian scholar G. Morris Carstairs describes the goddess Mataji in equally terrifying terms: "everyone worships the Mataji, the Goddess, who is a protective mother to those who prostate themselves before her in abject supplication, but who is depicted also as a sort of demon, with gnashing teeth, who stands on top of her male adversary, cuts off his head and drinks his blood" (1967: 157). This female goddess has the appearance of an infernal figure with multiple arms, all wielding sharp weapons.

One who written at length about mythical beasts in Hindu scripture is the Sanskrit scholar Wendy O. Doniger. In her book, *Women, Androgynes, and Other Mythical Beasts* (1980), she points out that many demonic figures of Vedic and post-Vedic Hindu lore are conceived as androgynous or her-maphroditic. Even more take on a specifically female form. Most of the hor-rible female figures, in a perverse reversal of the maternal role, are supposed to eat children and drink blood. Reflected in these images, fear of the "bad mother," the devilish flip side of motherhood, is a common thread in Hindu liturgy. For example, there is the ogress Putana, who is said to be a "devourer of children," and who appears in a charming maternal form, only to change back into a hideous monster once she starts sucking the life blood from her victims (41). Monsterdom in India is, however, an equal-opportunity category. Male demons also abound and are often more destructive, some even challenging the gods. Two of these, Madhu and Kaitabha, are so presumptuous that they actually steal the holy Vedic books from the gods in heaven, carrying them off to Hell beneath the great ocean of cosmic waters. They do this in a particularly reprehensible fashion: they cast a spell on the gods, take the Vedas, chop them to pieces, and hide them at the bottom of the ocean (223). Demons are always dismembering things! It takes all the efforts of the gods to regain and to restore the holy texts.

TRIBAL MONSTERS: THE GARO

Awful monsters and their counterparts the epic heroes find expression out-side orthodox Hinduism. A case of monster preoccupation comes from the

Garo, an aboriginal non-Hindu tribe. They are a matrilineal people who live in the East and West Garo Hills District of the state of Meghalaya on the Bangladesh border. Divided into nine sub-tribes, the Garo are a major aboriginal group of this region of India, and while most remain animists, there are also many converted Christians among them. Some live over the border in Bangladesh (Burling 1963).

The Garo are firm believers in demons and goblins, especially in nasty spirits called *mite*, who they say abound in the forests and other marginal places and who are always biting people and causing sickness (Burling 1963: 54). They, too, have their foundation myths. For the Garo, the world as it is had to be safely secured in the beginning of human time by the reckless feats of a warrior-god who defeated the usual monsters. The monster-tamer in Garo folklore is Goera, who like his counterparts the Norse Thor and the Ugaritic Ba'al is the god of thunder and lightening. His first contest is with a giant monster-boar who has dominated the world since the beginning of time.

As described by Indian folklorist Dewan Singh Rongmuthu, who collected much Garo mythology in the 1950s, this primordial monster-boar was quite formidable. It was the biggest and mightiest being in the whole world in that distant epoch. Its body was as big as a Himalayan peak. Like so many other monsters, it had not one, but seven terrible-looking heads, furcated from one main neck; each head had seven sharp projecting tusks that looked like two-edged scimitars (Rongmuthu 1960: 156–57). To make it even more hideous, this beast, Cyclops-like, had one piercing eye in the center of each of its seven foreheads which shone as bright and as luminous as the full moon on a clear night. When the gigantic creature stood up, its huge proboscis touched the Dura Hill, miles to the north, while its tail lay submerged in the waters of the Songdu River to the south.

So immense was this creature that its body harbored worlds within itself. According to Garo mythology, on its great humped back there were seven clumps of sharp jati bamboos, seven plots of thatch grass, and seven stalks of bulrush plants. Seven perennial streamlets also flowed there. Together these protuberances formed a little forest world on the back of the enormous creature, where dwelled a pair of langur monkeys with their offspring, as well as seven pairs of moles.

Not surprisingly, the sight of this behemoth was awe-inspiring to humans. People trembled with fear at the mere mention of its name, and no one could stand up to it. Unopposed, the monster-boar roamed where it would without interference, as if it were the master of the whole world. It devoured all the crops and every living thing that crossed its path, wantonly destroying the works of man.

Naturally, however, even such a supernal brute was no match for a determined hero such as the Garo warrior Goera. After the usual titanic struggle, the hero killed the monster-boar and, opting for civilization, settled down, built a house, got married, and behaved like a proper family man, becoming a model for all. But his domestic inactivity was short-lived, as new challenges threatened the land. These appear, of course, in the form of new monsters and fresh ogres. According to the folklorist:

Goera did not remain long in his house. As he found a life of inactivity too stale and unprofitable, he wandered all over the world in search of fresh adventures. In the course of his ramblings on many a strand, he directed his exploits against a great number of hideous monsters, which were accustomed to play havoc with human lives, and systematically exterminated them all. He rescued his elder sisters, who had been carried off by Sheh-elja Wachingja, the patriarchal head of the dogs. Buga Raja, the patriarchal head of the mermen, who had decoyed Goera's elder sister Mehjakchi Kahsyndik, was defeated by the hero in a bloody encounter. But the girl was not rescued as she had been confined inside some impregnable rocks by Bugarik Bugasil, who was Buga Raja's servant. This Bugarik Bugasil was the progenitor of the giant aquatic serpents which are known as sangkinnies. They seldom appear out of water for fear of Goera. (1960: 156–57)

But still the work of Goera was not done. His next feat was to vanquish a female ogre, one of the "most formidable monsters which was numbered among those slain by Goera in his ramblings" (171). This demon, a gargantuan beast named Budangma, was as tall as the highest tree on earth, and resembled an extremely ugly, hideously deformed woman. According to legend, she had an enormously protruding nose, thick pouting lips, one piercing eye in the center of her forehead, and earlobes that reached down to her ankles. These last she used as her bed covering when she slept. Her strength was tremendous and she was the terror of the children of that age, for she used to come stealthily to the villages at night and carry them away in order to eat them alive. But the dauntless Goera completely overthrew her in single combat. He felled her with one blow of his formidable club and hacked her body into pieces.

Even after this great victory, Goera had to fight another formidable female monster. In one outer corner of the earth, Goera in his wanderings came across a cruel giantess named Noeri Simeri Jahpramma, who could make herself invisible when in pursuit of her human quarry. She had in her possession hammers of different sizes and patterns that she used to mow down her victims. Stealthily approaching her lair, Goera saw the wicked fiend sound asleep, so he picked up a massive hammer she used to kill elephants and hit her a violent blow on the forehead, splitting her head into two. Thus the Garo were made safe from monsters at the beginning of time. Or rather, they were made relatively safe; lesser monsters and sprites still trouble their sleep.

SINHALESE DEMONS

The island of Sri Lanka, formerly called Ceylon, lies just off the Indian subcontinent. The southern part of the island is occupied by the Sinhalese people, who are heirs to an ancient Asian civilization. Like the Hindus and the Garo to the north, they are preoccupied with fighting off legions of devils who threaten them at very turn. The Sinhalese, however, are Buddhists. Following scripture, they believe that the cosmos is built up out of three gigantic levels of space—"three worlds"—arranged in a hierarchical order. The top level belongs to the deities, who are largely beneficent and who can be called on by humans in need; the intermediate level is populated by normal human beings; the lower level is a shadowy and fetid domain swarming with misshapen demons called *yakku*, who are the incarnation of evil. The layered worlds that constitute the cosmos are conceptualized as spatially, morally, and spiritually distinct, but they still interpenetrate, meaning that movement is possible among them. Like other monsters we have encountered, the yakku take advantage of this permeability to rise up from their dark lairs and attack innocent people in the middle world—our world.

As in the case of the Mesopotamian monsters, these unprovoked attacks are especially effective when people are vulnerable. Such is the case when a person is in an unusual or unprotected situation or an unstable emotional state, for example when he or she is in mourning, sad, confused, frightened, or in a peculiar situation the Sinhalese call "being alone" (isolated from other people, either by design or accident, and bereft of human company) (Kapferer 1983: 50–51). Since in Sinhalese Buddhism these beings are irredeemably evil, their sole purpose to cause harm and disrupt order, to make people sick, to overturn the work of men and gods. Destructive, grotesque, and devouring, the yakku are indeed monsters. The Sinhalese spend much time and energy in complex rituals of exorcism meant to drive the yakku away.

The anthropologist Bruce Kapferer spent many years studying the relationship between people and demons in Sri Lanka. Based on ten years of close analysis, his book *A Celebration of Demons* (1983) describes in minute detail the rituals and curing ceremonies by which the Sinhalese rid themselves of these supernatural scourges. According to Kapferer there are a bewildering array of evil spirits, almost too many to number. Most are conceived of as gigantic, others smaller, but they all have enormous strength in their deformed bodies, enough to subdue any normal human being and, indeed, to challenge the deities above. No matter what their appearance, they are all fierce, bloodthirsty, and full of sexual desire; worse, they have an insatiable craving for human flesh (118). In colorful paintings and in molded clay images, local artists portray them as follows: the demons are usually dark in color, covered with coarse fur or hair, their bloodshot eyes bulge out of their sockets, their noses are pointy or animal-like, their nostrils flare, their lips are thick and everted, and from their wide open mouths protrude sharp curving tusks like scimitars. One of these demons, Kalu Yaka, carries two decapitated children whose heads he has apparently ripped off and grips in his awesome maw. These demons are all violent, unpredictable, and mischievous; they delight in playing tricks on humanity (119–20).

The main Sinhalese demons are four in number and are worth describing in detail. The first is Riri Yaka. In Sinhalese mythology he has a primary form and eight other manifestations. In most of his incarnations, he is a giant, towering above his human victims. In his main form, his face is blue and splotched with blood; he has bloodshot eyes and red rays radiate from them. Blood pours from his nostrils and smoke billows from his ears. His breath is foul and his mouth is filled with decomposing human flesh. His entire body is scarlet with dripping blood. He has a close connection with the evil spirit Mara (the Evil One, the Harbinger of Death).

Next comes Mahasona, one of the most feared of all the demons. He is tens of feet high and possesses awesome strength. He rides a wild boar, carries an elephant on his shoulders, and drinks the elephant's blood from its neck. Mahasona has the head and toothy maw of a bear, the trunk and legs of a human, and four mighty human arms. Smoke pours from his nostrils.

Then there is Kalu Yaka mentioned above. In one of his manifestations he is dark blue-black in color; he has four arms and rides a black bull. A cobra is wound around his waist. He wields a wooden club. One of his particularly nasty specialties is decapitating children and drinking their blood.

Finally there is Sanni Yaka, a composite of eighteen different satanic forms. This weird changeling has all the awful attributes of the other demons, to which is added a special twist. He is thought to be responsible for causing wasting illnesses and infirmities, including such symptoms as facial paralysis, tics, and deformities. So aside from the usual monstrous deformities, he is represented in images and masks with contorted facial expressions (123).

Each of these demons causes a specific form of somatic illness or madness. In particular, mental illness and associated abnormal behavior are said to be either caused or exacerbated by the attack of a demon. Any inordinate emotion can invite demonic attention, be it fear, rage, grief over a lost loved one, sexual desire—expressed or repressed—jealousy, envy, even an extreme food craving. All these states are evidence of mental imbalance and are symptomatic of demonic possession. Unbalanced emotional states reflect a weakness in mental attitude, and this renders individuals vulnerable to the malevolence of the malign supernatural monsters that await their chance to attack (50). Fear is the emotional state that most commonly beings on the onset of demonic illness.

All Sinhalese demons share certain characteristics that make them close kin to the other monsters we have looked at. First, Sinhalese folklore regards them as eternal, as having existed since the beginning of time; in this way they resemble the immortal gods. Also, like gods, they are giants, endowed with superhuman strength and power—used, however, for evil. Like the gods morphologically, they are shape-changers. In addition they are depicted as composite figures, with bizarrely fused animal and human parts or what Claude Kappler (1980) has called a monstrous superfluity of parts, such as four arms or three or more heads. Unlike gods, they are uniformly malevolent in disposition. Many are also portrayed as man-eating, and these are often shown feasting on human flesh in the images made by local artists and exorcists. The imagery abounds in putrefying flesh, headless victims, dripping blood, and other Grand Guignol effects.

Like other good monsters, the Sinhalese demons live in a dark underground world from which they emerge to harass humans. And last, as in the case of so many monsters, they are associated with human frailty and sin.

They are, in fact, externalizations—embodied metaphors—for dangerous internal emotional states such as anger and fear, which like a demon can be said to possess a person. The monsters appear in tandem with human pain and suffering, and especially, as components of human anger and aggression.

CHUKCHEE OGRES

We move north now from the subcontinent to the Asiatic reaches of the old Soviet Empire, where we find numerous preliterate tribes and diverse monster beliefs. The aboriginal peoples of Siberia are well known throughout Russia for their demonic figures. A classic example are the Chukchee of Siberia, who live in the Autonomous District named for them in the Magadan Province on the Pacific coast. They also live in the Lower Kolyma District of the Yakut Republic and the north of the Koryak Autonomous District. These regions are in the extreme northeastern reaches of Siberia, partly within the Arctic Circle. The Chukchee are reindeer herders and hunters who migrate over large distances with their herds. They practice an animistic religion and place much emphasis on shamanism and magical curing. They are deathly afraid of various kinds of monsters and ogres.

Their impressive fabulous bestiary was described by Russian ethnographer Waldemar Bogoras at the turn of the last century (1910). His accounts of other matters have proved solid, so we can assume that these descriptions are valid. In general evil spirits in the Chukchee language are called *ke'let*, a generic term. The worst of these are called *re'kkeñ*, a word that implies evil spirits that have taken on man-eating proclivities. These spirits are imagined as large hybrid beasts, bigger than the massive Siberian tigers, and they hunt humans as their only food. In the Kolyma country, where Bogoras lived for a time, a re'kkeñ is said to be such a monster with a bear's body and very large fangs and long ears. Although zoomorphic, these creatures have some dangerous human-like characteristics, especially intelligence and the ability to use technology. Bogoras continues:

I obtained several curious details about the supposed ways of the re'kkeñ tribe. They cannot fly. Even when pursued by a shaman, they only dive underground, making the earth near them soften and give way like water. They have red canoes, in which they ascend even the shallowest waters, also large skin boats with crews of eight oarsmen and a boat-master . . . after the manner of men. When hunting from these boats, they lay their nets for men, who are their only game. Their houses are underground dwellings. Their kettles are made of grass. Their fire is snow-white in the day-time and blood-red in the evening, when it may be seen in the west after sunset. (1910: 27)

There are many other types of Chukchee monsters. Borogas was told by the local people of several kinds of hybrid creatures, cryptomorphs, and were-animals, all said to be predatory on human beings. Among these were oversized demons in the shape of sea-birds that are said to turn into monstrous killer-whales at will. These shape-shifters are also called sea-were-wolves, and they hunt people for food. In the local language they are also called "long-nosed birds." In summer these aerial-aquatic creatures assume the shape of killer whales, and in winter they come to the shore, transform themselves into wolves, and hunt the Chukchee reindeer herds as well as people. In accordance with this belief, wolves are thought to be endowed with supernatural powers and are held in reverent awe by the Chukchee. Another ogre hunts lost Chukchee travelers. He makes a musical noise with his snout to beckon travelers to come to him. At the same time he calls with a wailing voice, in imitation of a distressed traveler who has lost his way. Anyone who hears these calls and approaches the monster will be immediately caught and devoured.

Yet another Chukchee monster is said to capture women for nefarious purposes. It keeps these poor female captives locked in a cabin, abuses them, and eats them if it likes. The long prehensile tail of this monster snakes around the cabin door and keeps the sleeping room of the cabin closed to shut off escape. But its reptilian body is so long that, even if any of the captive women get out, its head can overtake the fugitives and turn them back.

CHINESE OGRES

Now we turn to the great civilization of China. There, in textual and in pictorial forms, we see some similarities to Western and Middle Eastern lore. Again there is the chaos monster theme in which a local hero defeats a singular monster at the beginning of time. Like the other great traditions we have looked at, ancient Chinese mythology also conjures up such a primordial adversary that in the typical pattern stands astride and threatens the world.

However, there is a difference between China and the other literate traditions we have already visited. Unlike the European, Middle Eastern, and

Fire-spewing monster. Canopy. Ngor Monastery, Southern Tibet, nineteenth century. The Newark Museum/Art Resource, NY.

Indian primal monsters, the ancient nemesis is not conceived as a reptilian dragon-like being in China or any Oriental civilization. The Eastern dragon is not the gruesome monster of medieval European imagination, but the genius of strength and goodness, having been appropriated by elites as an emblem of good fortune. In China the dragon as a symbol represents the spirit of fertility and therefore of life itself. Dragons are often associated with good luck and with royalty in some Oriental traditions, including those of China, Japan, and Tibet (Shuker 1995: 86–87). So the Eastern dragon motif will not be specifically a subject in this book. The Chinese monsters take on other forms, usually simian, sometimes avian.

Despite the iconographic difference, the main Chinese origin myth is familiar to the Western variants as a foundation narrative. The tale is told in the great book of ancient myths, the *Shu Ching*, dating at least from 80 B.C. (D. White 1991: 168). According to the story of the world's creation given in this book, all was order and harmony until a great demon-monster

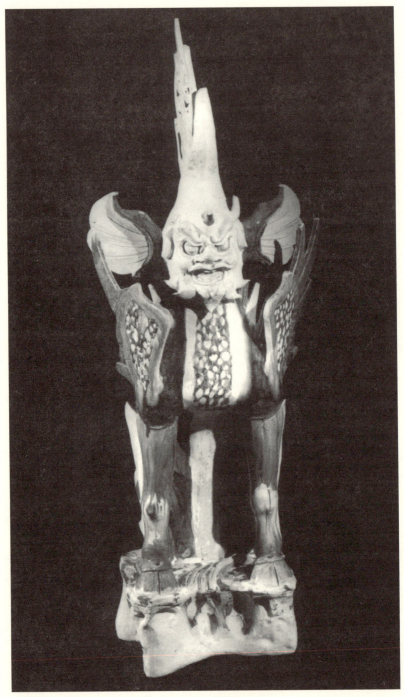

Chinese ogre. © Copyright The British Museum.

named Kung-kung rose up against the gods. This creature is said to look rather like a gargantuan ape or baboon and to have supernatural powers.

In the beginning of time, this ape-monster was close to the gods; he was in fact related to the five original sage kings who founded and began order on earth. However, Kung-kung was neither wise nor good like his brother gods, and his monstrous hubris turned him into a hideous giant with horns and a foul disposition. Thus transformed through sins, he was denied the gift of speech so that he is capable only of roars and screams. Thus punished, he rebelled against the world and soon took over. As Kung-kung is associated in Chinese mythology with the element of water, the earth is flooded under his illegitimate rule, and there is a danger that the raging flood waters of earth will rise up to the upper waters of heaven, thus confounding all and throwing the universe into a state of total chaos (D. White 1991: 168).

To prevent this calamity, the Chinese need a hero. One appears in the form of Chuan-hsü, the god of the wind. He is sent down to earth by the others gods to confront the giant ape-ogre and to rectify matters. Seeing this bold young hero advance, the seething monster positions himself upon the highest peak of the earth to do battle. Undeterred, Chuan-hsü attacks and after much struggle manages to throw Kung-kung down from the heights. When the great monster crashes into the chasm, bellowing and roaring, one of his huge horns smashes the base of the mountain, which collapses. With the shattering of this cosmic pillar, the planes of the earth become skewed, rivers flow up, the wind blows the wrong way, and everything is topsy-turvy. With the help of various deities, the warrior-god spends the next few eons correcting things, and finally order is restored. With the monster safely out of the way the world resumes in normal course.

OTHER CHINESE MONSTERS

Repeating the usual pattern, the primordial monster's death provides a brief respite for humanity, but once again many other dangers remain. As in the other traditions, the primal monsters never die, but live on to plague mankind forever. Chinese folklore is full of smaller but just as venomous and deadly ogres and bogeys. Like the people of India and Sri Lanka, the Chinese must remain vigilant against them.

As in India, such remnant monsters are linked to present-day outsiders and to the political portrayal of the barbarian foreigner. Thus, in the origin-of-the-world myth, when Kung-kung is defeated he and his monstrous hordes are said to be exiled to the furthest points of the globe. There they evolve into the non-Han savages (such as the northern Mongolian tribes) who constantly threaten the Middle Kingdom with invasion, rape, and pillage. This ancestral linkage between mythical monster and (real) threatening alien is indeed written into the Chinese language and orthography, as in Indian usage. The generic Mandarin term *kuei*, meaning such things as fear, strangeness, large size, cunning, and ghost of the dead and used generically for monster, also implies "people or race of an alien origin," that is, foreigners. In a further association, the written characters for the terms monster, chaos, and barbarian in Mandarin use the same radical; thus concepts for chaos and terror, the barbarian and the demon, the outsider and the monster were in fact semantically indistinguishable to the average literate Chinese (D. White 1991: 157).

The usual marine monsters also trouble the sleep of China. Being sailors and having many navigable rivers and a long coastline, the Chinese of course have the usual water spirits to contend with. One of these, the *bonze*, a classical sea serpent, patrols the waters off Hunan Island and is referred to with both familiarity and awe as Hai Ho Shang (D. Cohen 1970: 24). In one popular Chinese legend, the Chien Tang River was supposedly infested by a ferocious water monster known to local people as the Kiau. This beast was said to be like a chameleon in its ability to change colors and to camouflage itself during an attack on boats. In A.D. 1129, it is said, a local hero, no longer able to abide the suffering of his fellows at the hands of the Kiau, threw himself into the mouth of the river and did battle with the demon, emerging victorious after many days. Such legends are common in rural China, and this particular river has its share of stories. As far back as A.D. 488, an ancient writer reported for posterity that a local government official sailing on the Chien Tang River was attacked by a serpentine monster more than 300 feet long, which the observant official described as "dark black and having no scales" (Bright 1991: 4–5). Loch Ness (or perhaps Godzilla) in the Middle Kingdom!

Reports of terrible monsters were not confined to rural China, or to the rivers and seas of the far-flung Chinese empire. In the city of Nanking, a curious story attaches to the ruins of a celebrated pagoda made of porcelain. Located in the center of the city, this building was once topped by a great basin, thirty-nine feet in diameter, which filled with water when it rained. The legend relates that a large bird perched on the bowl's edge dropped a hideous-looking fish from the nether regions into the water-filled basin. This infernal fish then grew to monstrous proportions and soon began to exert such an evil influence over the entire neighborhood that the local thunder god was called in to dispatch the monster; in doing so, the god destroyed the pagoda as well (Bright 1991: 5).

As elsewhere, monsters and demons figure prominently in Chinese peasant folklore. In her book, *Shadow and Evil in Fairy Tales* (1983), the folklorist Marie-Louise Von Franz has collected numerous examples of ogre lore from the countryside. One particularly spine-tingling tale comes from oral peasant tradition in Kiautschou (123). Called "The Horse Mountain Ghost," it is rather typical of the genre in that it raises the possibility of running into a monster at any time. It goes like this:

At the bottom of the Horse Mountain there is a small village. There a peasant lived by selling corn. He always took his produce by mule to the next town to market and sold it for a good price. One day he returned from the market, swaying on his mule because he was slightly drunk from having stopped in a tavern to toast his good sale. Dusk was falling and the sky was getting black. As he rounded a bend in the path, he stopped short with a shock, for in front of him, barring his way, was the most horrible monster. Its enormous face was blue, and its awful eyes popped out like a grasshopper's or a crab's. The staring eyes were bright and shining like torches. The horrid mouth stretched from ear to ear and looked like a bowl of blood. Protruding from this foul orifice were rows and rows of very long and pointed teeth. The monster was twice as tall as any man.

Naturally, our peasant suffered a seizure of fright and started shaking uncontrollably, but luckily for him the monster had not yet seen him, so he stealthily rode off along an adjacent path, and galloped away as fast as he could spur on his steed. However, just as he turned a corner in the path, thinking he was safe, he was horrified to hear someone—or something— calling out his name. Paralyzed with fear, he looked back and saw that it was only his neighbor's son who had called out, so he paused, thankful for the human company. The neighbor's son said, "My father is very ill and doesn't think he'll live much longer, so he asked me to go to the market to get a coffin, and I am just on my way back home. Do you mind if I walk along with you?"

Much relieved, the peasant agreed. The young man then inquired as to why our peasant was going along this unused deserted path. The peasant replied, now becoming rather uneasy, that he had been going the usual way, but had run into a most terrible monster that blocked the way, and so he had ridden away with haste to save himself. At this, the neighbor said, "Old man, when you talk like that you frighten me too, and now I am afraid to walk home alone. Would you let me ride with you on the back of your mule?"

Thinking little of it, the peasant readily agreed, and the neighbor climbed up beside him. They want along for a while, and then the young man asked the peasant to describe the monster. The peasant, growing more and more uncomfortable, answered that he was still too petrified to speak of the monster's appearance but would tell his neighbor about it when they got home safely and he could collect his wits.

At this point, the peasant felt a chill. The neighbor then said, "Well, if you're too scared to talk, why don't you turn around and take a look at me and see if I look anything like that monster you saw." The peasant responded anxiously that he should not make such blasphemous jokes, for a human did not look like a devil. But the young man insisted and said "You must look at me!" He then grabbed the peasant's shoulder and with great force turned him around right there on the mule, and the latter, unable to avert his eyes, saw sitting right there behind him the very same monster he had seen at the stream. So great was his fright that he fell from the mule senseless and remained there without moving a muscle. The mule knew the way home and went along by itself, and when people saw that it had it returned without its master they suspected the worst, for they knew that monsters roamed the paths and byways. The villagers went out in groups and hunted up and down for their missing comrade. They found him lying unconscious where he had fallen and brought him home, but it was midnight before he recovered consciousness and could tell his neighbors the horrible adventure that had befallen him. So the story ends.

The visual and narrative motifs of this story are timeless and find echoes in many Western folktales in which monsters confront travelers. As always, the monster is associated with death and blood, sharp teeth, mystery, night, and fear. It threatens and pursues an innocent person. Its hideous face is a mixture of outlandish parts, part human and part animal; its mouth is wide and filled with sharp teeth; it is immense and powerful, and so on. Also common is the interdigitation of monster and man (a familiar person, the neighbor, becomes a loathsome monster). Equally familiar are the psychological ambiguities of the alien being juxtaposed to the close-to-home, and the dreamlike quality of being unable to get away from a horrible apparition.

Von Franz tells us that this classic story is found with only moderately altered details in peasant folklore from China to Europe to aboriginal America. She notes that the tale essentially has no point and no moral. Its purpose is only to induce shivers: "You know how those ghost stories make you feel in a way terrible and in a way wonderful; it is a gruesome wonder which many of you must have experienced in your childhood" (1983: 124).

ABOMINABLE APE-MEN

China is also the home of various simian cryptomorphs, the most famous of which, the Abominable Snowman or *yeti*, haunts the margins of Himalayan society and is a fixture of Western lore as well. Not all these weird two-legged creatures are depicted in Chinese culture as evil or malign, but they are all terrifying and not to be trifled with. Many are aggressive and hostile; others are shy and retiring. Perhaps *the* classic cryptomorph of modern times, the Tibetan yeti, described as powerfully built but reclusive, deserves a brief description. The following account, supplied by local Sherpas, derives from George M. Eberhart's 1983 book, *Monsters: A Guide to Unaccounted for Creatures*, and should probably be taken with a major dose of salt:

The profile of the yeti, based on the features most frequently given in Sherpa tales, goes like this: height varies between 4 ft. 6 in. and 16 ft. The head hair is long and sometimes falls forward over the eyes. The face is partially naked, often white-skinned, with features reminiscent of an ape or a monkey. Hair, predominantly reddish-brown to dark brown or black in color but lighter on the chest, covers the whole body. Shoulders are heavy and hunched, arms are long and extend to the knees or thereabouts. The posture is roughly man-like though slightly stooped. The walk is partly bipedal and partly quadrupedal. (117)

Yeti crazes pop up now and then in the Western media and produce the requisite shivers. As reported by the *Philadelphia Inquirer* in 1979, members of a British expedition on a slope in Nepal's Kunku Valley heard an eerie, high-pitched scream as they were looking at some ape-like tracks, some eight inches long, in the snow (December 25, 1979). They saw nothing else, as the creature apparently escaped without further incident. A Polish expedition to Mount Everest in 1980 also supposedly encountered the monster's footprints running along a single line and disappearing into the snowy distance (Eberhart 1983: 118).

While the yeti is native only to Tibet, Nepal, and the high peaks of western China, hairy ape-like monsters, known variously as *gin-sung* and *dzu-teh*, have been reported from several provinces of China since ancient times. In one case, in Zhejiang Province, the hands and feet of an ape-man were reportedly preserved in formaldehyde. This creature was apparently killed in 1957 in a fierce battle with local people after attacking a young girl. Its extremities were cut off and pickled by the village biology teacher. The feet supposedly have completely opposed big toes, and thus the beast, whatever it really may have been, was classified among the apes (Eberhart 1983: 118).

★ ★ ★

With their simian rather than reptilian cast, the monsters of China present one variation on the themes of structural fusion or organic superimposition and of primitiveness. Once again the visual model incorporates human-animal hybrids to convey a sense of alarm and shock as well as danger and disgust. Although the Asian monsters are of course as diverse as the huge continent itself, they all adhere to the basic template we have discovered underlying morphic variation elsewhere. Whether Chinese ape-demons, Indian shape-shifters, or the loathsome ogres of tribal peoples, they are terrifyingly large, awe-inspiring in their destructive powers, retrograde or devolved in conception, toothy, gratuitously malevolent toward humanity, fierce, and of course hungry for human flesh. Asian monsters are both male and female; some, as in India, are androgynous or hermaphroditic. In every case, they again invoke a sense of emanating from a distant past, a bygone era when humans were like infants, had no culture, and were helpless and vulnerable. Like their Western peers, Asian monsters are a combination of animal and human, a promiscuous mixture of animal parts; they are mute or inarticulate; they can only bellow, scream, roar, or, as in the case of the Chukchee demons, whistle. They are excrescences of pure emotion, blind id forces. Yet they are powerful, cunning, and formidable foes. Because of their mixed attributes, they are held in terror and awe, fear and reverence; reactions to them are complex and ambivalent.

Moving away from the Asian heartland, we now turn to the Pacific islands, starting with Japan. After surveying Japanese grotesqueries, we sail on to the archipelagos of the South Pacific: Micronesia and Polynesia. Finally we take a brief look at monsters down under.

JAPAN AND THE PACIFIC ISLANDS

Monsters are our children.
— *Jeffrey Cohen*, Monster Culture

ll the great civilizations boast grandiose monster repertories in their folklore and art, and especially in the myths that explain the world and humanity's place in it. Preliterate cultures are no less rich in monster mythology in their oral traditions. But none of the world's cultures—preindustrial, industrial, or postindustrial—have richer or more diverse monster imagery than Japan, the land of the behemoth known to all schoolchildren as Godzilla.

Terence Barrow, a Western scholar impressed with the variety of traditional Japanese "grotesqueries," argues that Japanese culture is "unprecedented" in the diversity of its demonic iconography. He provides the text for the thousands of examples in Nikolas Kiej'e's lavishly illustrated book on Japanese fantasy art (1973). An art critic who has studied the eerie and macabre in Japanese folk art, he states that monsters appear in Japanese art "in an abundance unequalled in any other culture" (7–8) and insists that in Japan monster imagery reaches an apogee encountered nowhere else on the planet. Considering the data presented in the present book, such a bald statement (like the others cited above proposing one or another culture as most imaginative) will not go unchallenged by the present reader. One thing we have seen again and again is how each authority regards his or her own case as unusually rich in monster imagery. But the truth is that a deep and abiding fascination with monsters is pan-cultural and such imagery flourishes everywhere. No single people has a monopoly on monsters.

But even if not unique in this respect, Japanese imagery is both impressive and unsurpassed in its range, diversity, and oddity. This proliferation may have something to do with the many foreign influences on the islands through the ages. Despite its geographic isolation, Japan at various times has been deeply influenced by ideas emanating from mainland Asia, including Buddhism, Hinduism, and Chinese religions and philosophies such as Confucianism and Taoism. It is almost a platitude to say that throughout their history the Japanese have been talented at adopting and synthesizing foreign ideas. And of course native Shinto ancestor-worship practices and beliefs have combined with these borrowings and graftings, along with recent Western notions (e.g., Hollywood horror films), to create a heady stew of supernatural evil-being imagery.

Any list of Japanese weird beasties is bound to be staggering. According to the art historians cited above, foremost among the many horrible creatures populating Japan are the so-called *oni* spirits, which Barrow believes may be imported wholesale from China (Kiej'e 1973: 18). Infesting the northern islands, these multifarious creatures are described as being hominoid demons that harass people at night, ruining their sleep and scaring innocents to death. Stealthy and treacherous, they look like humans at first glance, if one does not look too closely, and they are said to eat and drink like humans. But they have a devilish temper and can turn threatening at any moment. Japanese peasants describe them as of large size and of varying colors, usually turning a frightening deep purple or black when they reveal themselves. Some are said to have horns and beaks, others three sharp-clawed toes and fingers and three eyes. As well as being ugly, they are "malicious, cruel, and lecherous" (18) and their main activity seems to be gratuitously worrying, tormenting, and killing humans.

Already beset by these horrible shape-shifting oni, the Japanese people must contend also with a native-bred ogre they call *shokera*, a term that may be rendered "roof devil." More insidious than the oni, this evil spirit lurks on rooftops. Hideous and slimy, it has the nasty habit of spying on unsuspecting members of households from its perch, with an eye to mischief (Kiej'e 1973: 110). When it spies an opportunity, it drops into houses, writhes around, and scares the wits out of people, often causing heart-stopping seizures.

In addition to such domestic pests, there are legions of roadside monsters that wait patiently in woods and fields for passersby with which to make their next meal. Most are said to be reptilian and scaly, but, like Chinese ogres, some are simian in appearance, while others are insect-like.

In Japan more than elsewhere, weird creatures seem to enjoy haunting abandoned houses, particularly in the western parts of the main islands. Any empty house is likely to be inhabited by ghostly freaks and monsters who take delight in frightening or doing worse things to human beings. Some of these creatures have been endlessly depicted in native art, especially in woodcuts. Irksome and cunning, monsters never leave people alone in Japan. Even taking a bath at a public bathhouse, normally every Japanese person's sacred right, can be a risk. Horrible creatures are known to break into the public facilities with regularity and to grab some poor female victim and drag her away for rape or some other nefarious purpose.

Japanese people describe these pesky monsters as being both male and female. As in India, many Japanese demons are specifically female and have perverted feminine interests and traits. As in India, some of these female monsters turn motherhood into a foul parody by gobbling up children and sucking human blood. One of the worst of these female scourges is Nure Onna, or Wet Woman. In a diabolical manifestation, with long hair flying and reptilian tongue flicking out to taste the wind, she is said to be evil personified. Greatly feared by the fisher-people of the northern Japanese islands, she must be avoided at all costs or she will capture and eat her victims (72).

Another female demon is Hannya, a true baby-eater and possibly the most feared devil in all Japan. The story is that she was once a beautiful normal woman who one day went mad and became demonically possessed, becoming a fierce and implacable she-demon. She is the subject of much pictorial art and theater. As is common among female devils, in many Noh plays Hannya is noted for unusual cruelty toward young men and boys. She is often portrayed by artists as a demonic cannibal with pointed fangs, holding up a severed baby's head she is about to devour (172).

In rural Japan, among rice farmers, monsters frolic, disport, and threaten at every opportunity. Going to the market can be a risky adventure when the butcher-demons are on the prowl. One may encounter such terrible monsters purveying their diabolical wares at any turn of the path. In the deserted countryside at night, the faint tolling of a bell or gong is heard not as an ordinary ringing, but as a ghostly sound by a monster priest whose duty it is to toll regularly just to frighten people (108).

Monsters seem to be literally everywhere in Japan, even in holy places such as shrines and temples (like church gargoyles in Western Europe). They also infest the air above. Tengu, for example, a mischievous aerial monster of folklore, is depicted as a male humanoid with an enormous pointed nose, two pairs of eagle's wings, and heavy armor in the samurai style (Lehner 1969: 107). Another bird-like demon is Hai Riyo, the ancient dragon-bird, rather like the Sioux Thunderbird, envisioned as large and hawk-like, with sharp claws, a long reptilian snout containing fangs, and mandible tentacles. It also feeds children to its ravenous young.

If the Canadian Indians focus their fears on a single monster, the Windigo, in contrast many Oriental cultures, especially that of Japan, seem to deflect their fears into many types of monsters. As in India, these fractious, swarming monsters are, as we have seen, in every nook and cranny of the islands, haunting abandoned houses and jumping around rooftops in the cities, flying about, swimming in the oceans, and roaming the countryside looking for victims. Rather as in medieval Europe, when monster beliefs threatened to get out of hand and burst into full-fledged mass hysteria until repressed by the Church, the Japanese government in the Edo period (1615–1867) acted to dampen anxiety about these monstrous legions. During this epoch, preceding the modern Tokugawa period, tales of grotesque and frightful creatures reached epidemic proportions and began to cause actual panics among gullible people in the towns and villages. So extreme did the situation become that in 1808 the government passed legislation forbidding people to tell ghost stories that featured "flying heads, animal goblins, serpent monsters, fire demons," and suchlike terrors (Kiej'e 1973: 8). But one cannot legislate monsters out of the human psyche! As in Europe, this effort had little success.

We noted above that Japanese culture is synthetic and has borrowed a great deal from surrounding societies, especially China. However, as Barrow points out, Japanese grotesqueries have much in common not only with China and mainland southeast Asia (Indo-China, Thailand, Burma, and Malaysia), which one would expect, but also, curiously, with more distant islands of Polynesia and Oceania (16). This alleged convergence between Japan and the distant Pacific islands requires some discussion.

OCEANIA: OGRES AND ODDITIES

"Oceania," for current purposes will include all the Pacific islands, except Melanesia and Australia. We start with the Micronesian archipelago, which represents the island system closest geographically to Japan, and which spread out over vast stretches of water in the middle of the Pacific between Asia and America. As far as we know these islands, thousands of nautical miles from Tokyo, had had no sustained contact with the Japanese at any time during the past two millennia, aside from brief occupations during the Second World War. There is no evidence for cultural diffusion. Yet there are many parallels.

From these scattered Pacific islets we have good data on monsters and other evil creatures, much of the information coming from the careful ethnographies like that of anthropologist William Lessa (1961, 1980), which concerns Ulithi Atoll, an archipelago located smack in the middle of the Pacific. Lessa tells us that cannibal monsters are well known on Ulithi Atoll and "conform to the general type in folktales everywhere " (57). As elsewhere, for example, ogres on Ulithi are everywhere, infesting land, sea and air; they are, as is customary, cannibalistic, monstrously large, powerful, malevolent, and ill disposed toward humans. However, the diverse types and variations in Micronesia are as staggering as in Japan, requiring two weighty volumes to do them justice. As Lessa says in his second collection of folklore, bogeys and man-eating spirits are staples of folklore everywhere, but in the Ulithi islands they "find expression on a higher plane" than in other cultures, being virtually synonymous with folklore itself (1980: 79). As in Japan and many other places, an expert makes the claim that his subject people are more obsessed with monsters than anyone else— a supposition this book will surely dispel.

The most feared type of Ulithian ogres are called *legaselep*, a word Lessa translates as "mighty ogre" or "big spirit." Legaseleps are always depicted as male in gender. Their habitat is terrestrial and, like the Windigo, they prefer wooded places and deep caves, where they build nests and wait for passersby whom they can attack. Lessa has collected hundreds of tales that describe how such man-eaters trick or force humans into their lairs. The carnage among the poor islanders is monumental. In many stories entire villages are depopulated or sizable clans are eaten down to the last man just to make one dish in a monster's banquet. In many tales the entire population of a village pack up and sail away to avoid the rapacious ogres infesting their vicinity.

In one such story, related to Lessa by a very old man who said it occurred in the nineteenth century, a group of "big spirits" lived on a small island. One of these beasts was ten yards tall, the others somewhat smaller. These cruel giants preyed mercilessly on local people, and over time they ate almost the whole population of the village (1961: 57–59). Finally the few survivors all decided to emigrate to another island, leaving the place to the ogres and giving rise to a myth perhaps reflective of the island-hopping nature of Oceanic civilization in general. Could such venturesome travels of the Polynesian peoples be the result of fear of such terrible flesh-eating monsters? Were they forced to sail into distant seas in search of safe haven? Did fear of monsters populate the far-flung Pacific?

As is usual in monster lore, these Polynesian ogres are routinely defeated by local heroes after many years of communal suffering. In the myth above, for example, a young warrior finally shows up on the depopulated island and after innumerable scrapes manages to club all the ogres to death. In most cases in the Ulithi repertory, the archetypal hero is the youngest son of an old woman, whose other children have been dispatched by ogres. Having seen his older siblings fall prey, the remaining youth boasts that he will vanquish it, and goes out to the ogre's lair to confront it. After numerous adventures involving both fighting and trickery, the young warrior succeeds in carrying out his boast. In some other stories, it is one or more relatives of the victims who gather up their courage and defy the flesh-eating spirit. Such is the case in the tale, "The Ogre Who Ate Iöl's Daughter," retold by Lessa (1961: 62–63). A synopsis follows.

On the island of Mogmog lived three bog spirits (legaselep) who went around eating the people there with impunity. One of these monsters lived at the east end of the island, the second in the middle, and the third at the west end. So voracious were they that after a time only two people were left on the entire island—Iöl and his daughter. All the rest had been eaten. It came to pass one day that the old man went fishing by himself, and although he warned his young daughter to be careful so as not to meet the fate of all the others, the ogre came in through the window and swallowed up the girl before he could do anything about it. Angry enough to overcome his fears, the distraught man went to the ogres' lairs one by one and asked if they had killed his child. All three denied it; however, the third ogre, the one who lived at the west end of the island, looked rather funny to the old man—its stomach was suspiciously distended and it appeared to be suffering from some sort of indigestion.

Emboldened by the monster's enfeebled condition, the old man approached and saw his daughter's legs protruding from the monster's mouth. The legs were kicking, which meant she was still alive. So Iöl attacked the ogre while it slept, killing it with powerful spear thrusts and cutting off its hideous head. He then opened the belly and found his poor daughter, somewhat the worse for wear but still alive. "He then removed her from the spirit's belly and took her home" (1961: 63). Thus ends the tale. One will of course notice the similarities to Western folktales, especially "Little Red Riding Hood." The difference is mainly in the large-scale depredations of the Micronesian ogres, which seem to gobble up entire villages rather than a granny or two.

As we can see from such legends, these Ulithian ogres are always eating people until stopped by a hero or a guileful girl. Another local monster on the atoll, Rolá, also likes to eat young girls, perhaps revealing an erotic impulse. In one tale this monstrous spirit captures two young sisters and eats them one by one. But the girls are smart: knowing the dangers of living on a monster-infested island, they are prepared for such a fate. They had hidden sharp sea-shells in the folds of their dresses when they went out to gather food. When they find themselves in the ogre's stomach, they use the shells to cut open the monster's belly and make their escape.

Having survived, the girls appropriated the ogre's homestead: "The girls came out from his stomach and went to take a bath, and they went back to the langaselep's house and lived there" (Lessa 1980: 82). Writing about Oceania in general and the Hawaiian Islands as well, another researcher, Martha Beckwith (1970: 347) says that the sisters' heroic feat is just one example of "the common folktale trick of allowing [oneself] to be swallowed by a monster and then cutting [one's] way out." Then the heroes claim ownership of the monster's possessions, house, or ill-gotten gains. These are common themes indeed throughout the world, as we know from Western folktales.

MORE ISLAND MONSTERS

Although all are violent and tend to mutilate or eat humans, other Micronesian ogres differ in the nature of their depredations. One was said to be a vicious eye-gouger. Once upon a time this monster terrorized the island of Fais, a small fly-speck in the Ulithi chain, taking out people's eyeballs and keeping them for later use—as snacks or perhaps toys, the tale does not specify. In one tale, this eye-popping beast attacks a single family and rips out the eyes of each member until only the absent father is left with sight. The monster "leaped at the last child and took out its eyes, too. . . . Then he leaped at the mother and took out both her eyes. He put her face downward and then jumped up to the rafters and waited there" for the man (1980: 83). The father, however, is no easy mark but a true hero, and when he returns he fights and finally subdues the eye-gouging ogre, stealing back the missing eyes and restoring sight to his family.

In many cases in Oceanic folk stories, the hero who kills the ogre is made a chief or king. As in other areas of Oceania, the charismatic monster-slaying hero is often the youngest son of an old widowed woman. According to Lessa, this "Ogre-Killing Son" who is made chief is a common motif throughout Micronesia, Polynesia, New Guinea, the Solomon Islands, the New Hebrides, the Loyalty Islands, and as far afield as Malaysia (1980: 86).

Moving south and west from Micronesia to nearby Polynesia, we find the islanders contending with all manner of ogres, were-animals, water-monsters, sea serpents, giant cannibals, and suchlike. In a fascinating collection of Polynesian folklore, Bacil Kirtley (1971) provides much information about Polynesia monster lore. He tells of a giant "demon octopus" in the Marquesas that ravages the islands, a sea serpent near New Zealand that overturns canoes and eats the occupants, and a man-eating giant who lives in a cave on the island of Rotuma. He also notes were-animals as were-sharks, were-swordfish, were-eels, were-crabs, were-reptiles, and were-lizards. The were-shark motif reaches a pinnacle in Hawaii, Tonga, Java, and the Fiji Islands (171), where the seas and waterways are full of such terrors, all biting and snapping.

In the water off Tahiti (formerly French Polynesia), there is said to be a gigantic sea serpent that demands human sacrifices annually (120). On Tonga and also on some of the Hawaiian islands, there are what are described as "devastating dogs" (116). Like the monstrous Latin American canines, these beasts are said to grow to immense size and to prey upon children, chasing them down and tearing them apart. On the island of Kauai in the Hawaiian archipelago the people believe in hybrid spirits that are even more horrible than these killer hounds. These beasts have the overall shape of giant water-rats, but they are equipped with a huge shark's mouth on their back which is full of razor-sharp teeth. The curious composites supposedly trick unwary people into the water and then eat them using the shark's jaws on their backs.

One of these rat-shark hybrids is so well known that it has its own name: Kawelo, the demon fish. It lives in the region of Mana, on Kauai, and is well known in the vicinity for its savage depredations (Beckwith 1970: 140–41).

Human-into-monster transformations are a common theme in Polynesian folklore. On Fiji, for example, it is well known that a very bad man or a man said to have cannibalistic tendencies will turn into a huge snake, as "big as a coconut tree." Such vicious were-snakes dwell in the underbrush in the forest and attack unsuspecting people for food (Hames 1960: 29). One should point out, as an ethnographic fact, that the authors of these collections make it quite clear that these beliefs are still current, even among relatively sophisticated people.

FLAMING TEETH

As if all these terrors were not enough for the islanders to contend with, the island of Rotuma is also host to one especially horrid ogre called "Flaming Teeth." The tale of this incendiary creature has been reported by folklorist Inez Hames (1960: 38–39). What is most interesting about the way Flaming Teeth is conceived is that it improvises upon the usual monstrous-maw motif, creating a fiery new way to envision the monster's oral aggression aside from the usual swallowing and chewing effects. Here the teeth are on fire and burn the victim to death before being eaten. The tale goes like this:

Once in Rotuma, long ago, when monsters prowled the land, there lived a terrible giant in a great cave, and everyone was terrified of him. His teeth, the tale-teller says, were really coals of fire, burning all the time. How terrible he looked, when he opened his mouth, and there were red-hot teeth with flames spurting out of his mouth. "What a frightful fellow this cruel giant was. No wonder the people hid in their caves when he stalked the land" (38). Sometimes this fire-breather emerged from his cave and caught people and ate them right up without pause; sometimes he saved them for a treat later on. "Oh, if only Giant Flaming Teeth were dead," the people cried, "then our village would be a happy place." But it was not to be, and the attacks continued. Finally, two brave heroes tricked Flaming Teeth into a house and used a huge stone, which they had set up in the rafters, to drop on his head and kill him. The burning-tooth ogre was dead, and peace and joy reigned at last in the land.

But the most monster-infested place in all the wide Pacific may have been the two islands comprising New Zealand. There, the aboriginal Maori peoples were obsessed with evil beings. The earliest Europeans to visit the islands, from Captain Cook in the eighteenth century on, were quite impressed with local monster lore. Admiral Cook learned from them of "lizards of an enormous size" which supposedly burrowed into the ground and sometimes seized and devoured people. Another explorer, Antoine Nicholas, who was in New Zealand with the Rev. Samuel Marsden in 1814, gathered information of a similar kind. According to folklorist Johannes Andersen, who collected this material: "Early explorers often had pointed out to them places where these monsters were said to have dwelt" (1969: 139). Much of their belief system has been recorded and many of their pre-contact beliefs still have currency. One of the fiercest of the Maoris' imaginary monsters was a water-serpent that inhabited a lake near Tongariro. Such water-serpents, generically called *horomatangi* in Maori, were supposedly legion in all the lakes, streams, and ponds of New Zealand, making life miserable for the natives (Rose 2000: 181). These monsters were huge, hideous creatures that preyed on people when they went hunting or fishing. Grendel-like, they were said to resemble a cross between a reptile or giant lizard and a man, and to be always hungry for human flesh.

Interestingly, many Maori tales feature warrior-heroes who enter fearlessly into the watery haunts of these amphibian beasts to do underwater battle. The main Maori hero, a young warrior called Pitaka, is very much like the young Beowulf, slaying his share of riparian monsters. The resemblance has duly been noted by Maori folklorists; "Pitaka is like Beowulf in that he undertakes the destruction of more than one beast-enemy of man; and like Beowulf, he attacks one of them in its watery lair, and with the same equanimity as on dry land" (Andersen 1969: 139). Like Grendel's mother, some Maori ogres are rendered as female.

There are of course many other Maori monster-slayers for each locality boasts of its own. Another famous hero, hailing from the Manukau Heads area of New Zealand, is named Tamure. His epic battle with a notorious water monster (called by the generic term *taniwha*) is justly cited as perhaps the Maoris' finest hour. Typical of its genre, this tale of derring-do bears repeating.

Not so long ago, when the earth was relatively young, the native tale begins, there lived in an underwater cave at Piha, north of the Manukau Heads, a dreaded taniwha named Kai-whare. He was a monstrous cross between man and reptile and was feared as a voracious man-eater. He was more clever than most taniwhas: he hunted with cunning, not just brute force. On quiet nights he would lie patiently just beneath the waves outside the harbor bar until he saw the glow of the torches of the fishermen wading in the shallow waters trying to spear fish; or until the canoes drifted down with the tide as the fishermen tossed their nets overboard to catch the plentiful snapper and flounder. The monster would then swim swiftly but stealthily into the harbor and seize a man or woman preoccupied with spearing fish or pull an unwary fishermen from a canoe. He would sink his awesome teeth into the victim and drag him away to his watery lair for a leisurely meal. Such predation went on for a long time; the people were unable to do anything about it. It became a matter of utmost urgency in the land because virtually everyone was too terrified to go fishing. Fishermen no longer dared approach the best fishing grounds, and the food supply for the entire community began to dwindle to dangerous levels. It was time for a hero to intercede.

Kai-whare had eaten so many fishermen, the tale continues, that it was decided that help must be obtained, for no one dared to face the powerful taniwha (Reed 1963: 322). Faced with such calamity, the learned elders got together and anxiously exchanged ideas. Most of them were aware that at the village of Hauraki there lived a giant of a man named Tamure, who had already won renown as a brawler. Taller and broader than any other man on the island, he possessed a gigantic war club so powerful that a single blow would kill any taniwha. Once alerted to the problem by a messenger, Tamure strode from hilltop to hilltop, over lakes and marshes, just a few of his mighty steps taking him to Piha, where the people were gathered to greet their hoped-for savior. Many men offered their services, for everyone was anxious to assist in slaying the monster.

However, because he was so confident, Tamure refused all help and decided to destroy the taniwha alone. Wasting no time, he strode in a few steps to the rolling sand dunes by the seashore, leaving huge footprints that are still visible to this day. He took two more great steps and found himself on the southern shore of the Manukau Harbor, the place where the taniwha was reputed to dwell. The crowds assembled there told the hero how Kai-whare had devoured their friends, and how the monster swam silently into the harbor when they began to fish (322).

In response, Tamure made a short speech. "I shall deal with this tani-wha," he said in a booming voice. As the people clamored, he refused all help and asked only for information as to the monster's tactics and where-abouts. Once he understood how the monster preyed upon the people, he devised a plan. "When night comes I want all the fishermen to go out in their canoes to the beach and spear the patiki [fish]. Don't be afraid, Tamure will protect you" (322).

The following day, as planned, the hero strode resolutely out to the bay and waited for the creature to make his appearance. Having been starved of human meat for some time, the beast smelled prey and came crashing out of his underwater cave. Tamure heard a rumbling on the sea bed as rocks were thrown aside and giant waves dashed upon the shore. The taniwha's hideous head rose above the water. As the beast was preoccupied looking for victims, Tamure unleashed a powerful blow of his mighty club upon its head, so violent a blow that the waters flew upward to the sky and the world shook. Mortally wounded, Kai-whare thrashed about in agony, and the waves pounded against the cliffs, sending pillars of foam and water. The tail of the huge taniwha flung rocks and cliffs into the sea, leaving a clear-swept area of smooth rock that can be seen to this day. His work done, the hero strode back inland. The monster, being so huge and powerful, was not killed outright by the blow, but it was so weakened forever afterward that it became harmless to mankind. Its massive wounds prevented it from crossing over the sandbar at the mouth of the harbor, and its diet was forever confined to the crayfish and octopus found on the sea coast; in other words, was reduced to the status of a "normal" animal.

There are several versions of this legend and of the battle scenarios, which purport to explain many of the geological features of the coastline in this part of New Zealand. In some of these variants, the monster is defeated by a pair of giant twins, as happens in the Hopi tales. In other stories, it is the efforts of whole clans, or united tribes rather than a few heroic individuals that subdue him. It is important to note also, that in many Maori myths the monster is depicted as having a close relationship with the people it terrorizes. In one myth, for example, the sea monster Kai-whare is said to be kin of its victims, and at one point it is referred to as "the ancestor of the tribe." So the relationship between man and monster is again somewhat ambiguous, with vague relations and narrative twists and turns. Indeed, the hero Tamure, like Beowulf, can be said to be a kind of mirror image of the monster in his rather monstrous exceptionalism: he inspires awe because of his superhuman physical power, abnormal size, and unbridled violence, and because he transcends all the bounds and limits set by the culture on normal humans.

OTHER MAORI OGRES

As in ancient Greece, terrible monsters also fouled not only the waters but also the air of aboriginal New Zealand. Living in the hills between Rotura and Waikato was an aerial creature described by natives as a black monster with bat-like wings stretching twelve feet from tip to tip; his great head, set on a long supple neck, ended in a sharp snout. His jaws, as usual, were full of dagger-like teeth, and the talons on his feet and shoulders were as sharp as scythes (Reed 1963: 305). Like the Harpies and the American

Indian Thunderbird, such aerial creatures were said to attack humans and carry them off to their nests to feed to their young.

In aboriginal New Zealand, land monsters are just as numerous and vicious as those of the sea and air. Terrestrial monsters are divided into two kinds: *tipua* (goblins) and *taniwha* (the same term used for the sea monsters described above). The former are nocturnal, smaller, and more mobile: like vampires, they suck blood and cause diseases and other mischief; they live in crevices in the earth, forests, and wastelands. The latter are larger and are merciless killers and cannibals, preying on travelers and lost souls. Both are the embodiment of fear—of the dreaded, the imagined, the unknown—and, like monsters everywhere, they assume whatever shape may happen to be given to them by fear and by the indefiniteness of imagination awakened by the unmotivated terror of which people are capable. Whatever form they take—anthropomorphic or zoomorphic—most of these Maori land beasts have repulsive appearances, cavernous mouths, and an insatiable appetite for human flesh, in the words of ethnographer A. W. Reed (1963: 301). Many such monsters live in dark caves, emerging at night to attack. One such was the taniwha of Rotorua called Hoto-puku, one of the most horrible figures of Polynesia.

Even in a land haunted by so many demonic creatures, Hoto-puku was notorious for its cruelty. Once, in the not so distant past, an entire tribal war party was caught unaware by the demon. As the men walked across the Kaingaroa plain near the Waikato River, the scent of human flesh reached the monster's nostrils. Hoto-puku sprang out of his cave and bounded upon the men, catching them unprepared. On the open plain they had neglected to make precautions against such an ambush, and they had no weapons at the ready. So, the monster had the advantage and the seasoned warriors fled in confusion, for Hoto-puku had the appearance and power of a moving mountain. The spiky spines and protuberances on its back had the horrid appearance of growths on a sea monster, and it put the fear of the devil into the terrified warriors. In the confusion, some were trampled to death; others were taken in the cavernous mouth and swallowed whole by the beast (299).

The men fought back, some flying for help, and reinforcements soon arrived. The fresh troops were led by the famous hero chief Pitaka, who offered his services. Following the hero's directions, the brave men surrounded the taniwha, who retreated to his lair. They lured him out of his cave with various tricks, and, after a bloody battle lasting days, killed him by inflicting thousands of wounds on his tough hide. Curious, they wasted no time in cutting him open in order to examine the contents of his belly. Monsters being monsters, the warriors were not surprised the find the belly bursting with the decomposed bodies of their own men, women, and children, along with separated limbs, torsos, and heads. Beyond this, the monster's stomach was quite a treasure trove, containing innumerable objects and many precious possessions like garments, cloaks, cooking utensils, ornamental feathers, fat domestic animals, and useful weapons like darts and clubs.

After their victory, Pitaka and his men celebrated by indulging in a rather monstrous ritual of their own. Taking revenge for the monster's devastation, the heroes quickly dismembered the dead taniwha, rendered the fat from its vast body, and cooked and ate the rest. "And by this means they expressed their contempt, and celebrated their victory over the enemy which had killed their friends" (300). Killing and eating cannibal monsters is an oft-encountered motif in Maori folklore. Man and monster feed off each other as a general rule.

SOME OBSERVATIONS

The connection between man and monster in all the South Seas is, once again, complex, ambiguous, multifaceted, and in the end rather intimate. The boundaries between man and monster, between evil and good, are in each case shifting and permeable. For one thing, in many of the Maori and Polynesian tales the ogres are killed by heroes, as one would expect, but the victors often take a strange, and indeed monstrous, revenge on their slain victims afterward. Not content to kill the bogeys, these great heroes of the South Seas, as we have seen in the case of Pitaka, sometimes cook and eat their monstrous carcasses with great relish, in what for Westerners may appear a shocking role reversal. So complete is this reversal that one folklorist who has examined hundreds of Polynesian tales, A. W. Reed, tells a few myths in which it is hard to tell which is the cannibal monster and which the human victim. A startling example of this man-monster gastronomic mutualism is the following.

This curious myth recounts what happens after men kill a taniwha named Peke-haua. In Reed's translation, "The taniwha was cut open and . . . was found to contain a vast heap of bodies, garments, weapons, and other implements. The death of Peke-haua was an occasion for rejoicing. Its flesh was roasted and broiled, some parts being eaten immediately, and others preserved in calabashes in its own fat" (1963: 301). Indeed, monster fat and flesh seems to be a staple of the Maori diet, as these two tales and many others show. When battling monsters, take care not to become a monster yourself, as the adage goes. Eat *and* be eaten.

I should make one final point relating to the genealogical, if not behavioral, affinity between man and beast in the Pacific archipelagos. Throughout the islands, but especially in New Zealand, monsters and humans are related. Either they are brothers—twins spawned simultaneously by the gods who then go their separate ways—or the monsters are direct lineal ancestors to humans as we have specifically seen in the case of the ogre Kaiwhare (Reed 1963: 297). That is, they give rise to humanity in one way or another, by actual birth, totemistic parthenogenesis, or vomiting up swallowed proto-humans, spitting them out, or defecating them.

Elsewhere, for example in Hawaii and Tonga, all the were-animals we have spoken of have an even more immediate kinship, not to mention an organic unity, with humans, as people turn into monsters and back again. So once again the idea of what is monstrous and inhuman, notions that purport to encompass the opposite to all that is wholesome and good, turns out to be quite close to home. Not only are we often the descendants of monsters, as is so often the case in New Zealand mythology, but, as the saying goes, we are what we eat. The Maori diet in metaphorical terms includes a healthy dose of monster meat.

DOWN UNDER: BUNYIPS AND BOGEYS

Weird monsters also populate the biggest island of all, Australia. The following is an early (1822) account of an encounter between an early British settler in New South Wales named E. S. Hall, and a mysterious water beast. The incident occurred at Lake Bathurst:

In December last [1822] Mr. Forbes and I were bathing in the East-end of the Lake, where an arm runs among the honey-suckles. As I was dressing, a creature, at the distance of about 130 or 150 yards, suddenly presented itself to my view; it had risen out of the water before I perceived it, and was then gliding on the smooth surface with the rapidity of a whale-boat, as it appeared to me at the time. Its neck was long, apparently about three feet out of the water, and about the thickness of a man's thigh. . . . The head was rather smaller in circumference than the neck and appeared surrounded with black flaps, which seemed to hang down, and gave it a most striking and novel appearance. . . . It dived and was seen no more. (cited in M. Smith 1996: 4)

Unhurt but astonished by the experience, and trying to gain information from the local aborigines about the creature, Hall was frustrated by the fact that the natives refused to approach the area or even talk about it. The aborigines claimed that the black, serpentine "devil-devil" seen by Hall had previously taken and eaten their children. It turns out that Hall was among the first white settlers in the antipodean continent to encounter a bunyip—the native term for monster or demon. The Australian aboriginals had a long history of deadly experiences with these malignant beasts by the time of European migration.

No one knows when the word bunyip entered English—nor is any linguist certain from which native language it originated; possibly the aborigines picked it up from the whites, thinking they were speaking English, and the whites in turn assumed it was a native term. It therefore may have, like the word *kangaroo*, moved from language to language, and so the original source is long forgotten. However, by mid-century bunyip had become established throughout Australia with the English sense "monster" and was a household word in both the white and aboriginal communities.

The term first actually appears in print in the *Sydney Gazette* of 1812, when correspondent James Ives described a large black amphibious creature, native to southern Australia, "with a terrible voice which creates terror among the blacks" (M. Smith 1996: 4–5). Travelers and ethnographers have collected numerous native drawings and representations of bunyips from all over the continent; some resemble large marsupials, others look like bats or dinosaurs. According to Australian Malcolm Smith, a self-styled cryptozoologist who has investigated bunyips and other reported Australian bogeymen for years, belief in monsters lurking in the depths of lakes, is, or was, rife throughout the continent like everywhere else in the Pacific. He presents his findings in an entertaining and open-minded book called *Bunyips and Bigfoots: In Search of Australia's Mystery Animals* (1996).

One particularly fierce bunyip described by Smith was well known as a man-eater throughout south Australia. Called *katenpai* by the natives, it was described from native accounts gathered by explorer William Hovell, who traveled around 1840 to the Murrumbidgee River, also in New South Wales. The natives told Hovell of a mysterious and terrifying aquatic animal the size of a large bullock, with the head and neck of an emu, a huge mane of hair, the tail of a horse, four legs, and three sharp-clawed toes at the end of each foot (M. Smith 1996: 10). As usual, it feasted upon lost children. Soon stories were filtering from the bush about such man-eating

Yara-Ma-Yha-Who. From *Myths and Legends of the Australian Aboriginals* by W. Ramsay Smith (1930).

bunyips all over Australia, sending chills down the backs of both whites and blacks, who, if they agreed on nothing else, shared the same fascination and fear of monsters. Another such creature, as reported by the indefatigable A. W. Reed (1963: 87), resembled nothing so much as the Windigo. Called the Wulgaru by the aborigines, this monster was also described as a cannibal giant, with a distinctly "Frankenstein-like" appearance (according to acculturated natives), which roamed about the land seeking humans to attack (see also Rose 2000: 398–99). Like the kangaroo, the mysterious bunyip, in all its myriad incarnations, has become a symbol of Australian faunal oddity.

AUSTRALIAN SEA MONSTERS

The universal tradition of sea serpents is also a staple of the Australian imagination. The most famous sighting in Australian history dates from 1893, when a white schoolteacher named Miss S. Lovell (no first name given in the reports) reported in a letter to the English journal *Land and Water* about a monstrous sea creature seen off the coast of Queensland. Her account begins: "We have had a visit from a monster turtle fish," and she goes on breathlessly to describe a slithery beast looking like a cross between a giant turtle and a marine dinosaur, the body being "dome-shaped and about eight feet wide, with a long neck and large head." She estimates its length at about thirty feet or more, and speaks of a cavernous mouth full of either dagger-like teeth or "serrated jaw-bones," not being sure exactly what she saw. Not known for either having a fertile imagination or lying, the entirely respectable schoolteacher provided an account that was taken quite seriously by local authorities, giving rise to numerous searches and a mild mass hysteria in the area.

Later that year and on into 1894, there were additional sightings of aquatic beasts by other equally dependable Europeans, and with the stir it was making, the matter was taken up with the local aborigines. Queried by reporters, the natives expressed no surprise at the sightings and stated simply that the whites had seen was fast-moving sea-dragon *moha-moha*, or "dangerous turtle," which they claimed was amphibious and could exit the water at will, travel on its hind legs, and attack people miles inland. In fact, the local aborigines, having had a few bloody encounters with the Queensland monster that same year (one man reported having been bitten on the leg by the beast), had already abandoned their coastal villages and decamped inland for safety (M. Smith 1996: 26–27). Like the famous bunyips, this serpentine moha-moha has become a household term in Australia, akin to the Loch Ness monster and a source of much folklore and mythology.

One interesting aspect of the moha-moha legend bears repeating. When asked about the creature's nature and habits, the local inhabitants said that the monster had preyed on their people for centuries, and was well known to have an insatiable appetite for human flesh. So, like the other peoples of the Pacific, they tended to blame the moha-moha for unexplained disappearances, particularly of children, for which the beast was said to have special fondness. But they also told reporters that they themselves returned the favor—by killing and eating the moha-moha whenever they could. They added that its flesh was fatty and tasty and that one could feed an entire village for weeks. So, at least in aboriginal lore about monsters, it was not uncommon, "for the aborigines liked to eat it, and it in turn, liked to eat aborigines" (M. Smith 1996: 29). As in Polynesia, there is the odd feature of reciprocal commensalism: man-eating monsters and monster-eating men.

But the moha-moha is not all there is to frighten the imaginative soul down under. Using Australian newspapers and other news media as sources, Malcolm Smith compiled an impressive list of Aussie monster lore. In particular, unauthenticated sea monster sightings number in the thousands since records on the subject began in the early part of the twentieth century. One of the most famous incidents occurred in 1870 off Nepean Island, a tiny islet off the coast of Norfolk Island, near Tasmania. It was reported in a signed and sworn affidavit by a Captain Marcus Lowther, a man incapable of telling an untruth, according to his contemporaries:

The boat shot within a yard of it, and there it was, a veritable Sea Serpent. . . .
When first seen it must have been asleep, for its head was lying flat on the surface of the sea, and it body coiled up. The tail of the monster I saw plainly,
hanging some three of four fathoms below the surface. . . . Its length I cannot
tell you . . . but as far as I could judge, it must have been thirty or forty feet.
(M. Smith 1996: 27)

Such sightings continued through the years. In 1931, another horrible
sea monster was sighted off the south coast, again by an awed white fisherman, who retreated in terror. The "most surprising features" of this
demonic marine being, the fisherman reported to police after having
regained the power of speech, "were the creature's eyes, which were protruding and appeared to be as large as saucers, and its teeth, which were
saber-like, were fully six inches long." In 1935, another witness reported
seeing this same marine demon, and reported that its cavernous maw was
wide open and the lower jaw "studded with about 48 teeth." Monstrous
mouths and deadly dentition again!

Additional reports continued until at least until 1995, the year before
Smith's book went to press. Many accounts come from entirely reasonable
people, not otherwise known to be frauds or hysterics, and who are members of all ethnic groups and races in the southern continent. In September
1995, an unsigned letter was thrust under the door of the weekly *Isis Town
and Country* in Childers, Queensland. It read:

During the first week of September a friend and myself were fishing from a tin-
nie [little boat] . . . when I spotted something unusual. I called my companion's
attention to it and for what seemed about a minute we watched what appeared
to be an enormous snake with a bulbous head. I really do mean enormous: the
neck/body was upright out of the water and was topped by a head the size of
a Labrador dog, while the neck seemed about half the girth of a timber power
pole.

The letter goes on to say that they were not attacked or otherwise bothered
by the strange beast, which did not seem to notice them and which slipped
unhindered beneath the waves and was gone from sight. Other respondents
reported similar sightings. The unknown sea monster became known as the
Burrum Beast after a local landmark (M. Smith 1996: 63). Like Windigo it
fades obscurely into the shadows of the landscape of the mind.

ISLAND LORE

In Australia, as in the Pacific Islands and Japan, man and monster live in the closest proximity, swim together, walk together, fight, and eat each other. While we should not overemphasize the paradoxical everyday closeness of man and monster in the above material, it does give one pause to reflect upon conceptual boundaries. We are food to each other, in every possible meaning of the term. In Japan, the South Pacific, and Australia, among both aboriginals and Europeans, monsters and ogres are seen to be everywhere, infesting all the elements, as they were in the ancient Mediterranean world—in air, skies, and waters—and are grotesquely large or moderately man-sized (none are smaller than men). They inhabit a parallel and intersecting dimension, interacting with us on a daily basis. So we are left with a sense of organic unity between natural and supernatural, a mutualism, a permeable boundary in mental geography as well as moral universes. In a sense, then, one may say the in the eastern hemisphere as in the western, people and monsters are mutually dependent members of a family: blood relatives, united in mutual predation, yin and yang, soulmates, inseparable enemies. The monsters represent the cast-off part of the self, the inner negative, the violence and aggression within; but they are restless beasts, always returning from their fitful exile in the dark shadows.

RITUAL MONSTERS

*If monsters appear in all civilizations, in all epochs, and
in the thoughts of "normal" people as well the fantasies
of neurotics, it is because monsters perform a* natural
function*!*

—*Claude Kappler,* Monstres,
démons et merveilles à la fin du Moyen Age

 e have already encountered *ritual monsters*, by which I mean scary effigies or statues used in public festivities: figures of a horrible mien that are brought out to frighten or to instruct people, that is, ceremonial para- phernalia. Such would include the hideous masks the Sri Lankans use to exorcize devils and the colorful Kachina costumes the Hopi use to frighten neophytes during initiations. The ubiquity of such *rite fright* shows that the awful visions of the mind are wont to take concrete form and to engage with humans under controlled circumstances.

We have seen that since prehistoric times the monster's therapeutic func- tion is to give shape to deep-seated fears in objectified, manipulable forms, pictorially, as dramatis personae in theatrical productions, or as automated effigies that can interact with humans in choreographed narratives. In this way we reify the inner demon: magically make the monster real, external- ize it, animate it, and persecute it. Ritualized monsters of this sort are one way a culture can work to sublimate instinct, just as in modern America we have celluloid extraterrestrials and Halloween ghouls.

MAN-MADE MONSTERS: NDEMBU

One of the first anthropologists to explore the ritual realm of monsters was Victor Turner, whose groundbreaking works have become classics known to every graduate student. In a famous book on symbolism in tribal Africa, he analyzes demonic figures in the ceremonies of the Ndembu, a horticultural tribe of northwestern Zambia. Employing Van Gennep's insights, Turner argues that the rites-of-passage of such preliterate peoples create what he calls a *liminal time*, an out-of-the ordinary "betwixt-and-between" period (1967: 93) when the rules are overturned and anything can happen. In times of liminality, neophytes are subjected to special shocks designed to awaken them to the meaning of their culture. For example, they may experience bizarre visions arranged by their elders: lurid masks and effigies that cavort menacingly. Prime among such oddities in Ndembu culture are costumed monsters: half-human creatures of threatening aspect.

According to Turner, the sudden appearance of these monsters traumatizes the neophytes and causes them to wonder and reflect. This enacts a cognitive transformation by which the young can reenter the world with greater understanding and a deeper commitment to their culture. Upon examining the ritual paraphernalia of the Ndembu, for example, Turner remarks he was often struck by the grotesqueness of the costumes worn by the actors. The young people are confronted by a cavorting half-human, half-lion figure that lunges wildly as if to devour them. Other oddities abound in the Ndembu *sacra*: hideous zombies, semi-human creatures with tiny heads and misshapen genitals, ugly ghouls sporting disproportionately large or small limbs, wraiths without heads, frightening zoomorphs, and the like.

Earlier anthropologists—such as J. A. McCulloch in a pioneering article on "Monsters" in the *Hastings Encyclopedia of Religion and Ethics*—also noted the richness of African monster imagery. Like others at the time, McCulloch ascribed the African masks and costumed monstrosities to "hallucinations, night-terrors and dreams," which he supposed tribal Africans were prone to. Extrapolating further, McCulloch argued that such images reflect the mental differences between civilized and primitive peoples: "as man drew little distinction [in primitive society] between himself and animals, as he thought that transformation from one to the other was possible, so he easily ran human and animal together. This in part accounts for the animal-headed gods or animal-gods with human heads" (cited in Turner 1967: 104–5).

Disagreeing with this ethnocentric reasoning, Turner argues that the monstrous figures are not merely nightmares proceeding from the primitive brain but rather didactic devices. Lovingly constructed by local artists, they are used to teach the neophytes to distinguish clearly between the different elements of reality, as it is conceived in their culture (1967: 105). For Turner, as for others who have embraced his insights, the African costumes and *sacra* represent the people's inherent need to deal with and control the unimaginable and unknown in the world—that which exists "outside" the culture. From this standpoint, the use of the grotesque and monstrous images in such ceremonies may be interpreted as a means not so much of terrorizing young people (although this happens) as of awakening them to their own values and moral traditions: making them vividly and rapidly aware of what may be called the factors of their culture.

Thus the young people learn about the constituent elements of their world, and they are alternately forced and encouraged to think about their society, to consider the known cosmos and the powers that give them sustenance. For Turner, ritual monsters are metaphorical devices to encourage reflection and insight, ways of breaking down the normal into its component parts and reassembling them in new, exciting, even liberating ways. Effigy ogres are therefore not just fright masks, but the very stuff of the creative process, providing an experience necessary to human cognitive development. The terrible Ndembu were-lion encourages the observer to think about real lions, their habits and qualities, their metaphorical properties, religious significance, and so on. Even more than this, the relation between human beings and the real lion itself, and between the empirical and the metaphorical, may be speculated upon, and new ideas developed. Turner argues that monsters in the liminal period of the Ndembu ritual break, as it were, "the cake of custom" (106).

Although effigy monsters of this sort are perhaps represented most richly in the world's preliterate cultures with their ritual repertories, they are not unique to tribal folk. This kind of outré ritual object also abounds in the heart of western Europe—especially in rural areas—even today. Ritualized monsters and demons are particularly pronounced in the parochial village festivals of southern France and Spain, paramount among which is the Spanish Tarasca (Tarasque in French), the monster-serpent of Catholic demonology. Its cult reaches an apogee today in northern Spain in the region of Catalonia.

AN EXOTIC BESTIARY

Before getting to the Spanish Tarasca, we must take notice of the hundreds of demons, devils, and other kinds of costumed monsters that cavort and threaten during village festivals throughout Spain—a colorful Catholic mumming tradition that goes back at least to medieval days and shows the staying power of monstrous forms and images. Spain is in fact known throughout Europe for the persistence of its ritual clowns and devilish effigies, for which there are faint echoes in the rest of modern Western Europe, where perhaps science fiction literature and films have taken over this function. Many religious rituals in the rural Spanish pueblos feature mythic demons, "mimetic creatures," in Girard's words, and weird cryptomorphs such as minotaurs, menacing giants armed with spears and swords, cannibal ogres, outsized rams and goats, or deformed bulls (given the Spanish obsession with tauromachy). At the high point of these festivals, such figures (usually local men in costume, although sometimes mechanical devices are used) burst out of dark corners, set violently upon the bystanders, symbolically "eat" children, reducing the little ones to tears, and are finally defeated by a choreographed counterattack of the villagers—in the typical epic-hero mold we have seen so many times above. Some students of Spanish culture, like Carrie Douglass (1997) and Timothy Mitchell (1988, 1990, 1991), have even seen the Spanish *corrida*, the bullfight itself, as a reenactment of man-against-monster motif of classical antiquity. After all, the Spanish fighting bull is in some ways an unnatural and even monstrous creation, artificially outsized, produced through centuries of selective breeding and imbued with an abnormal ferocity. Mitchell (1988, 1990) refers to this tendency in Spanish culture as the "festival canalization of aggression," which he argues is the underlying national genius of liminality in rites and celebrations. Based on these persuasive observations, one may argue that the inner logic of the Spanish man-against-beast rituals parallels the therapeutic and restorative functions of the monster legend in oral and written folklore the world over. Let us briefly examine some of these events in calendar order.

Our first stop is the town of Riofrío de Aliste, in Zamora Province in northwestern Spain, where on the first day of each year people celebrate the festival of La Obisparra, or the Mock Bishop's Parade. This New Year's event features jumping devils and demons called *garochos*, armed with gigantic pincers tipped with goat horns, that prance about town until surrounded and defeated by the villagers. On both January 1 and 6 there is a similar event in the nearby town of Montamarta. A devilish figure called a *quinto* (literally a recruit, but here meaning a local man playing the monster) goes around town chasing people, pretending to eat children, and generally behaving like a wild animal. After a full day of this bedlam, the quinto is surrounded and symbolically dispatched by the populace.

In southeastern Spain, in the small town of Piornal (Cáceres Province, Extremadura) the people celebrate a similar fiesta called Jarramplas (Devil-

Carnival Minotaur figure "La Vaca Bayona," Pereruela de Sauyago, Extremadura, Spain. Photo by María del Carmen Medina.

Clown) on January 19 and 20. In this persecutory masquerade, which is held in honor of Saint Sebastian, the *jarramplas* (a local term) is a similarly attired monster figure. Wearing a horned mask and a multi-colored devil's costume, this hybrid beast goes around town playing a drum and frightening people by engaging in mock violence. According to ethnographer Javier Marcos Arévalo, who has studied zoomorphic imagery in Spanish festivals, the jarramplas figure has the special function of attacking all those who cross its path during the liminal festival period, "especially young people, and in particular young girls," thus lending the celebration a distinctly erotic excitement (2001: 18). The jarramplas masquerader sports a padded head-to-toe costume to protect him from the avalanche of rotten fruit and vegetables that the townspeople hurl at him as he cavorts. Local people say that the monster represents all the evil in the world and must be "killed" by the barrage of objects—a symbolic stoning by which the villagers get rid of their sins for one year.

Another demonic fiesta takes place in the town of Arbancón, in Guadalajara Province in northern Spain. This event, called El Botarga de la Candelaria (the Devil of Candlemas), takes place annually on the first Sunday in February. On a similar note of communal expiation, it features grotesque demons and zoomorphs (local volunteers in costume) who fight the villagers and pretend to eat children. They also go around town stealing objects and behaving with atavistic abandon. As in the events described previously, they are once again defeated by the multitudes in a ritual death symbolizing the defeat of all evil and the renewal of hope for the new year.

Later in February the various pre-Lenten carnivals in Spain also feature a plethora of demonic images and scary paraphernalia. Although carnival celebrations occur throughout Catholic Europe and Latin America, Spanish pueblo carnivals stand out because they often feature hideous creatures that ramble around town attacking or challenging people and enacting all sorts of nasty depredations. The carnivals of Bielsa (Huesca Province), Frontera (El Hierro), and Fuentes de Andalucía (Seville) are good examples of this symbolic aggression. All three have traditions of unbridled devils and frisky, brutish monsters in their celebrations. In the Bielsa festival masked demons wearing huge horns and armed with stakes and poles attack the townspeople, sending the children into gales of hysteria. During the carnival of the village of Frontera in the Canary Islands, there occurs the liminal period called Los Carneros, or the Rams. In this event, local youths disguise themselves as monster-rams, wearing sheepskins, placing wicker baskets on their heads to

form a huge sheep's head with great, pointy horns, and painting their arms
and legs black. They run up and down the streets attacking young boys and
girls (García Rodero 1992: 275). The children are duly impressed, many
bursting into tears at the sight of the threatening creatures.

In the Andalusian town of Fuentes, which I studied personally for many
years (Gilmore 1998), carnival masquerades feature monstrous female figures that look something like a cross between a witch and a demon, and are
armed with various weapons. These horrible apparitions march up and
down through the winding streets at night seeking victims to attack, which
they do with a ferocious mock violence bordering on the real, as well as a
battery of verbal assaults. Sometimes a number of them will surround a
bystander, making menacing feints and hurling invective until the victim is
reduced to tears. Vampire-like, they always disappear at the light of day.
Another form of goblin in Fuentes is the all-white ghost, or *carpanta*, a
man or women entirely swathed in heavy cloths or linens. The carpanta's
face is always covered and featureless so that the effect is one of a cipher, a
shapeless, disembodied ghoul. The festival resembles the American Halloween in some ways, but these demons do not ask for treats; their only
function is to attack and discomfort.

Another wild event featuring pretend goblins takes place in Acehuche in
mid-winter and is known as Las Carantoñas, a word that can be translated
as Ugly Faces or Ogres. According to the protagonists of this madcap festival, its object is for everyone in town to dress up in outlandish costumes, to
appear on the streets looking "as fiendish as possible," and to assume the
look of fantastic evil beings or half-human ogres (Marcos Arévalo 2001:
20). Joining in enthusiastically, the entire town put on grotesque masks and
homemade outfits, with an emphasis on mythical beasts they call chimeras
and human metamorphs like werewolves, vampires, and minotaurs, and
then rush about town marauding and pillaging. According to the townspeople, their purpose in the aggressive masquerading is to bring all the evil
of the town to the surface in the most ugly form possible in order to sup-
purate it, expel it, and cleanse the field. All this brings us to the arch-fiend
of all southern Europe, the Pentecostal dragon, called Tarasque in France
and Tarasca in Spain.

LA TARASQUE

As in many matters of religion, Catholic Spain shares ceremonial traits with
neighboring France, one of which is a special liturgical monster. This is the

famous Tarasque, the dragon-serpent of Corpus Christi and of the Feast of Pentecost, which in Catholic imagery symbolizes evil, sin, the devil, or paganism fighting against holiness. Usually represented in statuary and pictures in both countries' art as a man-eating sea serpent or some variant of a medieval dragon complete with fire-breathing snout, it may have originated in the early Middle Ages in the Provençal town of Tarascon (population 8,000), from which it takes its name, although it may have Celtic roots and date from even earlier, pre-Christian times. The contextual legend of St. Martha, dragon-slayer, however, arose in the twelfth century in Tarascon and quickly spread to the adjoining areas of the Languedoc and over the Pyrenees to Spanish Catalonia; along with it came the image of the man-eating dragon as a metaphor for sin.

According to the ancient legends, the Tarasque was a huge amphibious beast resembling a horse in overall shape, but with a lion's head and toothy mouth, six bear's paws, a carapace studded with great spikes, and a viper's tail. One imaginative local historian describes the beast as resembling "a giant armadillo" because of the humped, spiked back in many local representations (Nourri 1973: 44). It supposedly originated in Asia Minor but parked itself along the Rhône River in the south of France for a long time (perhaps favoring the climate like so many other visitors), where, aside from impeding navigation, it made a nuisance of itself by preying on local people, mainly eating virgins, as is customary for monsters. Celebrating its man-eating proclivities, representations on the town crest of Tarascon always feature a beast with wide-open mouth from which protrude the legs of a half-eaten victim.

Finally, the people could stand it no longer and sought celestial assistance. A holy woman, St. Martha, having arrived in Provence by means of a fortuitous shipwreck—incongruously, she is today the patron saint of hoteliers and restaurateurs in France—put a stop to its depredations by drenching the Tarasque with holy water just as it was devouring a man. After this holy intervention, the monster supposedly lost its ferocity and became tame, even benevolent, acting rather like a devoted pet to the saint, who lashed the now tame beast to her girdle. But the local people did not trust the transformation and killed it just to be sure (Barber and Riches 1971: 434). Although the first mentions of the Tarasque in written documents date from the mid-fourteenth century, one text dated 1497 cites the holy monk Raban Maur (ca. 776–856), who wrote that between Arles and Avignon near the banks of the Rhône there flourished countless "ferocious beasts and formidable serpents," as well as a terrible dragon, "unbelievably long and huge; its breath is pestilential smoke, its eyes glare sulfurously, and its snout is lined with horrible sharp teeth" (cited in Nourri 1973: 52–53). Some authorities identify the latter with St. Martha's Tarasque, so the myth may have been current as early as the eighth century.

According to local historians, the cult of the creature became an integral part of local ceremonial traditions, its death at the hands of the Tarascon-nais being commemorated in rites on various religious holidays, including Corpus Christi in mid-spring, and especially during the feast of Pentecost, which takes place seven Sundays after Easter (Renard 1991: 5). Various other localities in southern France place emphasis on similar figures of "dracs" (dragons) of various kinds during fêtes and religious observances. For example, in the villages of Razilly and Samsur, not far from Tarascon, there are festivals featuring papier-mâché *gueules*, or snouts of dragons, while similar monster-serpents are featured on church architecture in the towns of Aix-Sainte-Marguerite, Draguignon (whose patron saint and name-sake is indeed a dragon), Saint-Mitre, Bourg Saint-Andéol, and others, including the provincial capital itself, Marseilles, whose cathedral boasts a famous "drac."

In Tarascon proper, the observation of the monster reaches its apogee under the auspices of a local foundation called the Order of the Knights of the Tarasque (l'Ordre des Chevaliers de la Tarasque) founded in 1474 by King René of Languedoc. There, using the ancient town seals as models, the people have constructed a huge mechanical effigy of the beast which is occa-sionally taken out for the procession during the Feast of Pentecost. Suc-ceeding previous incarnations dating at least back to 1465, the present statue was built at various times between 1840 and 1943, the great head dating to the earliest period (Dumont 1951: 49–50). Carried aloft by sixteen male members of the Order inside the hollow body (who represent the swal-lowed victims) and guided along the city streets by another eight (symboliz-ing the city fathers), the model is over twenty feet long and is constructed of wood and metal. It has numerous moving parts, especially its snapping jaws and a large spiked tail that swivels like a boom. According to Louis Dumont (1951), a French anthropologist who studied the effigy and its cult at mid-century, major processions took place in the years 1846, 1861, 1891, and after World War II in 1946; since the latter year, the ritual continues to occur on an annual basis largely as a tourist attraction, and having lost the reli-gious connection has been renamed the Fête de la Tarasque.

Dumont tells us that, at least in the 1946 parade, which he witnessed in person, the effect of the Tarasque effigy was to convey a sense of menace and supernatural power to bystanders. As manipulated by its carriers, its behavior along the route was consistently one of "aggression" toward onlookers as the effigy made feints and lurches toward people with its huge mouth ajar and its lethal tail flailing. The objective of the cult as a whole is to manifest the "malevolent power" of evil. The man-eating theme is apparent in the procession, as the huge beast makes as if to snatch up children in its mechanical jaws. However, despite all this pretend violence, both Dumont and other French observers have noted the keenly ambivalent attitude of the people of Tarascon toward their namesake monster. As in the myth, the beast represents infernal forces, of course, being a ruthless monster, but because of its association with the saint it also symbolizes the triumph of good over evil. So there are mixed feelings. It may be best to quote at length from Dumont's masterly (and little known) book on this point:

In summary, if the positive (sacred) prevails over the negative (evil), both are present. As in the myth [of St. Martha], what matters is not good or evil per se, but moral ambivalence: a spiritual dualism in the form of a dialectic which tends toward the positive. The Tarasque is a figure of blessedness paradoxically through its own purifying violence, or rather, *the procession of the beast exploits an ambivalent power and transforms it, through the means of symbolic violence, into an essential beneficence.* (1951: 121; italics in original)

Dumont argues that it is this "contradiction of good and evil," as he calls it, in the ritual observance and in the mix of emotions inspired, combined with the timeless appeal and mystery of monsters, that explains the survival of the Tarasque cult in southern France and northern Spain since the Middle Ages. Another observer, Jean Nourri, a Tarasconnais himself, suggests that the Tarasque had by the Renaissance attained the position of a "sacred animal" in Provence, rather like the bull in ancient Crete or the cow in India. Others have noted the "totemic" quality of the Tarasque both in the French Midi and in Spanish Catalonia (Noyes 1992: 314).

LA TARASCA: BERGA

Various localities in Spain have their own totemic monsters. Berga is a town of a few thousand in Spanish Catalonia, across the Pyrenees about fifty miles due north of Barcelona. The town boasts a famous celebration like that which occurs on Saint Martha's Day in Tarascon. The Spanish fiesta, which draws visitors from all over the region and abroad, takes place each year during the feast of Corpus Christi, usually in late May or early June, when in the Catholic calendar people celebrate the body of Christ and renounce sin symbolized by devils, demons, dragons, and other hellish effigies. The observation of Corpus Christi was instituted in 1264 by Pope Urban IV in the bull *Transiturus* as a way of reinvigorating faith; it was confirmed and made obligatory for Christians in 1311 by Clement V (for more on this, see Rubin 1991). From the fourteenth century on there was widespread diffusion throughout western Europe of various commemorative parades and processions, presenting allegories and masques of good triumphing over evil and representing the most solemn conjoining of civil and religious celebrations known to late medieval and Renaissance urban centers. By the seventeenth century the Reformation brought them to an end, except for this corner of southwestern Europe (Noyes 1992: 228–29).

The Berga celebration is called the Patum. Amid the prancing devils and demons, the people of Berga carry aloft a huge effigy in the shape of a monster-dragon and parade it through the streets in a kind of mock challenge to the community. The most striking characteristic of this fearsome beast is that its mouth is filled with fireworks that explode continuously during the festival. The Berga monster itself is of curious aspect: unlike the French effigy, which, as some have said, resembles a giant armadillo with a spiked carapace, this Spanish cousin combines the usual long-necked dragon shape with the overall structure of a large equine. Such curious hybrid figures in Catalan mythology are known generically as *mulassas*, meaning something like monstrous mules. There are references to such fabulous fauna in Catalonia going back to the twelfth century, but the first mention of the term Tarasca in this context dates from 1790, when the Berga city fathers used the term to describe their effigy to some curious Castilian visitors (cited in Noyes 1992: 319). Still cherished today, the Berga Tarasca, locally known as the *mulaguita*, or more commonly the Guita (a local word for a nasty, kicking mule), is constructed of wood and other materials. It is painted dinosaurgreen and has a long neck atop which is perched a saurian-like head with a long snout, giving it a certain resemblance to the Loch Ness monster (Warner 1998: 116). It has been described by a local historian as an "original monster," a creature of infernal evil, a prime example of the enduring ritual fauna of Catalonia. Half mule, half dragon, the effigy is as tall as a threestory building. Its mouth is stuffed to the brim with firecrackers and explo-

One of the fire-breathing Guitas of the Patum celebration, Berga, Catalonia, Spain. Photo courtesy Manel Excobet/Foto Luigi, Berga.

sives, with the effect that it spits plumes of fire and flame throughout its wanderings through the town (Armengou i Feliu 1994: 100–101).

The tradition made its way down the peninsula by the thirteenth century, the first mention of the Tarasca in a ceremonial context in the southern city of Seville, for example, dates from 1282, shortly after its reconquest from the Arabs. From there it spread to the rest of Andalusia, where, as an added fillip in some localities, the model would be mounted by a choirboy called a *tarasquillo* (a kind of junior tarasca), whose job it was to yelp, cavort, and snatch off the hats of bystanders (Rodríguez Becerra 2000: 158). In some other provincial capitals, such as Granada and Madrid, the tradition in the early modern period ripened into elaborate processions in which the pasteboard effigy invoked the Dragon of the Book of Revelation and carried on its back a woman playing the role of the Whore of Babylon or some other lascivious siren of the Bible.

The Tarasca of Toledo is one of the best known in Spain. Made of wood, cane, and plaster, over twenty feet long and six feet tall, this impressive piece of sculpture carries on its back a doll with a blonde wig representing Anne Boleyn—a tradition that derives from the English queen's innocent role in Henry XIII's rupture with Rome, when he broke with the Church to divorce Catherine of Aragon and marry her. Thus she represents by default all the monstrous evils of the Reformation, associated in Spain with paganism. Combining monstrosity with a dose of misogyny, these models were often worked by pulleys and, like the French Tarasque, were customarily hyper-aggressive in attacking bystanders en route. They are wedded to basic Christian symbolism but may also have specific local meanings (Noyes 1992: 313).

By the mid-seventeenth century the monster and its entourage had become the focus of the Corpus Christi festival in all of Spain, and had become so entrenched among the rabble that clerical and civil authorities felt the celebration had gotten out of hand. Accordingly, King Charles III, in a Royal Pragmatic issued dated June 21, 1780, prohibited further use of tarascas in the Corpus or Pentecost celebrations, declaring it a pagan, frivolous entertainment that imparted too much "folkloristic atmosphere" to what should be most solemn events (Sánchez Herrero 1999: 49). As in other cases of the legal interdiction of monsters, this edict was largely ignored. Tarasca parades have only died out in major cities in Spain since the civil war, partly due to the restricted finances of municipalities. There is today some evidence of a revival in certain areas (Rodríguez Becerra 2000: 159). For example, in the town of Las Hacinas near the city of Burgos, the Tarasca has been entirely detached from Corpus Christi and any religious significance, and integrated into the local carnival in February. Made of pasteboard and wood, the Hacinas figure is a crude, huge long-necked hollow monster, manipulated by five men, that tears about the town gobbling up young women, who then must remain in its commodious belly until freed by reciting magic formulae. The Hacinas beast is famous throughout the region for its unique ability to cavort with sinuous mobility and to jump a full three feet in the air during its maraudings—an acrobatic feat of which the townspeople are duly proud.

To get some of the flavor of Corpus today in Spain with its traditional Tarasca, let us take a closer look at the Patum celebration in Berga. It was observed firsthand in 1990 by the American folklorist Dorothy Noyes and reported on by her in exquisite detail in an unpublished PhD dissertation

Tarasca, Toledo, Spain. Note Ann Boleyn doll on spine. Photo by
Fernando Martínez Gil.

(1992). The following is based on Noyes's splendid work and also on vibrant descriptions by Marina Warner (1998: 114–25).

When the festival occurs, the entire town of Berga becomes a street theater and is host to throngs of local people and visitors. The name Patum itself derives from the sound of a preludial drumbeat—Pa-tum! Pa-tum!—that signals the start of the celebration and is also connected to the Catalonian term for a report or explosion, cognate to the English "petard." Noise and flame are paramount in the Patum: every night there is a raucous fireworks display and an extended salvo of rockets and Roman candles to climax the day's festivities. Aside from the fireworks, the feature of the Berga Patum is the emphasis on demons, devils, giants, animals, and monsters.

The festivities are akin to the medieval Carnival of Devils, in which local people would dress up as demons and other infernal figures and skirmish with the crowds during a full week of orchestrated mayhem. In Catalonia the tradition of dancing devils probably relates in a generic way to the myth of St. Michael fighting against Lucifer and his legions; in Berga the demonic aspect of the pageant seems to date from an early period, if not to the beginning of Corpus celebrations in the Middle Ages. According to local scholars, there seems to have been some modification of the ritual in the early seventeenth century; the first documentary accounts, dating from 1632 mention two devils specifically, and, interestingly, also a female devil, or *diablessa* (Farràs i Farràs 1986: 77). However, the latter must have caused too much controversy among the populace to become a fixture of the celebration; it was presumably a man in transvestite garb, as occurs in some other rites in southern Europe in which men cross-dress, especially in carnivals and political protests (Gilmore 1998; Sahlins 1994). So the lady demon disappeared, and after 1656 there the Berga records mention only male devils and the Archangel Michael.

According to Noyes (1992: 307–9), demons and other diabolical figures figure prominently in Catalan folk culture in a general sense, both in religious rites and in oral literature. They serve as the principal nemesis of Christianity and as symbols of sin and depravity, rather like the Moors in Castilian demonology, but also as geomantic and chthonic spirits, rather like the leprechauns of Ireland. Demonic figures also play a role in popular theater in Catalonia, from the mystery plays and morality dramas of the early modern period to the passion pageants and village shepherd's plays of the present. In all these productions devils and ogres virtually take over the role of representing evil and the base instincts. In the Berga case, these festival demons always carried large clubs or *maces*, which has the same meaning in Catalan as in English; aside from looking like lethal weapons to bystanders, these maces serve as a convenient platform for the pyrotechnics that are so prominent a feature of the Corpus rituals in Catalonia. An account from 1790 says that:

Two men dressed as Devils, who
with firecrackers in their maces,
hands, horns, and tails, go jumping
to the sound of the drum, and
shooting the firecrackers, another
who does the role of St. Michael
coming out to persecute them, who
with his lance assaults them and
acts as if he is killing one
of the two Devils. (cited in Noyes 1992: 309)

In the Berga event there are various stages of aggressive deviltry, when men and demons battle it out with noisy explosives. In one event, customarily taking place on the third day of the week-long festival, townsmen disguised as devils escaped from hell—by custom all men, for women do not normally play this role—run out into the central square and set off the usual firecrackers and rockets. The bomb-throwing masqueraders are made up so as to appear of great size, which makes them more intimidating, especially to the screaming children. They put on towering papier-mâché masks in the form of ogres' heads, and their bodies are swathed in dampened vine leaves that both heighten the wild-man effect and afford a modicum of protection from the explosives they detonate. Each of these tall devils is accompanied by an assistant called an *accompanyant*, who lights the fuses of the bombs. As the bombs explode and the noise and fury mount, the crowd surges forward and the entire town erupts into a wild scene of hell-raising and pandemonium. Flares shoot from the devils' horns and grapeshot bursts out in great plumes of yellow and red smoke. The night air is lit by sparks and rent by cries and shouts. Noyes, who was allowed to participate in the chaotic event as a devil (unusual for a woman), wrote of her experience.

Inside, she recalls, you climb in darkness to the upper level of the building where the equipment is stored; there a darkened face looks over a half-door: this sinister figure represents the gatekeeper of Hell. He murmurs something to shadows behind him, and after a pregnant pause, he hands you a devil suit and a mask to put on. Guitar and drum music swells and like the others you begin to jump up and down, the throngs pressing in, Roman candles showering you with sparks, the cinders all over your hands and flying painfully inside your mask. There are torturously loud explosions near your ears; a brief instant of open space and suddenly the air is filled with so much smoke and flame than you despair of regaining either your composure or your balance. Now tottering with the tumult and the noise, you follow your *accompanyant* until the procession comes to an end, and then your assistant removes your mask and the lights of the village come on, bathing the scene in an eerie glow (384–85). Afterward, the figure of the Angel appears and does ritual battle with the leaping exploding demons, who finally lie down in a docile manner in defeat.

The main event, however, is probably the march of the Guitas, the Tarasca-like effigies, of which there are two. Trained men working pulleys and wires manipulate the effigies as they move toward the throngs. About twenty feet long, their long serpentine necks are topped with glossy black heads complete with rolling glass eyeballs and mouths painted scarlet and full of sharp fangs. The heads appear small seen from a distance, but as the effigies approach, they are seen to be large and menacing, and the encrypted monstrousness of their appearance—the dragon-like teeth, the blood-red coloring of the mouth, the glassy stare of the eyes, makes them all the more terrifying. Warner provides a splendid summary of their role:

The *Guitas'* manipulators rush the crowd, dipping the beasts' heads all of a sudden on one group, sweeping furiously across it, showering the bystanders with sparks. Then they suddenly swerve and mob another section of the throng, moving at breakneck speed along the length of the front lines, the lighted fire-crackers in their monsters' jaws sputtering and hissing all the while. The crowd wears heavy cotton hats and coverings as protection of the fiery saltpeter, but the young participants want to confront the danger. Later they display the scorched and holey trophies of the encounters like battle scars. (1998: 116)

People chase after the fire-spitting figures, retreating only when the Guita turns toward them and issues a well-directed column of flame. Young people are very much in the forefront of these mock-heroic confrontations, and the Guita responds generously to the feints of youths who are holding out their hats or other garments of clothing to be burned as trophies of their acts of bravery. Like a demon-god, the monster engages in a coquettish play of advance and retreat with umbrella-wielding provocateurs who challenge its authority. Drawing back just before the climax, it celebrates its fire-cracker detonations with a vigorous shake of its long neck and a humping tremor across its green frame (Noyes n.d.: 3)

Meanwhile, as all this is going on, there appear in the square two pairs of giants, the famous pasteboard *gigantes* that are paraded in virtually all Spanish village fiestas, richly garbed and representing the battling Moors and Christians of the Middle Ages. The event is completed with the dance of the dwarves, or *cabezudos*, grotesque child-like figures with oversized heads, who gambol about like uncontrolled children. On the following days there are further processions and masquerades, featuring various symbolic figures representing motifs in Spanish and Catalonian history. The entire fiesta concludes with a furious fusillade of rockets, fireworks, and bombs.

★ ★ ★

Monsters and ogres perform a "natural function" everywhere they appear, as Claude Kappler says in the epigram at the beginning of this chapter, referring to their indispensable expiative and psychotherapeutic effects. In rituals like those above, and in others that occur in tribal Africa and Asia, the participants reify the monstrous as effigies and statues, turning fantasies into real things which then can be displayed publicly, manipulated by people demonized according to local norms and the aesthetic schemes of the culture, confronted and defeated by the concerted efforts of the community. The ubiquity of such cultural transformations and social processes is truly remarkable, again pointing to some deep need in the human psyche to objectify inner states as metaphors and living symbols, and thus to disavow the "bad" part of the self within, to deny complicity and find external scapegoats to blame, to exculpate through means of displacement and externalization—an existential need to defend the self from the self, a need that has always existed and will always exist. The monstrous metaphor as object becomes the critical touchstone for communal renewal and for individual redemption, the sacrificial victim, the scapegoated emissary from the unconscious. And thus the monster takes on all the power of that which is denied in the self, all that which is repressed, and is both worshipped and attacked in the smoke and flame of the eternal battle.

Extrapolating from all this, we also see a brilliant thread uniting the ear-

liest expressions of the imagination with the most recent, attesting once
again to the universality of the inner struggle. The first true documented
monsters appear in Franco-Cantabrian cave art. One of these, at Pergouset,
dating from at least 15,000 years ago and probably earlier, depicts a
dragon-like figure with a long neck topped by the head of a horse or deer,
looking very much like the present-day Tarasque of France and the Guita
of Catalonia. The so-called "sorcerer" in the cave of Trois-Frères, bears a
striking resemblance to the hybrid figures that cavort today in the Spanish
rituals we have described: man below, ogre above, half human and half
beast, part demon and part god. Perhaps its function was also similar. Possibly the weird image scrawled by the cave dwellers is a prehistoric artist's
rendition of a masquerader in some forgotten rite, a metaphorical figure
representing the terror and mystery of life, a mix of "everyman" and
"everybeast" who was symbolically killed by the hunters—Girard's
"mimetic victim" in the Stone Age. Likewise, the Tarasca, so beloved of the
French and the Spanish and so much a part of village festivities, resembles
nothing so much as the fire-breathing dragons of ancient times like the
Egyptian Apophis and the Mesopotamian demon goddess Tiamat, all the
"wyrms" of Anglo-Saxon and medieval literature, and the demonic extraterrestrials of contemporary cinema—a unified image that has captivated
man from the dawn of civilization to the present. The only thing missing as
our barbarian ancestors danced around the fire exorcizing and extolling
their monsters was the Roman candles of Berga, but some incendiary homage was no doubt present in the Paleolithic imagination.

OUR MONSTERS, OURSELVES

What seest thou else in the dark backward and abysm of time?

—*William Shakespeare*, The Tempest

ow that we have now looked at monsters in every corner of the world and seen their horrible shapes and depredations in all sorts of contexts—fantasy, mythology, oral folklore, rituals, and both primitive and modern art—what can we say about their commonalities? What do all these terrible figments have in common? And what might such convergences say about the human mind that makes up such horrors everywhere in the world and at all times in history? Let us return to our original hypotheses and see how the data support our premises.

GIGANTISM

The first attribute that stands out is great size. No matter how monsters differ otherwise, no matter where they appear, monsters are vastly, grotesquely oversized. Looming intimidatingly, they pose a special challenge. Size relates in a generic sense to all animals, not only to humans, for large size means superior strength, which translates into the power advantage in confrontations. Indeed, "monster" in most modern usages refers to anything outstandingly big, as in the retailer's term "a monster sale." *Webster's Unabridged Dictionary* (1979 ed.) gives as a primary definition of *monster* anything "of enormous or extraordinary size." Yet physical enormity is not semantically implicit in the English word, which originates from roots meaning sign or portent, so we have to consider why the mind imposes such an attribute. There are two observations that are pertinent here.

The first is what bigness (especially height) means in the eyes of the observer. Monsters are always depicted *looming over* small, weak, and overshadowed humans. Can we point to anything common to the human experience that makes for such a consistent and powerful distortion? Aside from the size = power equation common to all animals, there is a connection to a perspective in which everything appears oversized, great, overwhelming and dangerous. Since monsters are undoubtedly connected to childhood fancies (Beaudet 1990; Warner 1998), we may look to the psychoanalysis of childhood for some direction, for monsters are children's alter egos, their inner selves.

Here we may turn to the work of psychiatrist Percy Cohen, who has written about size and height distinctions in childhood (1980). Cohen holds that such a view has to do with the retention of a juvenile perspective of helpless inferiority. Spatial deformations derive from the unconscious blueprint inherited from a time when the observer was indeed tiny relative to others, especially in relation to the parents, who must have seemed to scrape the skies. To express present emotions of fear, awe, and dread, such as felt by a small, weak child in a world of giants, the psyche dredges up perceptual residues of the time when such feelings of danger were experienced in pictorial terms. Cohen writes of this psychic conversion process:

All men have experienced childhood; and all children have experienced adults as more powerful, more prestigious, and more experienced than they are; all children have also experienced adults as higher than they are and have come to recognize or, at least, to suppose that greater height has much to do with greater advantage. (P. Cohen 1980: 59)

To this, of course, we must add that the same physical distortion implied by gigantism also conveys the child's fear of the overwhelmingly large (and advantaged) adult, whose vast bulk must translate into omnipotence.

The other ingredient here concerning gigantism involves the affective ambivalence sparked by an acuity of perceptive inferiority. We have seen throughout our discussion how the great monsters of world folklore are all perceived in divided sentiments. On the one hand they are objects of terror, but because of this physical asymmetry, because they are so enormously outsized (and in this way like the gods) and as a consequence irresistibly, supernaturally powerful, they are also objects of awe, even of reverence that borders on the religious—feelings that again can only derive from fantasies of parental omnipotence. Much like the parent to the child, of the punishing God of the Old Testament, the Qur'an, and other holy texts, the giant and mysterious power has a demonstrably bifurcated impact on the observer, conjuring up both terror and admiration, and invoking deep ambivalence toward the what the philosopher Rudolph Otto in his book *The Idea of the Holy* (1958: 3) has called the *mysterium tremendum et fascinans*, the presence of the sublime, the supernatural: the Great Terror of that which is unfathomable.

MALEVOLENT MAWS

Closely related to physical immensity is an organic synecdoche: the continual visual emphasis on the colossal mouth as organ of predation and destruction. However else they are rendered in anatomical terms, monsters are depicted has having yawning, cavernous mouths brimming with fearsome teeth, fangs, or other means of predation. These anatomical assets are used to rip and tear humans, to bite and rend and devour. Thus the behemoth of Christian lore is depicted as the "chewing animal" (Williams 1996: 186), the celluloid bogeys we have examined always threaten to bite and tear, as in *Jaws* or *Jurassic Park*, and the ritual demons always attack with their mouths stretching open like pools of blood, as in the Chinese folktale. Or else the monsters swallow their victims whole, as in the case of the biblical leviathan, which in contrast to behemoth is the "swallower" in scripture (187), or in the more familiar Jonah story in which the natural, great-mouthed whale takes the place of a supernatural beast.

However it is emphasized in biblical lore, a chewing or swallowing motif finds expression in all the world's folklores in similar tropes. For example, in Celtic mythology monster-slayer Finn McCool is swallowed by a monster of indefinite form, only to be spat out whole (Campbell 1968: 91). Among the Blackfoot Indians, the culture hero Kut-o-yis is swallowed by "a great fish," and in other American Indian tales culture heroes are routinely swallowed by sea serpents, ogres, or giant birds of prey. Among Plains Indians such as the Crow, Pawnee, Hidatsa, Arapaho, and Wichita, the "Swallowing Monster" is the motif most frequently encountered in heroic mythology and in folktales. The Hidatsa, for example, believed in a monster of unspecified shape called only "Big Mouth," which simply opened its maw, drew a large breath, and swallowed all the men and animals within sight (M. Carroll 1992: 300). We saw that the main, in fact defining, feature of the legaselep of Micronesia and taniwha of Polynesia is that they gobble people up, often ingesting them whole—so that the miraculous escape from the belly is possible. The theme of the enveloping, ingesting maw is found in every culture, every tradition, almost to a monotonous degree (Campbell 1968: 247).

Consequently, we may conclude that this theme betrays a universal

"Quint in Rage," original storyboard by Joe Alves for the movie *Jaws*.
Courtesy Joe Alves. (*above*)

Sinner about to be devoured by water monster, illustration from
nineteenth-century book. (*below*)

obsession with oral aggression. Monsters are always "Big Mouths." Compare, for example, the early nineteenth-century German woodcut depicting a marine monster with the cinema image of the monster shark attacking Quint in *Jaws*: in almost identical scenes, imagined more than one hundred years apart, artists have focused upon the central image of the oversized mouth of the attacking creature arising from the depths and dwarfing the defenseless human victim. Comparing various monster-dragon representations from Western sources, we see that in almost every case visual emphasis is obsessively upon the mouth as weapon, along with constituent assemblages of teeth, fangs, jaws, tongue, gulping throat.

This oral-alimentary obsession appears in most other cultures in various ways to similar effect. The Japanese serpent woman is depicted as a "ghastly eater" with protruding fangs and a gigantic mouth. The Greek Cyclops eats sailors; other monsters in Greek mythology, like the Harpies, tear and mutilate with their mouth, teeth, and jaws. The American Indian Windigo is depicted as having an enormous lipless maw dripping with blood. The pre-Columbian giants were voracious man-eaters, ingesting still-palpitating hearts just ripped from bodies. The American Thunderbird and the monster-avians of east Asia and the Pacific feed human victims to their wide-mouthed young. The Hopi kachinas are often depicted with ear-to-ear mouths, bloody fangs, and snapping jaws. Most other monsters in world cultures, no matter how envisioned, from Buddhist demons in Thailand to the jinn of the Muslim Middle East to the ogre-heads of "Monster Park" in Italy to the Devil himself in Christian eschatology, are depicted with the fierce apparatus of oral aggression. In village Spain today, as we have seen, the various ritual demons all attack children with gobbling jaws, pretending to eat them. The French Tarasque is depicted with the legs of a human victim protruding from its capacious mouth.

In most cultures, too, the monster's mouth shows stunning diversity as a weapon. In the West, medieval dragons not only bit or swallowed men whole like the Asian and Aztec ogres, but they also spewed fire or shot lethal smoke or venom from their mouths. A prime example surviving into the present day is the Pentecost beast in Spain, which is commonly represented either as a fire-breathing dragon or as a composite of equine and dragon, as in the case of the Guita of Berga in Catalonia and elsewhere in northern Spain and southern France. In each case, the ritual statue has no anatomical weapons aside from a mouth filled with big teeth or noisy firecrackers spitting flame and smoke.

Vampire. Publicity still from *Bram Stoker's Dracula* (1992).

In non-Western cultures, once again, the oral cavity in such effigies appears as a deadly weapon in a remarkable variety of ways, not only by biting, chewing, and swallowing but also by emitting noise, smoke, and fire. For example, Sinhalese demons are often depicted with wide-open bloody mouths of the usual man-eating variety. But in one remarkable case the demon Kalu Yaka is often depicted with a red hibiscus flower for a mouth, out of which protrude two flaming cloth torches representing the demon's tusks (Handelman and Kapferer 1980: 47). In Rotuma, Polynesia, the giant ogre known as "Flaming Teeth" has glowing coals for teeth. The Native American Windigo uses its mouth not only to kill and devour like a predatory animal, but also to issue thunderous screams and roars that uproot trees and cause catastrophic whirlwinds. The Cherokee utkena kills by its poisonous breath, one whiff of which is enough to fell a man (Hudson 1978: 62). The Swedish lindorm spits poisonous liquid.

Even the shape-shifters of modern fiction fit the pattern of polymorphous oral aggressiveness. Take, for example, vampires, whose mouths are often normal size in Western lore. As depicted in films and fiction, vampires always reveal themselves by oral clues: protruding canines. In addition, they destroy their victims with their mouths: draining dry, biting, devouring, dismembering, swallowing (Dundes 1998). Reviewing the literature on European vampires, psychoanalyst Richard Gottlieb notes that, despite the wide variety in the ways they are portrayed in Western folklore, they regularly destroyed with their mouths, whether by blood-sucking, flesh-eating, dismemberment, necrophilia, or simply "tearing apart" (1991: 469). The gaping, tooth-lined, flesh-tearing mouth is a universal synecdoche for monstrous predation. All this naturally brings us to the main point of all this oral depredation: cannibalism.

CANNIBALISM: PSYCHOLOGICAL INTERPRETATIONS

We see then that monsters by general agreement have rapacious mouths, which are indeed their main weapons. Monsters are almost by definition also man-eaters, using their dentition to dismember and devour humans—that is what monsters do. To fully understand the meaning of this complex and its attendant anxieties, we must delve into cannibalism and oral-aggressive fantasies, because it would appear that, whatever else it is, the monster is a cannibal fantasy.

The study of anthropophagous imagery and its social meaning starts in the psychoanalytical literature with Freud. In his early work, *Three Essays on the Theory of Sexuality* (1905), Freud shows an unusual interest in the subject. Writing about early psychosexual development, he introduces the concept of an oral-aggressive stage, primary to the anal, phallic, and genital sequences. Freud felt that cannibalistic urges at the oral stage were universal, but were not simply destructive, because they were also an attempt to incorporate the beloved maternal figure as part of the nascent self in order to gain possession and control over the external world and to make up for inevitable loss of the comforting object. Freud writes:

The first of these [stages] is the oral or, as it might be called, cannibalistic pregenital sexual organization. Here sexual activity has not yet been separated from the ingestion of food; nor are opposite currents within the activity differentiated. The *object* of both activities is the same; the sexual *aim* consists in the incorporation of the object—the prototype of a process which, in the form of identification, is later to play such an important psychological part. (1905: 198)

However, like other authorities of the time, Freud also assumed that a purely aggressive cannibalistic element was present in the male sexual orientation as an innate and evolutionary aspect of the libido:

The history of human civilization shows beyond any doubt that there is an intimate connection between cruelty and the sexual instinct. . . . According to some authorities this aggressive element of the sexual instinct is in reality a relic of cannibalistic desires—that is, it is a contribution derived from the apparatus for obtaining mastery. (1905: 159)

For Freud and his followers, cannibalism is the ultimate form of sadism and indeed of human aggression itself, because it is the original form. The wish to tear with the teeth, rend, and swallow is the primary focus of all aggressive urges that follow in later life.

Freud's follower Karl Abraham made some important contributions in a series of papers on character development (1942a, b). In his analysis, he concluded that the unexpectedly frequent cannibalistic symptomatology he encountered in clinical sessions revealed unconscious wishes to bite the mother's breast as a revenge for infantile disappointments and frustrations during the breast-feeding stage of life (Freud's oral stage). Like Freud, Abraham felt these aggressive wishes were universal, not just present in neurotics. However, going beyond Freud, Abraham divided the primal oral stage into two parts.

Occurring right after birth, the preliminary stage was objectless, without ambivalence, and characterized by a sucking and nutritional aim. The second stage arose once the teeth erupted and the jaw muscles developed to the point where the child could bite. This stage, spurred on by oral discomfort, was cannibalistic and ambivalent, reflecting mixed feelings toward the mother: on the one hand there are love and a wish to incorporate the maternal object, as Freud noted; on the other there is hate: the wish to bite and devour and destroy. This split in affect follows the natural development of the child toward the parental figure as the anal stage is reached and the parents become more frustrating and punishing as well as loving and nurturing.

Shortly afterward, Melanie Klein gave oral sadism a prominent and decisive role to play in her theories of the mental evolution of the child. She argued that the child undergoes a stage shortly after weaning in which its sadistic destructiveness reaches its maximal intensity, and that this stage is never fully extinguished in the mental apparatus of the adult. In later works (collected in a volume published in 1975), Klein revised the onset of this oral sadistic stage to just after birth, making it the most primary of the psychosexual periods. The contents of these infantile cannibalistic fantasies, she postulated, consist of biting the mother's breast, tearing it apart, and sucking it dry (see Freeman and Freeman 1992: 344 for a review).

Klein seems quite aware of the role of the monster as an allegory in this fantasy. She writes that

the man-eating wolf, the fire-spewing dragon and all the evil monsters out of myths flourish and exert their unconscious influence in the phantasy of each child, and it feels itself persecuted and threatened by those evil shapes. (1975: 249)

She adds that the real objects behind those imaginary, terrifying figures are the child's own parents, and that those dreadful shapes reflect the features of its father and mother, however distorted and fantastic the resemblance might be. The evil and distorted cannibals were not realistically arrived at by perceptions of the parents' real behavior, but were seen as deformed by projection onto them of the child's autonomous fantasies of oral violence against the parents, against which they want to retaliate. If these early the-

Detail from *Last Judgment* by Fra Angelico (ca.1387–1455), showing the Devil devouring sinners. Alinari/Art Resource, NY

orists are correct, it is clear that in standard psychoanalytic treatment, oral sadism is a constituent part of normal psychosexual development, present in most or all humans, and superseded by the usual overlay of repression.

In addition, the oral-sadistic fantasies in Klein's theory are regarded by her an her followers as derivatives of the death instinct—what Freud originally postulated as an innate aggressive drive, so that oral sadism is a mixture of libido and aggression and represents a primary—if not *the* primary—mode of human destructiveness. The cannibalistic fantasies direct the death instinct toward the external object—the mother's body—and away from the ego, as a means of warding off disintegration. Also important in Klein's theory is the emphasis on affective ambivalence, present also in Freud and Abraham, in relation to the oral-sadistic impulse. According to all three, the wish to eat the parental object and to rend the mother's breast results not from a simple antagonism, but from mixed feelings, from a basic ambivalence, love and hate. Freud and Klein agreed that the cannibal fantasy is part destructiveness and part a desire to retain or incorporate the victim as an integral part of the self (see Gottlieb 1991). Thus identification with the victim also plays a part, as in the old adage "you are what you eat"; and the basic ambivalence is "whether to eat or be eaten" (Sagan 1974: 34). The monster narrative, in which one is attacked by a cannibal beast, can then be said to incorporate both a projection of primary aggressive impulse onto an external object, and, at the same time, a demonstration of guilt or atonement—that is, of victimization: the fantasist is both subject (eater) and object (eaten). The dual fantasy implies both a cannibalistic urge and a wish to be eaten (that is, physically punished, torn apart, mutilated).

At the same time it gives vent to infantile oral aggression, the violent monster of the imagination also embodies the sadistic parent that murderously punishes transgression with dismemberment. In this light, we may see the cannibal component of the monster, which, as an inevitable mental aspect, implies being torn asunder in order to be consumed, as a manifestation of Oedipal guilt and castration anxiety displaced onto the body. Thus the monster derives its incredible psychic power from its ability to unite different forces and opposed processes within the unconscious. One may label the monster the primary universal and multivalent symbol of the human psyche: it conflates the entire range of conflicts comprising the unconscious.

ANTHROPOLOGICAL VIEWS OF CANNIBALISM

Given its power over the mind, cannibalism has been a subject of much discussion in cultural anthropology too. In the past few years there has been a
major reconsideration of the phenomenon and a rather acerbic debate
about its occurrence in primitive societies. In a controversial book published in 1978, anthropologist William Arens argues that alleged instances
of cannibalism among primitive peoples, as reported by travelers, missionaries and the like, have been vastly exaggerated—they are the products of
misinformation, ethnocentric distortion, or plain prejudice. After debunking numerous such cases cited in the anthropological literature (many truly
dubious), he insists that cannibalism never in fact existed as a culturally
acceptable phenomenon in any culture, although he admits that it may
have occurred as a desperate (reluctant) resort to fend off starvation after
catastrophes, as in the case of the Donner party. Arens's argument here is
absolute: accusations of cannibalism are always false. They are always ethnocentric inventions to demonize or dehumanize another group. This is
actually not too far-fetched an idea, if one considers how often such allega-
tions have been used to defame enemies throughout history.

Nevertheless, Arens's passionate denial of cannibalism as an empirical
fact has, in turn, been subjected to severe criticism by anthropologists who
cite evidence as to its occurrence as a culturally approved phenomenon and
its frequency in primitive cultures. An example is the edited volume by
Paula Brown and Donald Tuzin (1983). Debunking the debunker, the con-
tributors to this text demonstrate fairly convincing examples of anthro-
pophagy among the aboriginal peoples of New Guinea, Oceania, and other
areas. Joining the debate, other anthropologists have argued that archeo-
logical and literary evidence of ritual cannibalism among such people as the
Aztec is virtually incontrovertible. However, in virtually all these substanti-
ated cases, man-eating is a highly formal ritual event, taking place as part
of funeral rites with some symbolic and spiritual significance. Man-eating
is virtually never a nutritional practice. No tribes have ever killed and eaten
other humans for food, at least as far as we know.

PRIMARY HUMAN AGGRESSION

Regardless who is right in this debate, my own view is that everyone
involved has missed the point. The central issue is not whether cannibalism
existed (it no doubt did in many pre-literate societies if only as ritual), but

rather that the fantasy of cannibalism is so widespread as to be a true human "universal" (Brown and Tuzin 1983: 4). The *fantasy* of man-eating, in all its gory glory, not the acting out, is what counts. As psychology has taught us, people do not always act out their impulses, which nevertheless represent a mixture of wishes and fears percolating just beneath the surface. Indeed every society known to humanity shows evidence of cannibalism as a fantasy, and, indeed in many cases an obsession: either in the form of a preoccupation displaced into accusations against an enemy group ("those savages are cannibals!") or as a label attached to despised groups within the society (as in accusations in Medieval Europe that the Jews drank the blood of Christian children)—and, of course, in the case of imaginary monsters.

If people do not practice man-eating themselves, one may be sure that they accuse others of doing it, or they invent horrible ogres who safely act out their repressed wishes, as among the Algonquians with their Windigo psychosis. There is no society in which cannibalism does not prey upon the mind as phobia. Arens's desperate effort to deny that cannibalism ever existed is itself an example of the power of this obsession: a mania that takes its place in the repertory of the mind as the most ubiquitous nightmare, the ultimate horror, shared by all, primitive and civilized, old and young, male and female alike. It thus invokes the most intense disgust and the most ardent denials. Eli Sagan (1974) is probably right to call cannibalism the primary form of human aggression. This observation goes a long way in explaining the motif of man-eating in monster imagery.

The psychically primal status of the cannibal impulse also helps us understand oral components of monster imagery, especially the association with juvenile anxieties. No matter in what form or context they appear, the monsters we have met are wordless, speechless. Even the Frankenstein monster, although like a man in other respects, cannot articulate beyond a rudimentary level. Like others of his ilk, he roars, stammers, and shrieks. Not silent, but bellowing like Windigo, Tiamat, Vritra, Kung-kung, and "Flaming Teeth," or hooting like the Jersey Devil or the Hopi "Monster Woman" Soyok Wuhti, monsters are emanations from the primitive preverbal stage of mental development. They are incapable of meaningful articulation but only use their mouths to issue the shriek or hoot of the animal or the wail and cry of the baby. They are pure affect in nonverbal form—in this they are like figures in dreams.

Monsters are thus rooted in the primary organization of the time before

speech: in this primordial world there are only sounds, images, and emotions. And this wordless world is experienced through the mouth. This oral
primacy that also explains the *form* of aggression associated with monsters:
the tearing and rending, the gobbling mouths, the gnashing teeth, the cavernous maws, cannibalism itself, and the overwhelming sense of eating and
being eaten as simultaneous experiences—all aspects of oral sadism, of the
incorporation and destruction that are characteristic of the ambivalent
infantile omnipotence, as well as infantile helplessness. Dispensing with
even a modicum of disguise, the Indians in the Hudson Bay area conceive
of Nulayuuiniq as a giant cannibal infant (Rose 2000: 234). In a sense, as
these Eskimos have surmised, infants *are* cannibals: they eat and drink
their mothers, both literally and figuratively. The monster is, in part, a
mental remnant from that primordial stage.

PALEOLITHIC PREDATORS?

In addition to all the above, we may also look to phylogeny as well as
ontogeny on this score. Could it be that some of the power of this man-
eating terror derives not as a product of the individual's experience, but as
a collective memory from our own infancy as a species? Could the fear of
being eaten by a huge and pitiless carnivore stem from our experience with
predators in the infancy of human consciousness? As the fossil evidence
makes abundantly clear, Paleolithic man-eaters were gigantic, and, given
the primitive level of technology at the time, surely formidable foes. The
mighty cave bear (*Ursus spelaeus*) that infested Europe, for example, stood
ten or more feet high at the shoulder (Kurtén 1976); and at the time the
cave paintings were made in Europe, when men were battling these monsters for living quarters, humans were still prey to saber-toothed tigers,
lions, wolves, and other large carnivores. In addition, our ancestors were
much smaller at that time, the men averaging not much over five feet, the
women slightly less, making the disparity in size even more terrifying
(Churchill et al. 2000: 35). Other dangerous animals, even herbivores like
the wooly mammoth and wooly rhinoceros, were immense in size and
deadly threats as well, even if they did not eat humans. The mastodon stood
twelve feet at the shoulder and the woolly rhinoceros at least six. As Cawson (1995: 18) says, the very word *monstrous* "has the suggestion of size,
recalling the great animals that were once everyday enemies of our ancestors." Although this is pure speculation, it is certainly something to keep in
mind when considering the deathless fascination of monsters.

Sea-serpent seen by Hans Egede in 1734, off the south coast of
Greenland. From *Mythical Beasts* by Charles Gould (1886).

Based on the above, we can say that the monster, whatever else it symbolizes, is also a metaphor for retrogression to a previous age and time. The
monster is a trip to the Shakespearean "dark backward and abysm of
time," on a number of different levels. First, the monster, always bestial in
appearance and primitive in behavior, signals a return of the primeval reptilian cerebellum, the lowest animal instincts in man. Monsters often have
reptilian traits, or else, in the case of the ogres and demons of China and
the Far East, simian qualities. Sometimes, as in pagan Scandinavian lore,
monsters are "worms"; elsewhere they have insect or arachnid characteristics; sea monsters have fish-like or amphibian traits. This morphological
convention represents a form of regression in a bioevolutionary sense: devo-
lution to lower levels, a return to the infancy of life itself, to the primal ooze.

Second, monsters reflect primary process thinking and the oral sadism of
the human neonate, which equal regression in the psychodynamic sense:
the return of the individual to prior states of development. Further, in all
the world's folklore (especially among American Indians), monsters are said

to be remnants of a distant geophysical past, revenants, or vestiges of the epoch before culture, when humans were helpless and vulnerable—that is, like newborns, like infants. Monsters are thus also regressive in a mythic-religious sense, predating the gods and good spirits. What all this regressive imagery suggests, of course, is that every human carries within him- or herself the entire primitive past of the species as a set of undying fantasies, and that humans are all alike in this regard. Thus the cultural displacement mechanism of the monster in folklore: a universal metaphor for the unwanted backward-leaning retrograde self.

This regressive component also might explain the consistent watery imagery in monster lore, the fact that monsters inhabit murky waters, lakes, ponds, fens, and marshes, and that they are portrayed as slimy or amphibious in appearance and behavior. Like the neonate leaving the womb in birth, monsters *emerge* from the deep and nurturing waters to bellow and shriek. The water that surrounds and shelters the monster symbolizes not only the amniotic fluids of the womb, but also the primal element from which all life emerged.

HYBRIDS, HORRORS, AND HEROES

Next, we must consider the feature of formal hybridization in monster imagery. Perhaps none of our original propositions has been borne out as resoundingly as this one: in whatever culture, monsters are bizarre composites, made up of pieces of a reassembled reality. Promiscuously, they combine human with animal features, or mix living and dead tissue, or conflate ontological realms like the hydra and the manticore, or are amalgams of discordant parts from a variety of organisms like the Greek chimera or the Asian ogres with their ape-like traits. Monsters do indeed challenge—"reshuffle" (Harpham 1982: 5)—the very foundations of our known world. Challenging our cosmological assumptions and perceptions, monsters are cognitively as well as physically challenging.

What does this mean about the human mind? Are Douglas and Turner correct in assuming that the mind needs monsters to awaken it to unknown possibilities? Can the perceptual deformations involved in the creation of monsters have a positive mental purpose, aside from the obvious therapeutic function of giving vent to and externalizing instincts and fears? Are monsters like dreams in this regard: are they necessary for normal mental functioning?

It is clear, first of all, that Freud's concept of dreamwork is perfectly suited to the understanding of the cognitive process of monster-making. The anatomical pieces of the monster are captured by the imagination from empirical reality, as a form of nightmare *bricolage*, or opportunistic scavenging by day, but imbued with powerful emotional content that informs their shape and context as dark forces. The organic components constituting the monster are symbolic manifestations of emotions displaced, or projected in visual form. When we speak of monster images conflating such feelings into a complex, animated amalgam we are employing the Freudian concept of imagistic—or structural—condensation that he proposes as an explanation for the creativity of dreams, art, and fantasies. In addition, we may see this process as occurring in a trans-temporal as well as pictorial dimension—just as Freud argued about dream images. Like dreams, the monster's body combines everyday reality with powerful repressions emanating from past experiences and sense impressions from the unconscious; the monster always has this oneiric quality (Andriano 1999: 49). Monsters are seen vaguely, fleetingly, and are then shielded again by the darkness; indistinctly observed like dreams.

But there is also a paradoxical sense in which terrifying images, like those in bad dreams, are cognitively useful, not simply as outlets for repressed emotions, or as a way of letting off steam or literally "waking us up," as nightmares do, but acting as salutary spurs to the imagination, waking us up to new ideas, for example. As anthropologists like Turner and Douglas have argued, our monsters indeed help us to think and to imagine; they facilitate thought and they encourage us to confront deep fears. Monsters are our guides, our entrée into the mysterious worlds that lie both outside of us and within us. Therefore, although like the unknown itself, they frighten us, monsters also contribute to the development and growth of the imagination. As such they are indispensable in dealing with the challenges of life.

Many psychologists of childhood such as Denyse Beaudet (1990) and Jean Piaget (1962: 229) have surmised this important imaginative function of dream images. Piaget says that such freewheeling unconstrained mental operations as creating imaginary monsters provide *Spielraum*, an imaginary play-space in which young people can experiment with revolutionary ideas and images, or as Erik Erikson as put it (1972: 165), a means to infuse reality with imaginative potentiality. As Bruno Bettelheim has said, this form of creative mental play permits children to give their anxieties a "tangible form" that then can be distanced and defeated (1976:120). This projective process of course continues in adulthood, not only in dreams and fantasy, but, as we have seen, in community rituals. As Heinz Mode puts it,

It is in no small measure that they [monsters] have contributed towards bringing primeval fears into the bright light of living day, giving visible shape to creatures of the imagination, and thus bringing them out of mystical concealment and unfathomable eternity on to the brief stretch of earthly life, making them mortal. (1973: 232)

Hence there is always a non-fixed boundary between men and monsters. In the end, there can be no clear division between us and them, between civilization and bestiality. As we peer into the abyss, the abyss stares back.

Indeed, many of the most revered culture heroes have qualities that are unsettlingly similar to those of the monsters they fight. Beowulf is disturbingly like Grendel: he is outsized, aggressive, fearless, and has the same superhuman powers and limitless stamina. Like Grendel, he mutilates his vanquished foes in battle, even the females, decapitating Grendel's mother and displaying the grisly remains as a trophy. The language of the poem makes this closeness of hero and monster unequivocal. In the Anglo-Saxon, Grendel is described as "monster," "demon," "fiend," and so on, but he is also called "warrior" and "hero." Both the monster and the monster-slayer in the original verses are called "awesome" and "awe-inspiring," and "formidable" (Orchard 1995: 32–33). In like measure, the Yurok hero Pulekukwerek is even described as looking, as well as acting, like a monster: he is grotesquely large and sports a huge horn growing out of his buttocks—a virtual man-beast. The Indian hero Goera is also a mutilator; he chops his beaten monster-foes into tiny pieces. The mythic warriors of Polynesia, like Tamure and Pitaka, not content with simple victory, gleefully butcher and eat the ogres they kill. So in all this mutual blood and gore, who is the monster, who the victim?

OF MONSTERS, GODS, AND ANIMALS

Of course this ambiguity helps explain the consistent bestial imagery in monsters, as well as the human-into-beast transformations in werewolves, vampires, and the like. This mixture of human and animal is a direct consequence of a profound ambivalence shared by all people: a simultaneous terror and fascination with the beast within, the impulsive need to both deny and acknowledge that, no matter how exalted, we humans are members of the animal kingdom and heir to violent instincts. Like other animals, humans retain an atavistic side as a result of the retention of a primitive cerebellum. Coping with our dual impulses, murderous and compassionate at the same time, we make a deity of the good within us and a monster of the bad. We think in terms of polarized opposites, rather than admit the dualism and internal division, although neither side can be purified and is always contaminated by the other. Thus we decide the issue by making the monster the killer-sadist, the cannibal within which we can then cast out as an alien being. The monster remains as the reminder of the primitive nature of the psyche and its animal origins. The beast-monster is the pictorial, animated reflection of age-old human obsession with the fact of incomplete evolution.

The same may be said about the place of monsters in the physical world. As we have seen monsters emerge from a kind of metaphorical exile, from borderline places. As David White puts it (1991: 1), monsters occupy "peripheral space" in all cultural traditions. We have seen this in each and every case from the Australian bunyips to the Jersey Devil: whatever the people in a particular culture demarcate as wilderness, as noncultural space, as unexplored territory, there are monsters. As well as cognitively, in this spatial sense the monster demarcates not only between the real and the unreal, but between the permitted and the forbidden. The irruption of the monster into human affairs represents the arrival of that which is denied in the self, distanced metaphorically speaking—those traits that have been renounced and consigned "out there." Thus we construct both the exile and the alien territory to which he belongs.

Promiscuously combining incongruent organic elements, the monster also unifies the moral opposites that comprise human comprehension. Ugly and malevolent, the monster is demonic of course, but it is also paradoxically divine: in its mystery and power, god-like and unfathomable, an object of reverence, and of admiration—even of identification—as well as of fear and loathing. "Evil is not without its attractions—symbolized by the mighty giant or dragon" (Bettelheim 1976: 9). Monstrous attributes inspire mixed emotions. Raw animal power is admirable as a means, if not an end.

Uniting both tendencies in the human heart, monsters are viewed with a sharp and undisguised ambivalence in most cultures. The Congolese Mokele-Mbembe is literally worshipped as a "beast-god" (Nugent 1993: 241) and is offered sacrifices, as is King Kong in the movie. The Babylonian Tiamat is both divine and demonic. The Windigo and the Wechuge are objects of veneration bordering on worship; the ancient chaos-monsters like Apophis are always depicted as having godlike traits or are portrayed as having some perverted kinship to the gods. The French and Spanish festival dragon is a "beloved" and revered as well as hated image (Rodríguez Becerra 2000: 158). In Tarascon the dragon even takes on the added value as a "beneficent" source of civic pride and personal identification (Dumont 1951: 121). As well as mixing cognitive categories, all these monsters unite the extremes of the moral universe, and are always imbued with what Beaudet calls a "god-demon duality" (1990: 88). It is no surprise then that in the Middle Ages, monsters were sanctified by theologians like St. Augustine, and holy persons and even God himself were sometimes represented as "monsters" (Strickland 2000: 45). The Park of Monsters in Italy is also known as the Sacred Wood. No matter how awful, the monster comes through "as a kind of god" (Campbell 1968: 222).

THE SUPER-ID

We have seen that imaginary monsters embody a variety of inner states, many sharply contradictory. One of these states stems from fear, a fear not only of the dangerous external world, but of the self. The monster embodies, also, the sense of guilt. For the child, the monster represents the punishing Oedipal parent, and the cannibalistic threat is a simile for castration. Yet the child also identifies with the monster, for it embodies his or her own "bad self." Children wish to be good, that is, to conform to the ideals propagated by parents and society, but they know that they are not, that they harbor hostile, erotic, and aggressive impulses, so they invent the monster and drive it into the unconscious. Self-knowledge contradicts the self-image they strive to attain, subverts their efforts to be good, and therefore makes them, in their own eyes, a monster. What child, after being found out and punished, has not experienced the feeling of being evil and horrible, of being cast out of the human community—like a monster? As Leslie Fiedler (1978: 30) puts it, any child is bound at some time to feel "some monstrous discrepancy" between his or her impulsive nature and the role expectations of the era. The vulnerability to such self-doubt is carried into adulthood.

This fact of course explains the common interchangeability of human and monster, why in most mythologies people can so easily turn into monsters, and why most monsters retain human characteristics and the worst of human traits. Characterologically speaking, monsters are fully human: their unmotivated malice and destructiveness are human, not animal traits.

My own theory of monsters stems from this "double projective mechanism," as Kappler calls it (1980: 259). Granted, the monster embodies the raw id. But, Protean and ambivalent, the monster also represents the superego. More precisely, it represents that part of the psyche that Freud called the conscience. In various places in his work, Freud allowed as how the conscience could ally with and absorb the powerful sadism of the id in order to punish the self for imagined transgressions; in fact, this is his basic approach to sadomasochistic perversions. For Freud, the aggressive energy appropriated by the superego to punish the ego has roots "deep within the id" (Brenner 1955: 131).

I think this standard psychoanalytic formulation can be taken further. The data above show that the monster is both a powerful universal symbol and the product of a compulsive fascination that can be explained only in its own terms. The monster's unequaled hold over the human mind requires an explanation that acknowledges the autonomy of the mental processes involved and, as we suggested earlier, points to the existence of a fourth component in the psyche. Like the ego and superego, this supernumerary agency, which I will call in the absence of any existing term the "super-id," is a spin-off from prior stages of development, but it unites the extremes of the mental apparatus from which it has emerged, taking on a life of its own. Energized by the unbridled power of id, infused with guilt, morally empowered by masochistic identification, the monster unites, as does no other single trope, metaphor, or symbol, the totality of the psyche in all its grotesqueness, contradictoriness, whimsey, and dynamism. The monster is the super-id.

The power of monsters is their ability to fuse opposites, to merge contraries, to subvert rules, to overthrow cognitive barriers, moral distinctions, and ontological categories. Monsters overcome the barrier of time itself. Uniting past and present, demonic and divine, guilt and conscience, predator and prey, parent and child, self and alien, our monsters are our innermost selves.

REFERENCES

Abraham, Karl. 1942a [1924]. "A Short History of the Development of the Libido, Viewed in the Light of Mental Disorders." In Abraham, *Collected Papers on Psychoanalysis*. London: Hogarth Press.

———. 1942b [1924]. "The Influence of Oral Eroticism on Character Formation." In Abraham, *Collected Papers on Psychoanalysis*. London: Hogarth Press.

Ames, Michael M. 1980. Epilogue. In *Manlike Monsters on Trial: Early Records and Modern Evidence*, ed. Marjorie Halpin and Ames, 301–15. Vancouver: University of British Columbia Press.

Andersen, Johannes C. 1969. *Myths and Legends of the Polynesians*. Rutland, Vt.: Charles E. Tuttle.

Andriano, Joseph. 1999. *Immortal Monster: The Mythological Evolution of the Fantastic Beast in Modern Fiction and Film*. Westport Conn.: Greenwood Press.

Armengou i Feliu, Josep. 1994. *La Patum de Berga: Comilació de dades històriques, amb un suplement musical dels ballets de la Patum*. Berga, Spain: Columna l'Albí.

Atwood, Margaret. 1977. "Canadian Monsters: Some Aspects of the Supernatural in Canadian Fiction." In *Canadian Imagination: Dimensions of a Literary Culture*, ed. David Staines, 97–122. Cambridge, Mass.: Harvard University Press.

Bann, Stephen. 1994. Introduction. In *Frankenstein: Creation and Monstrosity*, ed. Bann, 1–15. London: Reaktion Books.

Barber, Richard and Anne Richies. 1971. *A Dictionary of Fabulous Beasts*. London: Macmillan.

Barrow, Terence. 1973. "Ghosts, Ghost-Gods, and Demons of Japan." In *Japanese Grotesqueries*, comp. Nikolas Kiej'e, 7–28. Rutland Vt.: Charles E. Tuttle.

Barton, Carlin A. 1992. *The Sorrows of the Ancient Romans: The Gladiator and the Monster*. Princeton, N.J.: Princeton University Press.

Bauer, Henry H. 1986. *The Enigma of Loch Ness: Making Sense of a Mystery*. Urbana: University of Illinois Press.

Beaudet, Denyse. 1990. *Encountering the Monster: Pathways in Children's Dreams*. New York: Continuum.

Beckwith, Martha W. 1970 [1940]. *Hawaiian Mythology*. Honolulu: University of Hawaii Press.

Bennett, Lynn. 1983. *Dangerous Wives, Sacred Sisters*. New York: Columbia University Press.

Bettelheim, Bruno. 1976. *The Uses of Enchantment: The Meaning and Importance of Fairy Tales*. New York: Knopf.

Bishop, Charles A. 1975. "Northern Algonkian Cannibalism and Windigo Psychosis." In *Psychological Anthropology*, ed. Thomas R. Williams. The Hague: Mouton.

Blundell, Susan. 1986. *The Origins of Civilization in Greek and Roman Thought*. London: Croom Helm.

Bogoras, Waldemar. 1910. *Chukchee Mythology*. Chukchee Texts, Part I. New York: E.J. Brill.

Bottig, Fred. 1991. *Making Monstrous: Frankenstein, Criticism, Theory*. Manchester: Manchester University Press.

Brandes, Stanley H. 1992. "Spatial Symbolism in Southern Spain." In *The Psychoanalytic Study of Society*, vol. 18, ed. L. Boyce Boyer, Ruth M. Boyer, and Stephen M. Sonneberg, 119–35. Hillsdale N.J.: Analytic Press.

Bredekamp, Horst. 1985. *Vicino Orsini und das Heilige Wald von Bomarzo: Ein Fürst als Künstler und Anarchist*. Photos by Wolfram Janzer. Worms, Germany: Werner.

Brenner, Charles. 1955. *An Elementary Textbook of Psychoanalysis*. New York: International Universities Press.

Bright, Charles. 1991. *Sea Serpents*. Bowling Green, Ohio: Bowling Green State University Popular Press.

Brightman, Robert A. 1988. "The Windigo in the Material World." *Ethnohistory* 35: 357–79.

Brown, Paula and Donald Tuzin, eds. 1983. *The Ethnography of Cannibalism*. Society for Psychological Anthropology Special Publication. Washington, D.C.: Society for Psychological Anthropology.

Buckley, Thomas. 1980. "Monsters and the Quest for Balance in Native Northwest California." In *Manlike Monsters on Trial: Early Records and Modern Evidence*, ed. Marjorie Halpin and Michael M. Ames, 152–71. Vancouver: University of British Columbia Press.

Bulfinch, Thomas. 1970 [1855]. *Bulfinch's Mythology*. New York: Thomas Y. Crowell.

Burling, Robbins. 1963. *Rangsanggri: Family and Kinship in a Garo Village*. Philadelphia: University of Pennsylvania Press.

Butturff, Douglas R. 1968. "The Monsters and the Scholar: An Edition and Critical Study of the *Liber Monstrorum*." Ph.D. dissertation, University of Illinois.

Campbell, Joseph. 1968 [1948]. *The Hero with a Thousand Faces*. 2nd ed. Princeton, N.J.: Princeton University Press.

Campbell, Joseph with Bill Moyers. 1988. *The Power of Myth*. New York: Doubleday.

Carpenter, Carole H. 1980. "The Cultural Role of Monsters in Canada." In *Manlike Monsters on Trial: Early Records and Modern Evidence*, ed. Marjorie Halpin and Michael M. Ames, 97–108. Vancouver: University of British Columbia Press.

Carroll, Michael P. 1992. "Folklore and Psychoanalysis: The Swallowing Monster and Open-Brains Allomotifs in Plains Indian Mythology." *Ethos* 20: 289–303.

Carroll, Noël E. 1990. *The Philosophy of Horror, Or Paradoxes of the Heart*. New York: Routledge.

Carstairs, G. Morris. 1967. *The Twice Born*. Bloomington: Indiana University Press.

Cawson, Frank. 1995. *The Monsters in the Mind: The Face of Evil in Myth, Literature and Contemporary Life*. Sussex: Book Guild.

Churchill, Stephen E., Vincenzo Formicola, Trenton W. Holliday, Brigitte Mattholt, and Betsy A. Schumann. 2000. "Hunters of the Golden Age: The Upper Paleolithic Population of Europe in an Evolutionary Perspective." In *The Mid Upper Paleolithic of Eurasia, 30,000–20,000 BP*, 31–58. Leiden: University of Leiden Press.

Cohen, Daniel. 1970. *A Modern Looks at Monsters*. New York: Dodd, Mead.

———. 1982. *The Encyclopedia of Monsters*. New York: Dodd, Mead.

Cohen, Jeffrey J. 1996. "Monster Culture (Seven Theses)." In *Monster Theory: Reading Culture*, ed. Cohen, 3–25. Minneapolis: University of Minnesota Press.

———. 1999. *Of Giants: Sex, Monsters, and the Middle Ages*. Minneapolis: University of Minnesota Press.

———, ed. 1996. *Monster Theory: Reading Culture*. Minneapolis: University of Minnesota Press.

Cohen, Percy. 1980. "Psychoanalysis and Cultural Symbolization." In *Symbol as Sense: New Approaches to the Analysis of Meaning*, ed. Mary LeCron Foster and Stanley H. Brandes, 45–68. New York: Academic Press.

Cohn, Norman R. 1993. *Cosmos, Chaos, and the World to Come: The Ancient Roots of Apocalyptic Faith*. New Haven, Conn.: Yale University Press.

Colarusso, John. 1980. "Ethnographic Information of a Wild Man of the Caucasus." In *Manlike Monsters on Trial: Early Records and Modern Evidence*, ed. Marjorie Halpin and Michael M. Ames, 255–64. Vancouver: University of British Columbia Press.

Coleman, Loren and Jerome Clark. 1999. *Cryptozoology A to Z: The Encyclopedia of Loch Monsters, Sasquatch, Chupacabras, and Other Authentic Mysteries of Nature*. New York: Simon and Schuster.

Colombo, John R. 1997. Windigo: *An Anthology of Fact and Fantastic Fiction*. Saskatoon, Saskatchewan: Western Producer Prairie Books.

Colton, Harold S. 1949. *Hopi Kachina Dolls: With a Key to Their Identification*. Albuquerque: University of New Mexico Press.

Courlander, Harold. 1971. *The Fourth World of the Hopis*. New York: Crown.

———. 1982. *Hopi Voices: Recollections, Traditions, and Narratives of the Hopi Indians*. Albuquerque: University of New Mexico Press.

Cresti, Carlo and Matteo C. Cresti. 1998. *Mostri, e altri prodigi di fantasia nelle architetture del manierismo e del modernismo*. Florence: Angelo Pontecorbo.

Daniel, Howard. 1964. *Devils, Monsters, and Nightmares*. London: Abelard Schuman.

Daston, Lorraine and Katharine Park. 1998. *Wonders and the Order of Nature, 1150–1750*. New York: Zone Books.

Derrida, Jacques. 1995. *Points: Interviews, 1974–1994*. Ed. Elisabeth Weber, trans. Peggy Kamuf et al. Stanford, Calif.: Stanford University Press.

Desparmet, Joseph, ed. 1909. *Contes populaires sur les ogres*. 2 vols. Paris: Ernest Leroux.

de Waal Malefyt, Annemarie. 1968. "Homo Monstrosus." *Scientific American* 219: 113–19.

Doniger, Wendy O. 1980. *Women, Androgynes, and Other Mythical Beasts*. Chicago: University of Chicago Press.

Douglas, Mary. 1966. *Purity and Danger*. London: Routledge and Kegan Paul.

Douglass, Carrie B. 1997. *Bulls, Bullfighting, and Spanish Identities*. Tucson: University of Arizona Press.

Dumont, Louis. 1951. *La Tarasque: Essai de description d'un fait local d'un point du vue ethnographique*. Paris: Gallimard.

Dundes, Alan. 1998. "The Vampire as Bloodthirsty Revenant: A Psychoanalytic Postmortem." In *The Vampire: A Casebook*, ed. Alan Dundes, 159–75. Ann Arbor: University of Michigan Press.

Eberhart, George M. 1983. *Monsters: A Guide to Information on Unaccounted for Creatures, Including Bigfoot, Many Water Monsters, and Other Irregular Animals*. New York: Garland.

Erikson, Erik. 1950. *Childhood and Society*. New York: Norton.

———. 1972. "Play and Actuality." In *Play and Development: A Symposium*, ed. Maria W. Piers, 127–67. New York: Norton.

Farràs i Farràs, Jaume. 1986. *La Patum de Berga*. Barcelona: Edicions de Nou Art Thor.

Fernandez, James W. 1986. *Persuasions and Performances: The Play of Tropes in Culture*. Bloomington: Indiana University Press.

Fiedler, Leslie. 1978. *Freaks: Myths and Images of the Secret Self*. New York: Simon and Schuster.

Flusser, George and Eric S. Rabkin. 1987. *Aliens: The Anthropology of Science Fiction*. Carbondale: Southern Illinois University Press.

Fogelson, Raymond. 1965. "Psychological Theories of Windigo 'Psychosis,' and a Preliminary Application of a Models Approach." In *Context and Meaning in Cultural Anthropology*, ed. Melford E. Spiro, 74–99. New York: Free Press.

———. 1974. "Windigo." *Encyclopedia Americana*, 4–10. New York: Americana Corp.

———. 1980. "Windigo Goes South: Stoneclad Among the Cherokees." In *Manlike Monsters on Trial: Early Accounts and Modern Evidence*, ed. Marjorie M. Halpin and Michael M. Ames, 132–51. Vancouver: University of British Columbia Press.

Freeman, Ruth and Thomas Freeman. 1992. "An Anatomical Commentary on the Concept of Infantile Oral Sadism." *International Journal of Psycho-Analysis* 73: 343–47.

Freud, Sigmund. 1900. *The Interpretation of Dreams*. Standard Edition, vols. 4, 5, ed. and trans. James Strachey. London: Hogarth Press.

———. 1905. *Three Essays on the Theory of Sexuality*. Standard Edition, vol. 7, ed. and trans. James Strachey, 125–248. London: Hogarth Press.

Friedman, John B. 1981. *The Monstrous Races in Medieval Art and Thought*. Cambridge, Mass.: Harvard University Press.

García Rodero, Cristina. 1992. *Festivals and Rituals of Spain*. Text by José M. Caballero Bonald. New York: Harry Abrams.

Geertz, Armin. 1994. *The Invention of Prophecy: Continuity and Meaning in Hopi Religion*. Berkeley: University of California Press.

Gilmore, David D. 1998. *Carnival and Culture: Sex, Symbol and Status in Spain*. New Haven, Conn.: Yale University Press.

Girard, René. 1972. *Violence et le sacré* (*Violence and the Sacred*, 1972)

Gottlieb, Richard M. 1991. "The Legend of the European Vampire: Object Loss and Corporeal Preservation." *Psychoanalytic Study of the Child* 49: 465–80.

Gould, Charles. 1969. *Mythical Monsters*. Detroit: Singing Tree Press

Graburn, Nelson H. 1980. "Man, Beast, and Transformation in Canadian Inuit Art and Culture." In *Manlike Monsters on Trial: Early Records and Modern Evidence*, ed. Marjorie Halpin and Michael M. Ames, 193–210. Vancouver: University of British Columbia Press.

Grady, Frank. 1996. "Vampire Culture." In *Monster Theory: Reading Culture*, ed. Jeffrey J. Cohen, 225–42. Minneapolis Minnesota: University of Minnesota Press.

Grant, John. 1992. *Monster Mysteries*. London: Grange Books.

Grimm, Jakob. 1882. *Teutonic Mythology*. Trans. James Steven Stallybrass. London: George Bell.

Guthrie, W. K. C. 1965. *A History of Greek Philosophy*. Vol. 2, *The Presocratic Tradition from Parmenides to Democritus*. Cambridge: Cambridge University Press.

Hallowell, A. Irving. 1974. *Culture and Experience*. Philadelphia: University of Pennsylvania Press.

Halpin, Marjorie M. and Michael M. Ames, eds. 1980. *Manlike Monsters on Trial: Early Records and Modern Evidence*. Vancouver: University of British Columbia Press.

Hames, Inez. 1960. *Legends of Fiji and Rotuma*. Auckland N.Z.: Watterson and Roddick.

Handleman, Don and Bruce Kapferer. 1980. "Symbolic Types, Mediation and the Transformation of Ritual Context: Sinhalese Demons and Tewa Clowns." *Semiotica* 30: 41–71.

Harpham, Geoffrey G. 1982. *On the Grotesque: Strategies of Contradiction in Art and Literature*. Princeton, N.J.: Princeton University Press.

Hay, Thomas H. 1971. "The Windigo Psychosis: Psychodynamic Factors in Aberrant Behavior." *American Anthropologist* 73: 1–19.

Heaney, Seamus. 2000. *Beowulf: A New Verse Translation*. New York: Norton.

Heuvelmans, Bernard. 1990. "The Metamorphosis of Unknown Animals into Fabulous Beasts and of Fabulous Beasts into Known Animals." *Cryptozoology* 9: 1–12.

Hogarth, Peter J. and Val Clery. 1979. *Dragons*. New York: Viking.

Holiday. F. W. 1973. *The Dragon and the Disc: An Investigation into the Totally Fantastic*. New York: Norton.

Hudson, Charles. 1978. "Uktena: A Cherokee Anomalous Monster." *Journal of Cherokee Studies* 3: 62–75.

Huet, Marie Hélène. 1993. *Monstrous Imagination*. Cambridge, Mass.: Harvard University Press.

Isla, Alejandro. 1998. "Terror, Memory and Responsibility in Argentina." *Critique of Anthropology* 18: 134–56.

Jackson, Rosemary. 1981. *Fantasy: The Literature of Subversion*. London: Methuen.

Jeffrey, David L. 1980. "Medieval Monsters." In *Manlike Monsters on Trial: Early Records and Modern Evidence*, ed. Marjorie Halpin and Michael M. Ames, 46–64. Vancouver: University of British Columbia Press.

Jones, Ernest. 1971 [1951]. *On the Nightmare*. New York: Liveright.

Kapferer, Bruce. 1983. *A Celebration of Demons: Exorcism and the Aesthetics of Healing in Sri Lanka*. Bloomington: Indiana University Press.

Kappler, Claude. 1980. *Monstres, démons, et merveilles à la fin du Moyen Age*. Paris: Payot.

Kassovic, Julius S. 1980. "The Familiar and the Grotesque: The Roots of Monster-Making in a Mexican Indian Village." In *Manlike Monsters on Trial: Early Records and Modern Evidence*, ed. Marjorie Halpin and Michael M. Ames, 187–92. Vancouver: University of British Columbia Press.

Kennedy, John G. 1970. "Aman Doger: Nubian Monster of the Nile." *Journal of American Folklore* 83: 438–45.

Kiej'e, Nikolas, comp. 1973. *Japanese Grotesqueries*. Text by Terence Barrow. Rutland Vt.: Tuttle.

Kirtley, Bacil F. 1971. *A Motif-Index of Traditional Polynesian Narratives*. Honolulu: University of Hawaii Press.

Klein, Melanie. 1932. *The Psychoanalysis of Children*. London: Hogarth.

———. 1975. *Love, Hate, and Reparation, and Other Works*. London: Hogarth Press.

Kurtén, Björn. 1976. *The Cave Bear Story: Life and Death of a Vanished Animal*. New York: Columbia University Press.

Lascault, Gilbert, 1973. *Le Monstre dans l'art occidental: Un problème esthetique*. Paris: Klincksieck.

Law, John. 1991. *A Sociology of Monsters: Essays on Power, Technology, and Domination*. New York: Routledge.

Leach, Edmund. 1982. "Anthropological Aspects of Language: Animal Categories and Verbal Abuse." In *Reader in Comparative Religion*, ed. William Lessa and Evon Vogt, 206–20. New York: Harper and Row.

Lehner, Ernst and Johanna Lehner. 1969. *A Fantastic Bestiary: Beasts and Monsters in Myth and Folklore*. New York: Tudor.

Leroi-Gourhan, André. 1982. *The Dawn of European Art: An Introduction to Paleolithic Cave Painting*. Trans. Sara Champion. Cambridge: Cambridge University Press.

Lessa, William A. 1961. *Tales from Ulithi Atoll*. Berkeley: University of California Press.

————. 1980. *More Tales from Ulithi Atoll: A Content Analysis*. Berkeley: University of California Press.

Luciano, Patrick. 1987. *Them or Us: Archetypical Interpretations of the Fifties Alien Invasion Films*. Bloomington: Indiana University Press.

Magaña, Edmundo, ed. 1988. *Les Monstres dans l'imaginaire des indiens d'Amérique latine*. Paris: Lettres Modernes.

Malotki, Ekkehart. 1983. *Hopituwutsi/Hopi Tales: A Bilingual Collection of Hopi Indian Stories*. Tucson: Sun Tracks, University of Arizona Press.

Marano, Lou. 1982. "Windigo Psychosis: The Anatomy of an Emic-Etic Confusion." *Current Anthropology* 28: 385–412.

Marcos Arévalo, Javier. 2001. "Roles, functiones y significados de los animales en los rituales festivos (La experiencia extremeña)." *Jornada de Religiosidad Popular* 3: 3–18. Almeria: Instituto de Estudioes Almerienses, Diputacion Provincial.

Mayor, Adrienne. 2000. *The First Fossil Hunters: Paleontology in Greek and Roman Times*. Princeton, N.J.: Princeton University Press.

McCloy, James F. and Ray Miller. 1976. *The Jersey Devil*. Wallingford, Pa.: Atlantic Press.

Mitchell, Timothy. 1988. *Violence and Piety in Spanish Folklore*. Philadelphia: University of Pennsylvania Press.

————. 1990. *Passional Culture: Emotion, Religion and Society in Southern Spain*. Philadelphia: University of Pennsylvania Press.

————. 1991. *Blood Sport: A Social History of Spanish Bullfighting*. Philadelphia: University of Pennsylvania Press.

Mode, Heinz. 1973. *Fabulous Beasts and Demons*. New York: Phaidon.1973.

Moon, Mary. 1977. *Ogopogo: The Okanagan Mystery from Indian Lore to Contemporary Evidence, the Facts About the Legendary Monster of British Columbia's Okanagan Lake*. Vancouver: J. J. Douglas.

Moretti, Franco. 1983. *Signs Taken as Wonders: Essays in the Sociology of Literary Forms*. Trans. Susan Fischer, David Forgacs, and David Miller. London: NLB.

Mully, Wilfreda A. 1980. "The Unwanted Possession: The Origin of Monsters from a Psychoanalytical Point of View." In *Manlike Monsters on Trial: Early Records and Modern Evidence*, ed. Marjorie Halpin and Michael M. Ames, 37–46. Vancouver: University of British Columbia Press.

Napier, John. 1972. *Bigfoot: The Yeti and Sasquatch in Myth and Reality*. New York: Dutton.

Nigg, Joe. 1999. *The Book of Fabulous Beasts: A Treasury of Writings from Ancient Times to the Present*. New York: Oxford University Press.

Norman, Howard. 1982. *Where the Chill Came From: Cree Windigo Tales and Journeys*. San Francisco: North Point Press.

Nourri, Jean Paul. 1973. *La Tarasque, qu'es aco? Le roi Réné, le jeux de la Tarasque, le monstre*. Tarascon: Editions "Le Commercial."

Noyes, Dorothy. 1992. "The Mule and the Giants: Struggling for the Body Social in a Catalan Corpus Christi Festival." Ph.D. dissertation, University of Pennsylvania.

———. n.d. "Fire in the Plaça." Unpublished manuscript in author's possession.

Nugent, Rory. 1993. *Drums Along the Congo: On the Trail of the Last Living Dinosaur.* Boston: Houghton Mifflin.

Orchard, Andy. 1995. *Pride and Prodigies: Studies in the Monsters of the* Beowulf-*Manuscript.* Cambridge: D.S. Brewer.

Otto, Rudolph. 1958. *The Idea of the Holy.* Trans. John W. Harvey. London: Oxford University Press.

Parker, Seymour. 1960. "The Wiitiko Psychosis in the Context of Ojibwa Personality and Culture." *American Anthropologist* 62: 603–23.

Parsons, Elsie Clews. 1969 [1936]. *Hopi Journal of Alexander Stephen.* New York: AMS Press.

Pender, Stephen. 1996. "'No Monsters at the Resurrection': Inside Some Conjoined Twins." In *Monster Theory: Reading Culture,* ed. Jeffrey J. Cohen, 143–67. Minneapolis: University of Minnesota Press.

Peniche Barrera, Roldán. 1987. *Bestiario Mexicano.* Mexico City: Panorama Editorial.

Piaget, Jean. 1962. *Play, Dreams, and Imitation in Childhood.* New York: Norton.

Pliny, the Elder. 1971. *Natural History.* Trans. H. Rackham. Cambridge, Mass.: Harvard University Press.

Preston, Richard J. 1980. "The Witiko: Algonkian Knowledge and Whiteman Knowledge." In *Manlike Monsters on Trial: Early Records and Modern Evidence,* ed. Marjorie Halpin and Michael M. Ames, 111–31. Vancouver: University of British Columbia Press.

Pryde, Duncan. 1972. *Nunaga: My Land, My Country.* Edmonton: M. G. Hurtig.

Reed, A. W. 1963. *Treasury of Maori Folklore.* Wellington, N.Z.: A.H. and A.W. Reed.

Renard, Louis. 1991. *La Tarasque: Le temps retrouvée.* Marguerittes: Equinoxe.

Ridington, Robin. 1976. "Wechuge and Windigo: A Comparison of Cannibal Belief Among Boreal Forest Athabaskan and Algonkians." *Anthropologica* 18: 107–29.

———. 1980. "Monsters and the Anthropologist's Reality." In *Manlike Monsters on Trial: Early Records and Modern Evidence,* ed. Marjorie Halpin and Michael M. Ames, 172–86. Vancouver: University of British Columbia Press.

Rodríguez Becerra, Salvador. 2000. *Religión y fiesta: Antropología de las creencias y rituales en Andalucía.* Seville: Signatura Demos.

Rongmuthu, Dewan Sing. 1960. *The Folk-Tales of the Garos.* Calcutta: University of Gauhati, Department of Publications.

Rose, Carol. 2000. *Giants, Monsters, and Dragons: An Encyclopedia of Folklore, Legend, and Myth.* Santa Barbara, Calif.: Oxford University Press.

Rowland, Beryl. 1987. "Harpies." In *Mythical and Fabulous Creatures: A Source Book and Research Guide,* ed. Malcolm Smith, 155–61. New York: Greenwood Press.

Rubin, Miri. 1991. *Corpus Christi: The Eucharist in Late Medieval Culture.* Cambridge: Cambridge University Press.

Sagan, Eli. 1974. *Cannibalism: Human Aggression and Cultural Form*. New York: Harper and Row.

Sahlins, Peter. 1994. *Forest Rites: The War of the Damoiselles in Nineteenth-Century France*. Cambridge, Mass.: Harvard University Press.

Sánchez Herrero, Juan. 1999. "Crisis y permanencia: Religiosidad de la cofradías de Semana Santa de Sevilla, 1750–1874." In *Las Cofradías de Sevilla en el siglo de la crisis*, ed. León Carlos Álvarez Santalo. Seville: Universidad de Sevilla.

Scafella, Frank A. 1987. "The Sphinx." In *Mythical and Fabulous Creatures: A Source Book and Research Guide*, ed. Malcolm Smith, 179–91. New York: Greenwood Press.

Shuker, Karl. 1995. *Dragons: A Natural History*. New York: Simon and Schuster.

Skal, David J. 1993. *The Monster Show: A Cultural History of Horror*. New York: Norton.

Smith, Malcolm, ed. 1996. *Bunyips and Bigfoots: In Search of Australia's Mystery Animals*. Alexandria, N.S.W.: Millennium Books.

South, Malcolm. 1987. *Mythical and Fabulous Creatures: A Sourcebook and Research Guide*. New York: Greenwood Press.

Strickland, Debra. 2000. "Monsters and Christian Enemies." *History Today* 50: 45–51.

Suttles, Wayne. 1972. "On the Cultural Track of the Sasquatch." *Northwest Anthropological Research Notes* 6: 65–90.

———. 1980. "Sasquatch: The Testimony of Tradition." In *Manlike Monsters on Trial: Early Records and Modern Evidence*, ed. Marjorie Halpin and Michael M. Ames, 245–54. Vancouver: University of British Columbia Press.

Teicher, Morton I. 1960. *Windigo Psychosis: A Study of a Relationship Between Belief and Behavior Among the Indians of Northeastern Canada*. Seattle: American Ethnological Society.

Tolkien, J. J. R. 1984. *The Monsters and the Critics and Other Essays*. Ed. Christopher Tolkien. Boston: Houghton Mifflin.

Turner, Victor. 1967. *The Forest of Symbols: Aspects of Ndembu Ritual*. Ithaca, N.Y.: Cornell University Press.

———. 1977. "Process, System, and Symbol: A New Anthropological Synthesis." *Daedelus* 106: 69–81.

Uebel, Michael. 1996. "Unthinking the Monster: Twelfth-Century Responses to Saracen Alterity." In *Monster Theory*, ed. Jeffrey J. Cohen, 264–91. Minneapolis: University of Minnesota Press.

Van Gennep, Arnold. 1960 [1908]. *The Rites of Passage*. Trans. Monika B. Vizedom and Gabrielle L. Caffe. Chicago: University of Chicago Press.

Von Frantz, Marie-Louise. 1983. *Shadow and Evil in Fairy Tales*. Dallas, Tex.: Spring Publications.

Wallace, Anthony F. C. 1972. *The Death and Rebirth of the Seneca*. New York: Vintage Books.

Warner, Marina. 1998. *No Go the Bogeyman: Scaring, Lulling, and Making Mock.* New York: Farrar, Straus and Giroux.

Waterhouse, Ruth. 1996. "Beowulf as Palimpsest." In *Monster Theory*, ed. Jeffrey J. Cohen, 26–39. Minneapolis: University of Minnesota Press.

White, David G. 1991. *The Myth of the Dog-Man.* Chicago: University of Chicago Press.

White, Hayden. 1972. "The Forms of Wildness: Archaeology of an Idea." In *The Wild Man: An Image in Western Thought from the Renaissance to Romanticism*, ed. Edward Dudley and M. E. Novak, 3–38. Pittsburgh: University of Pittsburgh Press.

Williams, David. 1982. *Cain and Beowulf: A Study in Secular Allegory.* Toronto: University of Toronto Press.

———. 1996. *Deformed Discourse: The Function of the Monster in Medieval Thought and Literature.* Montreal: McGill-Queen's University Press.

Wittkower, Rudolf. 1942. "Marvels of the East: A Study in the History of Monsters." *Journal of the Warburg and Courtauld Institutes* 5: 159–97.

Wright, Barton. 1973. *Kachinas: A Hopi Artist's Documentary.* Flagstaff Ariz.: Northland Press.

Wright, Pablo. 1988. "Pitet: le maître des os dans la mythologie Toba." In *Les Monstres dans l'imaginaire des Indiens d'Amérique latine*, ed. Edmundo Magaña, 115–21. Paris: Lettres Modernes.

INDEX